The Great Treasury Raid

For a raid of its magnitude, the time (high noon) and setting (the United States Treasury, a stone's throw from the White House) showed a breath-taking boldness of design and planning. From out of nowhere, it seemed, they appeared—old people and young, rich and poor, an oil millionaire here, a factory worker there, a real estate tycoon, a working mother, several well-known movie stars, some corporation presidents, even the chairman of a powerful Congressional committee. It was a mixed lot, all right, that converged on the Treasury Building that high noon. Into the building they strolled, gloriously nonchalant. No one stopped them; not a guard looked up to question them. Quickly and quietly they found their way to the vaults; opened them noiselessly with the special passkeys each had brought with him. Like clockwork, with split-second timing, each went to his appointed spot, picked up a bag and walked out as calmly as he had entered. At the exits the guards sat motionless. At precisely 12:04 it was all over. Each of the "visitors" had vanished into thin air.

So had forty billion dollars from the United States Treasury.

Who are these "visitors"? How did they get their passkeys? How much did each get? And why did no one try to stop them? That is the story of "The Great Treasury Raid."

The GREAT TREASURY RAID/

33765

by Philip M. Stern

Random House · New York

Some of the material in this book first appeared in the following publications: *Harper's Magazine, The New Republic, The New York Times Magazine, The New York Herald Tribune, The Washington Post, The Progressive.*

For Leni

Preface

During the past year, while writing this book, I have often characterized it, half-seriously and half-facetiously, as an effort to make the subject of tax "loopholes" intelligible to my wife.

My interest in trying to simplify this eye-glazing subject began, however, some years before she and I met. It began in the fall of 1951, when a group of political liberals in the United States Senate, led by Minnesota's Hubert Humphrey, made a concerted, though thoroughly unavailing, assault on tax "loopholes." As a research assistant to one member of that group, Senator Paul H. Douglas of Illinois, I peered for the first time into that dark and tangled jungle, the Internal Revenue Code. As I sat in the Senate chamber beside Senator Douglas during the nine days of that remarkable debate, I was introduced to the world of corporation "spin-offs" . . . two-for-one offsets . . . the "one-way-street" provision . . . net operating loss carrybacks . . . collapsible corporations.

As I listened, fascinated and bewildered by the jargon, I

was struck by the fact that the public must be almost wholly unaware of what was going on in the Senate chamber— unaware that the provisions being considered, and the tax favors being dispensed, involved millions, tens of millions, sometimes hundreds of millions of dollars. (As Harvard law professor Stanley S. Surrey* wrote in 1957, tax decisions "are largely fought out behind [a] technical curtain" that is "impenetrable to the newspapers and other information media.") Not only was the general public screened off from this debate; most of the senators seemed to have thrown up their hands in helplessness, abdicating tax decisions to the experts on the tax-writing committees.

This was in the period when, it was said, the Senate's tax policy was largely made by two men: Senator Walter George of Georgia and Senator Eugene Millikin of Colorado, each his party's ranking member of the Senate Finance Committee (which handles tax matters), each expert in tax matters—but neither man kindly disposed to the Treasury Department's efforts to tighten up tax preferences and prevent the creation of new ones. When they frowned on a Treasury proposal, the Senate frowned too. But when Senator George looked with favor on a provision to grant $2 million of special tax relief to movie magnate Louis B. Mayer (as he did that year—see Chapter 3), there were none to gainsay him. (Even the Humphrey band of tax rebels was unaware that the Mayer provision was nestled in the very bill they were criticizing.)

Nowhere, then, is the aphorism "knowledge is power" more graphically validated than in the writing of the tax laws. And because the knowledge is held by so few, so is the power.

It is generally supposed that the major "loopholes" are immutably imbedded in the tax laws. Congress' mauling of the Kennedy Administration's "loophole-closing" proposals in 1963 did nothing to shake that supposition, and the prospects are not likely to change, I believe, so long as millions of highly non-

---

* Since 1961 the Treasury Department's top tax official.

expert citizens like my wife remain unaware of who-gets-what-
from-whom—and also who suffers—because of the "loopholes."

Hence, this effort to make the subject intelligible. In the
process, however, I have tried not to gloss over the often painfully close questions of judgment involved in tax policy. This
is no field for quick, black-and-white portraits or judgments,
and I have tried to present the principal arguments on both
sides. Yet, while I have sought to give the reader a basis for
arriving at his own judgments, I have made no effort to disguise my own viewpoint.

The Great Treasury Raid is concerned with departures from
the uniform taxation of individual Americans. It deals, therefore, almost exclusively with the federal individual income
tax, very little with corporate, excise or other forms of taxation.
It purposely by-passes the question of whether government
spending is too high or too low, as well as the merits or demerits
of government deficits or surpluses. Nor does it debate whether
tax rates should be graduated (i.e., higher at higher income
levels—which I, personally, strongly favor) or flat—equal for
all incomes. This book takes the view that once Congress decides how much revenue should be raised, and adopts a rate
schedule of tax rates to achieve its goal, those rates should
be applied as uniformly as possible to all citizens.

Those who wish to lessen or eliminate their tax burden may
do so in two ways. They might practice tax *evasion;* but this
is not only inadvisable—since it is illegal and carries heavy
penalties—but quite unnecessary, since the same tax reductions
can usually be achieved entirely within the law, through what
is known as the art of tax avoidance. Tax evasion consists of
such transgressions as failing to file a tax return, deliberately
failing to report certain income, falsely claiming dependents,
or any other deliberate falsehood in the preparation of one's
tax return. On the other hand, tax avoidance, with which this

book is almost exclusively concerned, simply consists of arranging one's activities or investments so as to take advantage of the provisions of the tax law itself, and thereby reduce one's tax burden. (Some have called it "do-it-yourself tax-cutting.")

Tax avoidance sounds more sinister than it is. For example, putting one's money into state or municipal bonds (whose interest payments are tax-free) instead of federal bonds (interest taxable) could be considered tax avoidance. So might an investment in a no-dividend "growth" stock, in the hope of a large and lightly-taxed, capital gain, rather than investing in a high-dividend, but stably priced stock.

Some wonder if there is always a meaningful difference between avoidance and evasion,* but the courts have clearly held that no moral opprobrium should attach to tax avoidance within the law. As Judge Learned Hand once observed:

> . . . there is nothing sinister in so arranging one's affairs as to keep taxes as low as possible. Everybody does so, rich or poor; and all do right. Nobody owes any public duty to pay more than the law demands: taxes are enforced exactions, not voluntary contributions. To demand more in the name of morals is mere cant.

Senator Pat Harrison of Mississippi, former chairman of the Senate Finance Committee expressed it simply: "There's nothing that says a man has to take a toll bridge across a river when there's a free bridge nearby."

No criticism is intended in this book of taxpayers who avail themselves of these tax-saving features of the law, as Congress clearly intended they should;† indeed, I do so myself. It is at

---

* Ex-lawyer David T. Bazelon, in his book *The Paper Economy*, points out, for example, that frequently the law is so ill-defined that taxpayers are prompted to try "a whole passel of maneuvers which turn out to be avoidance or evasion only after the fact."

† Some have said, only half-facetiously, that when Congress enacts a tax concession for the purpose, say, of stimulating the economy, citizens are derelict in their duty if they fail to carry out Congress' intent—i.e. if they fail to exploit the tax concession to the hilt.

the law itself that fingers should be pointed, not at those who
follow it.

For experts and practitioners, the field of taxation is already
brightly illuminated by a massive amount of technical literature
which leaves me both humble and awed, and to which I do not
pretend to have added new knowledge. But for the average
citizen, this field is as dimly lit as any in the realm of public
affairs. This book is addressed to those who may have cursed
the darkness.

PHILIP M. STERN

WASHINGTON, D. C.
SEPTEMBER, 1963

---

*NOTE: The numerical illustrations and references to tax rates
in this book are based on the rates in effect before Congress
began consideration of a major rate change in 1963. Under any
new rate schedule, while the figures in the numerical illustrations would change somewhat, except where noted the principles would remain the same.*

Contents

1. The Tax Deviates   3

Who are the "tax deviates"? Five Americans with
incomes of over $5 million—yet paying no tax . . .
17 Americans with incomes over one million . . . one
with a $20 million income one year—yet paying no
tax . . . another multimillionaire who has not had to
pay a penny of tax since 1949. But the poor are "tax
deviates" too—they pay only half what the tax rates
seem to call for. *Why* the "tax deviates"? Because of
tax "loopholes"—tax preferences which, all told, cost
the Treasury $40 billion a year.

2. Ah, To Be an Oil Man   17

How can multimillionaires pay no taxes, year after
year? How can corporations with profits in the tens
of millions not only pay no taxes but receive tax
refunds? How can an oil man's chauffeur be worth
$17 million at his death? The reason: special tax

deductions for nonexistent investments, not only for oil and gas, but for about eighty-five other minerals (including oyster shells and clam shells)—all costing the American taxpayers nearly $2 billion every year.

3. *Ah, To Be Louis B. Mayer* 44

If you know the right congressman or senator—or the right lobbyist—you can have your own made-to-order tax-relief provision written into the law of the land, tailored to your own particular specifications (movie magnate Louis B. Mayer did it; why not you?). While it won't have your name or initials on it, your private provision can save you millions in taxes (Louis B. Mayer's saved him $2 million).

4. *Your Wife May Be Worth a Million* 62

Most husbands are probably ungratefully unaware of the true value—cash value, that is—of their wife. Chances are, too, that most wives are underselling themselves. But, thanks to a fiction in the tax law, a wife can be worth as much as $7 million! Infant children can also be useful as tax-savers. Some have even been made full-fledged business partners with their parents when they were only hours old.

5. *The Great Capital Gains Trial* 81

In the case of *People v. The Capital Gains Tax,* the "prosecutor" seeks to prove the 25 percent capital gains tax guilty of adding more unfairness and complexity than any other feature of the tax law. At the least, it produces some ridiculous results—including a special provision bestowing the favorable tax rate on Christmas trees! All told, nearly $20 *billion* wholly escapes taxation every year because of the capital gains tax.

6. Living High at the Taxpayers' Expense

108

Tax-deductible African safaris may be a thing of the past, and tax-supported yachts and hunting lodges may be more difficult to put on the "swindle sheet" since a 1962 law tightened up on expense-account entertaining. Even so, a lot of high living can still be partly charged to Uncle Sam—*if* you're among the lucky one-in-ten who has an expense account.

7. How "Show Biz" Wards Off the Tax Collector

126

For decades, Hollywood celebrities and the Internal Revenue Service have frequently found themselves eyeball to eyeball as show business luminaries have fought to keep their prodigious incomes from vanishing into the U.S. Treasury. Among their favorite techniques: the "collapsible corporation" . . . the "incorporated pocketbook" . . . and, of all things, cattle raising.

8. How To Get Rich Quick in Real Estate—With Uncle Sam's Help

143

Step into the Orwellian world of real estate "tax shelters," where profits become losses (on tax returns) and losses are highly profitable. Example: One company had $5 million cash profit, but reported a $1.7 million tax *loss*! The technique is simple: "fast write-offs" of buildings against 91 percent top-bracket rates . . . a quick sale, with profits taxed at only 25 percent . . . it's heads the taxpayer wins, tails the government loses.

9. Missing: $5 Billion

161

Through carelessness, ignorance, inadvertence—and, sometimes, a little cheating—$25 billion that should be listed on tax returns goes unreported every year. Cost to the Treasury: about $5 billion—enough to allow a ten percent tax cut for every taxpayer, *if* the

missing billions could all be found and collected.
Most of it can't be, but soon electronic sleuths working twenty-four hours a day (no coffee breaks) and
able to read 6½ million characters a minute will be
catching many a slip that now goes unnoticed.

10. *The Favored Few*   179

You will be surprised (or shocked) to learn how few
Americans make more than $10,000 or $25,000 or
$50,000 a year. Yet these "Favored Few" are the
main beneficiaries of tax preferences that cost the
Treasury hundreds of millions—even billions—every
year: items like tax-free bonds, stock options and the
preferential taxation of corporate dividends which
saves the average millionaire $40,000 a year.

11. *The Favored Many*   205

The rich and powerful have no monopoly on tax
preferences. The aged, the blind, veterans, home
owners, factory workers—all bask in the warmth of
one tax preference—or several. Hardly anyone
questions these tax boons to the Favored Many—
even though their annual cost comes to $25 billion.

12. *Some Moral Preachments of Our Tax Laws*   230

Do you believe that repairing a dented fender is
more important than fixing a broken arm? Or that
people should be discouraged from educating themselves for a better job? Or that they should be encouraged to go into debt rather than live within their
means? Or that people who work for a living are less
deserving than those who don't? Well, all those conclusions are in our tax laws—although not, of
course, in so many words.

**13. *'Tis More Blessed To Give—If You Work It
Right***   238

The way the law works—or, more accurately, the

way many taxpayers work the law—the charitable giver often turns out to be more blessed than the receiving charity. For instance, privately controlled "charitable" foundations have enabled their donors to keep control of companies and win corporate proxy fights. Art collectors have "given away" their paintings—but kept them for life. In fact, it is actually possible to *make* money by giving money away.

14. Tax Precautions To Take Before You Die   251

The estate or death tax is supposed to be "the great leveler"—that is, in theory it's supposed to break up the great fortunes as they pass from one generation to another. But the well-advised leave their money tax-free to their wives, or give it to their heirs (at cut rates) while still alive—or even manage to skip whole generations of estate taxes. Result: Behind the seemingly sharp bite of the estate tax rates lies a surprisingly docile bark.

15. Old "Loopholes" Never Die, They Just Get Bigger   267

In taxes, "equity" has been defined as "the privilege of paying as little as someone else." Thus, once a loophole has been granted one group, it becomes "inequitable" to deny it to other groups. Result: Loopholes are not only virtually imperishable; they enlarge with age. Example: Percentage depletion was once confined to oil and gas; now it covers sand and gravel, oyster shells and clam shells, ornamental stone—and flower pot clay.

16. The Heavy Odds Against Tax Reform   277

Judging by the regularity with which "loophole-closing" is spurned by Congress, the deck appears stacked against reform. Among the cards in the deck: inarticulate and diffuse pro-reform forces arrayed against highly focused, intensely vocal anti-

reform forces . . . the tax-writing power tightly held
by two carefully chosen congressional committees
. . . a complex tax law that baffles the general
public and endows the pressure groups and experts
with unusual power.

*17. What Should Be Done About "The Great
Treasury Raid"?*   300

The approach of putting partial-reform patches over
an already leaky tire hasn't worked. If there is a
hope of tax reform, it may lie in starting over with
an entirely new tire—in a simplified, broadly-based
system which taxes *all* income—but at rates about
half as high as the pre-1964 rates.

Appendix

   Acknowledgments   317
   Glossary   320
   Notes and Sources   328

Index   353

The Great Treasury Raid

"The Congress shall have the power to lay and collect taxes on incomes, from whatever source derived . . ."

—Article XVI, Amendments to the Constitution of the United States

SEC. 1. TAX IMPOSED.

[Sec. 1(a)]

(a) RATES OF TAX ON INDIVIDUALS.—A tax is hereby imposed for each taxable year on the taxable income of every individual other than a head of a household to whom subsection (b) applies. The amount of the tax shall be determined in accordance with the following table:

If the taxable income is:	The tax is:
Not over $2,000	20% of the taxable income.
Over $ 2,000 but not over $ 4,000	$ 400, plus 22% of excess over $ 2,000.
Over $ 4,000 but not over $ 6,000	$ 840, plus 26% of excess over $ 4,000.
Over $ 6,000 but not over $ 8,000	$ 1,360, plus 30% of excess over $ 6,000.
Over $ 8,000 but not over $ 10,000	$ 1,960, plus 34% of excess over $ 8,000.
Over $ 10,000 but not over $ 12,000	$ 2,640, plus 38% of excess over $ 10,000.
Over $ 12,000 but not over $ 14,000	$ 3,400, plus 43% of excess over $ 12,000.
Over $ 14,000 but not over $ 16,000	$ 4,260, plus 47% of excess over $ 14,000.
Over $ 16,000 but not over $ 18,000	$ 5,200, plus 50% of excess over $ 16,000.
Over $ 18,000 but not over $ 20,000	$ 6,200, plus 53% of excess over $ 18,000.
Over $ 20,000 but not over $ 22,000	$ 7,260, plus 56% of excess over $ 20,000.
Over $ 22,000 but not over $ 26,000	$ 8,380, plus 59% of excess over $ 22,000.
Over $ 26,000 but not over $ 32,000	$ 10,740, plus 62% of excess over $ 26,000.
Over $ 32,000 but not over $ 38,000	$ 14,460, plus 65% of excess over $ 32,000.
Over $ 38,000 but not over $ 44,000	$ 18,360, plus 69% of excess over $ 38,000.
Over $ 44,000 but not over $ 50,000	$ 22,500, plus 72% of excess over $ 44,000.
Over $ 50,000 but not over $ 60,000	$ 26,820, plus 75% of excess over $ 50,000.
Over $ 60,000 but not over $ 70,000	$ 34,320, plus 78% of excess over $ 60,000.
Over $ 70,000 but not over $ 80,000	$ 42,120, plus 81% of excess over $ 70,000.
Over $ 80,000 but not over $ 90,000	$ 50,220, plus 84% of excess over $ 80,000.
Over $ 90,000 but not over $100,000	$ 58,620, plus 87% of excess over $ 90,000.
Over $100,000 but not over $150,000	$ 67,320, plus 89% of excess over $100,000.
Over $150,000 but not over $200,000	$111,820, plus 90% of excess over $150,000.
Over $200,000	$156,820, plus 91% of excess over $200,000.

SOURCE: Sec. 11(a), 1939 Code.

—Section 1(a), The Internal Revenue Code of 1954, as amended

1 / The Tax Deviates

For a moment, examine the Sixteenth Amendment to the Constitution and the first section of the tax law of the United States* as if you were a visitor from a distant and isolated land, unfamiliar with the ways of American government and politics. To your untutored eye, these laws must appear severe indeed, providing for taking no less than a fifth of even the poorest man's earnings, "from whatever source derived," and for taking as much as 85 or 90 percent of a wealthy man's income. Your uninitiated scrutiny of the rate table leads you to believe that everyone with incomes of $2,000 or less pays 20 percent taxes. And, computing beyond the upper reaches of the rate schedule, you conclude, with a shudder, that everyone with a $500,000 income pays 78 percent of it in taxes, and that if a person

---

* This is the rate schedule in effect prior to Congress' consideration of a major rate change in 1963, i.e., the rates that were in effect when the various phenomena described in this chapter took place.

somehow managed to have $5,000,000 of income, more than 90 percent of it would go to the government.

So much for your visitor's view. Now look at the world as it *really* is.

In the real world:

—Five Americans in 1959 had incomes of more than $5,000,-000, and paid—not 90 or even 78 percent, but zero taxes. No taxes at all.*

—One American enjoyed an income of nearly $20 million in a recent year—and paid no taxes.

—Another, whose annual income has been close to $2 million in recent years, has not had to pay a penny of income tax since 1949.

—In 1961, seventeen Americans had incomes of $1,000,000 or more, and paid not a cent of it to the Treasury. Thirty-five persons had incomes of $500,000 or more, yet paid no taxes.

—A lawyer in Alexandria, Virginia, made out his own tax return and that of a wealthy client one April, and discovered that his client had six times as much income as he, and paid one-fifth as much tax.

—In 1960, a real estate corporation in New York had a "net cash return available for distribution to stockholders" of over $5,000,000, yet paid no taxes. In fact, on its tax return it showed a *loss* of over $1,750,000.

—A Mrs. Horace Dodge put her entire $56 million auto-fortune legacy into tax-free bonds, and thus was in a position to enjoy over $1,500,000 of yearly income *without even reporting it on her tax return.*

Not everyone with a $5 million income was as fortunate as the happy five who paid no taxes. There were, in 1960, thirty-seven people whose total incomes, including their presently untaxed capital gains, came to more than $5 million. Yet although the rate schedule, as viewed through an unpracticed

---

* Sources for these and other statistics, quotations and statements may be found in the Appendix.

eye, seems to call for them to pay more than a 90 percent tax, in fact these thirty-seven paid, on the average, *a little less than 25 percent tax.*

And although Section 1(a) calls for them to pay a far greater share of their income to the government than those with smaller incomes, they actually paid *less than half* as much in taxes, proportionately, as those with about one-tenth the total income.

The Sixteenth Amendment to the Constitution empowers Congress to tax all income, "from whatever source derived." Yet in 1960, Americans had total incomes of $400 billion, *but paid taxes on less than half of it.* Moreover, the average rate of tax on the half they *did* pay taxes on was little higher than the *lowest*-bracket rate of 20 percent.

Clearly, there are striking deviations between the real world and the uninitiated visitor's view of the Sixteenth Amendment as well as Section 1(a) of the Revenue Code.

Why these deviations? Because of the "tax deviates."

Let no one take offense—we are all tax deviates, to a greater or lesser degree. Every one of us; the richest and the poorest.

To illustrate, compare what the rate schedule in Section 1(a) seems to call for with what was actually paid in taxes in 1960:

The wealthy are obviously far more successful "tax deviates" than the less well-to-do.* While those in the under-five-thousand-dollar group pay, on the average, about *half* what the rate schedule calls for, *those in the over-five-million-dollar group typically pay about one-fourth what the rate schedule provides.*

---

* They are helped in this respect by the fact that the expenses involved in becoming accomplished "tax deviates" (i.e., their fees to tax lawyers and accountants) are themselves tax-deductible. Thus, not only is the Treasury obliged to accept the deprivations of revenue involved in tax avoidance; it is obliged to underwrite part of the cost that makes this possible!

TAKES AS PERCENT OF INCOME*

Income Group	Due per rate schedule	Actually paid
Under $5,000	20.7%	9.0%
$5–10,000	23.7	11.0
$10–20,000	29.4	14.8
$20–50,000	44.1	21.8
$50–100,000	60.8	31.1
$100–150,000	73.6	34.6
$200–500,000	84.1	33.3
$500,000–$1,000,000	88.6	31.1
$1,000,000 and over	90.1	32.3
$5,000,000 and over	90.7	24.6

The comparative dollar savings from being a "tax deviate" are also striking: the average under-five-thousand-dollar taxpayer saves $274. The average multimillionaire taxpayer saves $5,990,181.

A visitor from, say, Shangri-La might expect that persons with like income would pay like taxes, regardless of the source of their income. Yet here are four real-world men, each holding in his hand his entire year's income—$7,000.

Albert's $7,000 was earned over a year's time in a steel mill. Albert pays $1,282 in taxes.†

Bert's work was less strenuous: he just watched $7,000 in dividends from his corporation stock flow into his bank account. His tax is $992.30.

Charles merely picked up the telephone, told his broker to sell some stock and netted a $7,000 profit. Charles' tax: $526.

David's $7,000 came from interest on his state and local bonds. He paid no tax at all.

---

* "Income" includes presently untaxed capital gains, but does *not* include tax free interest on state and local bonds. Other notes on this table may be found in the Appendix.

† Under the pre-1964 rates.

And here are several other noteworthy gentlemen:

Edward and Frank each have one dependent: Edward supports a young bride, Frank, an aged aunt in a nursing home. A tax break enjoyed by wealthy newly-wed Edward is wholly denied the impecunious and celibate Frank.

George, sixty-five, is still active as a high-paid corporate executive and going strong; Henry, sixty-four, is in ill health and can't find work. George gets a tax concession (because he is sixty-five); Henry does not.

Isador, who grows and sells grain, pays more taxes than Jerome, who grows and sells Christmas trees. Ken, a poultry raiser, bears a heavier tax burden than Leon, a livestock raiser.

Mike and Norman have equally fertile imaginations. Mike's produces a major novel, Norman's a new macaroni maker, each of which sells for $300,000. Mike pays three times the tax Norman pays.

How do they do it? How do the under-$5,000 taxpayers manage to pay 9 percent instead of the 20 percent called for by the rate schedule? More intriguing, how do the multimillionaires succeed in paying less than 25 percent instead of 90? How, above all, does one person contrive to have nearly $20 million of income and pay no taxes at all? How, in short, does one go about becoming a tax deviate?

Well, there are several approved techniques. You can take advantage of the special oil deductions (Chapter 2); or split your income into separate, more lightly-taxed bundles (Chapter 4); revel in the glories of the favorable 25 percent capital gains rate (Chapter 5); incorporate yourself, and protect your income behind a corporate shield (Chapter 7, pp. 126–142); seek refuge in the warmth of a real estate "tax shelter" (Chapter 8); give paintings and other risen-value possessions to charity (Chapter 13); or—if you have proper access to a congressman (or lobbyist)—you can even have a tax-relief provision tailored to your very own specifications (Chapter 3).

Apparently, the techniques are being sharpened to an ever-increasing efficacy. Until 1955, none of those fortunate Americans with incomes of $1 million and over avoided taxes entirely. In 1955, however, there were four who managed to pay no taxes; and in succeeding years, the number of un-taxed millionaires has gone up steadily, to six in 1957, then to eight, then to fifteen, back down to eleven in 1960 (evidently a bad year for millionaires), and then up to seventeen in 1961.

Whatever the techniques used, though, it all boils down to this: you become a tax deviate by using tax "loopholes."

But what *is* a tax "loophole"? Many regard the oil depletion allowance as a "loophole"; but rest assured the oil industry and Texas oil millionaires do not. To the Eisenhower Administration, the dividend tax relief enacted in 1954 (see p. 197) was a long-needed reform; but to the Kennedy Administration, it was a "discriminatory and inequitable" tax concession. The National Tax Equality Association is certain that farm (and other) co-operatives enjoy a "loophole," but the Co-operative League of the U.S.A. is equally sure no "loophole" exists.

Is a "loophole," then, simply a provision a particular person doesn't happen to approve of (or doesn't happen to be able to use himself)? And what about a provision such as the tax deduction for charitable contributions that enjoys virtually universal approval? It costs the Treasury $2½ billion a year— is *it* a "loophole"?

To atone for its shortcomings, the word "loophole" has been sentenced, in this book, to live within quotation marks, and to defer to the term "tax preference"—preferences as viewed from the lowly and unhappy position of the most unpreferred and helpless taxpayers in America: the 7,192,100 unmarried persons who, in 1961, filed a "short-form" tax return. As a group, they come closest to paying the Section 1(a) tax rates, and there is little or nothing they can do about it.

A thumb-nail sketch of the typical unmarried "short-form" filer will show why:

His average income: $2902.77. Maximum income: $10,000.

Occupation: wage earner (or salaried worker) with virtually
no income outside what he earns on the job—no dividends, no
interest, no capital gains. He probably doesn't own his own
home; if he does, he gets no tax advantage from his mortgage
interest payments—*or* his medical expenses *or* his weekly contributions to his church, for that matter—since he does not
itemize his tax deductions. Instead, he contents himself with
the 10 percent standard deduction. But, aside from this and
the $600 personal exemption, he pays the taxes an unenlightened
visitor would expect, looking at Section 1(a) of the tax code.
Being unmarried, he is, of course, denied the more favorable
tax rates that come with filing a joint return.

When April 15 rolls around, no amount of fancy pencil work
or burning of the midnight oil can help him. He can't even
capitalize on the frailty of human memory in forgetting to
report those little odds and ends of dividend or interest income
that dribbled in through the year: his income has long since
been reported and his taxes withheld from his paycheck, week
by week—spirited away without his ever even seeing the
money. (Chances are, in fact, that too much was spirited away,
and he must depend on a government refund to set matters
right.)

Thus, as he and the other 7,192,099 like him see it, everything other than the personal exemption and the 10 percent
standard deduction is a "tax preference," and will be considered
such in this book. Even the standard deduction will come in
for some close questioning. Yet although our unmarried short-
form filer is comparatively unpreferenced by our tax system,
even he is not wholly unprivileged. He may receive some income he doesn't even have to report on his tax return, such as,
for example, his social security, veterans' or other government
benefits, or fringe benefits from his employer.

All of us are acutely sensitive to the cost of government outlays. There is always a slight shock (even though we have heard
the figures often) that the farm program costs $3 billion or

that defense costs $50 billion or the space program $4–5 billion. The annual repetition of these colossal expenditures makes us all too painfully mindful of them—year in and year out.

Each tax preference has *its* price tag, too: if the preference didn't exist, the Treasury would collect more revenue. Thus, each is a drain on the Treasury in just the same way as the farm or defense or foreign aid programs, and ought to be judged like any spending program—not only by the supposed benefits it produces, but also by its cost to the Treasury, *which is to say, its cost to all of us as taxpayers.*

This last point is crucial and too often overlooked. There is a lamentable tendency to regard the Treasury as some alien entity, and to slide over the fact that *when someone else pays less, the rest of us pay more.*

Well, you may say, when the cost is spread around among forty-eight million taxpayers, how much does it mean to each? A few cents—a few dollars, perhaps; not more.

But the cost *isn't* spread evenly among all taxpayers. Those who enjoy the fewest tax preferences—mainly wage earners and salaried professionals (teachers, doctors, lawyers)—bear the brunt.

Even more important, when you put all the tax preferences together, instead of considering them one by one, the cost isn't just a few cents or dollars per person. All together, these tax preferences are costing the United States Treasury—that is, costing all of us—*forty billion dollars a year* (see table, pp. 15–16).

If we eliminated all the preferences, we could reduce all tax rates by nearly half, and still raise the same amount of revenue. The final chapter of this book suggests a simplified, broadly-based income tax system in which the rates range from 11 percent to a maximum of 50 percent—in contrast to the 20- to 91-percent rates effective through 1963.

Thus, those who blame high tax rates exclusively on "excessive government spending" are, to a considerable extent, hissing the wrong villain. They should reserve at least some of their indignation for the prodigiously costly tax preferences. Those who so vocally extol the virtues of budget-balancing jealously safeguard each dollar of government outlays, but they are curiously silent about the $40 billion the Congress is indirectly "spending" through tax concessions. Were they to scrutinize the *income* side of the federal ledger with the same gimlet eye they reserve for the *outflow* side, tax reform might gain some new evangelists.

But they don't; and the leakages in the tax system are not only just as costly as direct outlays; they are far more pernicious, for the price tags are tucked inside the merchandise where they can't readily be seen. The farm subsidy, for example, has a public price tag ($2,851,657,000 in Fiscal 1963— anyone can find it on page 133 of the Budget of the United States); the oil subsidy program* does not. Year after year, this oil subsidy costs the Treasury a billion and a half dollars —although you can't find the billion and a half in the Budget; it isn't there.

The farm subsidy is combed over, attacked, defended and debated in Congress every year. The appropriations committees would never dream of according automatic, annual, rubberstamp approval to such a multi-billion dollar subsidy program. Yet this is precisely the effect of congressional *in*action on the depletion subsidy.

If Congress should fail to act on the farm subsidy appropriation in any year, the program would die. But when Congress fails to act on the *oil* subsidy, it is perpetuated because it's in the permanent tax law.

And so long as a tax preference is in the law, the decision as to its annual cost is largely out of Congress' hands. Who decides the cost? The taxpayers who choose to avail themselves of the provision. Many is the preference whose cost at first was innocently low but later ballooned. For example, the deduction

---

* Via the depletion allowance described in Chapter 2.

for interest payments, adopted in the original 1913 law, doubt-less cost, then, a few million dollars at most. Today it drains nearly $3 *billion* a year from the Treasury.

Of course, cost is only one element in assessing any govern-ment effort. If benefits outweigh cost, then clearly the price is right. But does the oil subsidy program, for example, give us taxpayers our billion-and-a-half money's worth? We are told, for example, that the subsidy is needed to encourage people to take risks and explore for oil. But when we are deliberately keeping out foreign oil and deliberately holding Texas oil wells to less than 30 percent of capacity, do we really need to spend a billion and a half a year to encourage finding more? And if the purpose of the subsidy is to encourage risk-taking, why give part of it to the passive land owner who risks nothing while others drill on his land? (Alas, there is no annual, or even regular periodic, occasion when questions such as this may be asked.)

And what of the tax concessions we grant the aged? They may ease our conscience, but do they provide the relief we think they do? What does our conscience say to the fact that *these tax concessions grant no help to four-fifths of all the elderly*—those whose incomes are so low as to be nontaxable in any event? Like so many tax concessions, these are upside-down subsidies: they are wholly denied the neediest, but their value goes up as income rises and need declines.

Each tax preference or subsidy comes complete with its own built-in justification. We are solemnly assured that this con-cession or that is urgently needed to, for instance, stimulate the economy; to create an "incentive" for—or, perhaps, remove a deterrent from—some publicly beneficial activity (such as exploring for oil or giving to charity); to relieve a "hardship" (when coal royalty contracts unforesightedly failed to allow for rising coal prices, a "hardship" was created and tax relief accordingly bestowed); or to correct an "inequity" (but, as you

will find in the chapter, "Old 'Loopholes' Never Die, They
Just Get Bigger," equity, in taxes, as Congress sees it, is "the
privilege of paying as little as somebody else"). These, of
course, are just the major stops on the organ, and they may
be played singly, in combination, or with almost infinite variations when background music is needed for the granting of a
tax preference.

Some uncharitable observers have been unkind enough to
suggest that these explanations—frequently technical and
complex—merely serve to becloud the real purpose of tax
preferences: to wit, lessening the tax burden of a select and
favored group of taxpayers. Tax concessions, these skeptics
argue, are nothing but a camouflaged flank attack on the steeply
graduated rate schedule of Section 1(a) of the tax law. The
oblique approach is used since a bold, frontal assault would
be too offensive to American economic folklore. The writers
of the tax laws, it is irreverently suggested, must at all costs
maintain appearances and satisfy the public that they are ap-
propriately soaking the excessively rich ("See the ninety-one
percent rate? Doesn't that prove it?"*) and redistributing their
income to those less well-fixed. All the while, though, it is
darkly contended, the tax writers are systematically undermin-
ing the steep rate schedule *in ways the public can not readily
understand*.

Perhaps this is an excessively harsh view of the *motives* of
those who fashion the tax laws, but not of the *effect* of what
they have done, as the table on page 15 eloquently confirms.
While the pre-1964 rates may seem, to the uninitiated, to ascend
to an over-all "tax-take" of 90 percent, in practice they only
manage to climb to 35 percent—little more than one third of
their supposed height—*and then, for the very wealthiest, drop*

---

* Curiously enough, when the Republicans finally gained control of the
White House and Congress, after two decades of out-of-power invectives
against "confiscatory" tax rates, they only lowered the top-bracket rate
from 92 to 91 percent.

back to less than 25 percent. Our tax rates, in short, bark far more sharply than they bite.

In some circles it is not thought polite to talk or think about taxes as a vulgar clash of groups or classes, or to mention the fact that one man's "loophole" is another man's cross—that when A pays less, B pays more. Yet that is the essence of the matter. As tax attorney Louis Eisenstein has felicitously observed,* taxes "are a changing product of the earnest efforts to have others pay them."

In 1895, defending the constitutionality of the income tax before the Supreme Court, Attorney James C. Carter put it this way:

> In every community those who feel the burdens of taxation are naturally prone to relieve themselves from it if they can . . . One class struggles to throw the burden off its own shoulders. If they succeed, of course, it must fall upon others. They also, in their turn, labor to get rid of it, and finally the load falls upon those who will not, or cannot, make a successful effort for relief.

He then went on to say:

> This is, in general, a one-sided struggle, in which the rich only engage, and . . . in which the poor always go to the wall.

Whether Carter, speaking nearly seventy years ago, was prophetically correct, you are invited to judge for yourself through the pages that follow.

---

* In his delightful book, *The Ideologies of Taxation.* Copyright © 1961 The Ronald Press Company, New York.

THE HIGH COST OF TAX PREFERENCES

These items . . .	*"Shrink" the tax base by . . .* (Billion dollars)	*. . . And cost the U.S. Treasury* (Billion dollars)
EXEMPTIONS*		
Extra exemptions for the aged and blind	$ 3.2	$ .9
EXCLUSIONS (Income not reported on tax return)		
Government payments (social security, unemployment and veterans' benefits, etc.)	11.9	3.6
Rent equivalent on owned homes	6.5	2.0
Fringe benefits	9.0	3.0
Interest on tax-free bonds	2.0	1.0
Interest on life insurance savings	1.5	.4
Sick pay and dividend exclusions	.9	.3
PERSONAL DEDUCTIONS		
Itemized deductions	43.0	11.9
Standard deduction	12.0	2.6
BUSINESS DEDUCTIONS		
Depletion deductions (corporations included)	3.7	1.5
Intangible drilling deductions (oil and gas)	——	.5
Travel & entertainment (estimated "excesses")	——	.3
Real estate depreciation	——	.2

* Sources for figures appear in the Appendix. Explanations of many of the terms may be found in the Glossary.

THE HIGH COST OF TAX PREFERENCES

These items . . .	*"Shrink" the tax base by . . .* (Billion dollars)	*. . . And cost the U.S. Treasury* (Billion dollars)
TAX CREDITS		
The dividend credit	—	.5
The retirement income credit	—	.1
CAPITAL GAINS		
The 50 percent of gains not reported on tax returns	6.0	2.4
The gains that escape tax at death	12-13	2.9
UNREPORTED INCOME		
Dividends and interest	3.7	.9
INCOME-SPLITTING FOR MARRIED COUPLES	—	5.0
T O T A L S	**$115 billion**	**$40 billion**

2 /

Ah, To Be an Oil Man

On March 15, 1945, American bombers blasted Hitler's headquarters, the RAF bombarded the Ruhr Valley, Tokyo was in a
panic because of U.S. fire bombs . . . and 4,000 Americans were
reported dead on Iwo Jima.

In the United States, it was income tax day, the deadline for
filing tax returns for the year 1944.

For Amanda Bailey, a $25-a-week charwoman in a California
defense plant, this meant little added work. Her $3.02 a week
had already been taken out of her paycheck. Her total 1944
earnings: $1,300. Her 1944 taxes: $157.00. Percent of her income
paid in taxes: 12.1 percent.

For J. Alton Shellborne, Houston oil investment advisor,
March 15, 1945, was even more painless. No fuss or bother (his
tax return was, of course, prepared by his accountant)—and,

more important, no tax. His total 1944 income: $2,035,000. His 1944 tax: zero. Percent of his income paid in taxes: zero.

For the Amerada Petroleum Company, the filing of a 1944 tax return was considerably less onerous than for most corporations struggling under the burden of the war-time excess profits tax. On the average, corporations that year paid 55 percent of their net profits in taxes. But not Amerada. Net profits for 1944: $5,511,000. Federal income tax: $225,000. Percent of net income paid in taxes: 4.1 percent.

While Amanda Bailey is a hypothetical character, the tax figures for her salary are real, and there were millions like her in World War II. In fact, so vast were the government's revenue needs that many making as little as $12 a week—half Amanda Bailey's pay—were paying taxes to help finance the war.

There is nothing hypothetical about Amerada Petroleum. It is a real company and the figures you have just read may be found in the 1945 issue of *Moody's Industrials*.

J. Alton Shellborne exists, too, and the figures about his $2,035,000 tax-free income are also real—taken from a Treasury Department case study, although the Treasury is legally forbidden to disclose his true identity.

Mr. Shellborne's $2 million of untaxed 1944 income was no one-year freak. In the succeeding three years, his income came to $1,703,000, $1,443,000 and $2,945,000, respectively—*yet in none of those years did he pay any federal income tax*. In fact, for the five years 1943 through 1947, his income totaled $10,583,000, and his taxes came to less than $44,000—4/10 of 1 percent of his income. (Amanda Bailey paid 12.1 percent of her 1944 income in taxes.) Another oil operator had income totaling $14,300,000 during that same period, only 6/10 of 1 percent of which went for taxes.

Nor are these feats strictly wartime phenomena. A recent Treasury study tells of a modern-day Shellborne, labeled Individual D, who in 1960 enjoyed *income* ("total reported economic income," in the Treasury's words) *of over $26 million** —*yet paid not a penny of federal income tax that year,* just as in at least two prior years (1957 and 1959). In fact, incredible as it may seem, his 1960 income tax return actually reported a *loss* of $846,330, much of which could be helpfully used to shield future-year income from taxation.

Another fortunate operator, identified as Mr. B, had total net income for the four years 1958 through 1960 of $9,419,000—*but paid no income taxes in any of those years.* Still another affluent gentleman managed to enjoy $5 million of income in one year without paying any taxes on it—including a full million of *non-oil* income. Finally, government officials tell of one oil and gas operator who had sold at least $50 million worth of oil in the last twelve years, whose income in the years 1958–60 was in excess of $5,500,000—*and who had not had to pay any income tax since 1949!*†

Nor was Amerada's 1944 good fortune an isolated, one-shot stroke of luck. The average tax paid by all U.S. corporations in 1961 was 49 percent of their net profits. By contrast, here is the percent paid in that same year by major U.S. oil companies, according to *Moody's Industrials*:

Texaco	13.2%
Sinclair	18.2%
Socony-Mobil	31.1%
Standard Oil (Cal.)	11.7%

Company W, an actual oil firm listed in another Treasury Department study, made profits of $65,700,000 in a six-year period —yet not only did the firm pay no income taxes, net; it actually got a $425,000 *refund* of previously paid taxes!

---

* See Appendix note.

† Such non-taxable oil operators enjoy a "fringe benefit." By contributing as little as $1 a year to charity they can make sure that if they ever wish to retire from the oil business, another avenue of total tax avoidance will await them (see p. 249).

Company A, over a fourteen-year period, had total profits of nearly $261 million. The average corporation would have paid taxes on such profits of around $130 million. But Company A is heavily in the oil business, so its actual tax bill was only $27 million. Thus, this single company enjoyed a total tax saving of over $100 million.

In 1957 U.S. corporations taken as a whole paid an average of 48.7 percent of their profits in federal and state taxes. But the large oil companies paid only 23.6 percent—less than half as much. *If these oil companies had paid the same taxes as the others, their tax bills would have been higher by one billion dollars in that year alone.*

Principal among the provisions of the U.S. tax laws that bring about such remarkable results is a feature known as "percentage depletion," which spares oil companies, oil investors and oil land and royalty owners the burden of paying *any* taxes on 27½ percent of their total oil income—or *half* the net profit from their respective oil properties, whichever is less.

In addition to this "depletion allowance," oil companies and investors are allowed large and immediate tax deductions of their so-called "intangible drilling expenses," in a manner not permitted other taxpayers. This has the effect of adding insult to the depletion injury suffered by the Treasury, for it permits oil investors, in effect, to use Uncle Sam's money to help them pyramid their oil holdings and *generate even more tax-favored income*. In fact, these special expense deductions played a far more powerful role than the depletion allowance in enabling J. Alton Shellborne to enjoy a $2,035,000 tax-free income at the height of World War II.

Percentage depletion also applies to more than eighty-five other minerals (ranging from sulphur, coal and iron ore to flower pot clay, ornamental stone and oyster and clam shells), but since about 83 percent of the depletion benefits emanate from oil and gas, this chapter will deal almost exclusively with them.

Percentage depletion alone costs the Treasury an estimated $1.5 billion per year. In addition, the special "intangible drilling expense" deductions cost several hundred million dollars a year, so the total annual cost of the tax preferences enjoyed by the mineral industries exceeds $2 billion.

This prodigious drain on the federal Treasury is frequently defended as an indispensable incentive to the costly and high-risk exploration for oil and gas. Some find this argument less than convincing in view of the deliberate policy of restricting Texas oil wells to less than 30 percent of their production capacity,* and, more especially, in view of the acknowledgement by a leading depletion *proponent* that we already "have enough oil" to meet our "requirements for the next hundred years," not to mention the "potential fuel in the known [oil] shale reserves [sufficient] to last this nation a thousand years."

Take booming industries such as oil and gas; add some lucrative tax advantages. The result: some spectacularly rich Americans.

For example, oil and its tax favors are largely responsible for the wealth of J. Paul Getty, who once estimated the worth of his holdings at several billion dollars, but then added, "But remember, a billion dollars isn't worth what it used to be."

Oil and its tax advantages—together with a borrowed $50 for a broken down drilling rig and some outstanding help from Lady Luck—raised H. L. Hunt from a barber-ranch hand-lumber jack to an oil tycoon worth between $2 and $3 billion. His income is estimated at roughly a million dollars a week.

The late Hugh Roy Cullen, who once worked in a San Antonio candy shop, later came to express his generosity and exuberance in grandiose fashion, presenting the University of Houston with a personal gift of $100,000,000. Originally, that was all he intended to give. But when the University scored an

---

* The regulation of oil production sprang originally from considerations of conservation, and also serves the purpose of allocating production evenly among all wells. But basically, the 30 percent production rate is set by the *demand* for oil.

upset football victory over Baylor, the elated Mr. Cullen added a "bonus" check of $2,225,000.

In 1958, two fabled oil multimillionaires—Clint Murchison and Sid Richardson—teamed up to contribute $20 million to help Robert R. Young gain control of the New York Central Railroad. Later it developed that there had been a misunderstanding on Richardson's part. He had thought the deal was for $5 million each instead of $10 million. He called up his partner, not to berate him for the $5 million misunderstanding, but simply to inquire, "Say, Clint, what was the name of that railroad?"*

In New Orleans, Dr. Martin Miller conducted a quiet practice of surgery and a side practice of investing in oil—so shrewdly that his income was once estimated at between $7 and $8 million a year according to *Fortune*.

In oil, there is plenty of money to go around. The chauffeur of oil man Michael Late Benedum originally had but one ambition in life: to be guaranteed $50 a week in his old age; but due to the generosity of his employer in cutting him in on oil deals, he was worth $17 million when he died.

Chances are your favorite movie star is dabbling in oil as a way of cutting down taxes on those Hollywood super-salaries. Bob Hope and Bing Crosby, mock enemies in their screen portrayals, once teamed up on an oil lease in Texas' Scurry County, and were delighted when the drillers brought in a 1,000-barrel-a-day well—their second in two months. Near Wichita Falls, Texas, Gene Autry had six such wells, but near Vernal, Utah, Jimmy Stewart had to be content with a well bringing in only eight hundred barrels a day.

The very wealthy consider oil investments almost a must. One industrialist, worth $85 million, confided to the *Wall Street Journal*, "When a fellow is in my income bracket, he automati-

---

* The Gettys, Hunts, Cullens, et al, are far from typical of the industry as a whole. Yet, with tax rates as high as they have been in the last twenty years, few who have not enjoyed the tax shelter of oil depletion have been able to amass wealth of Getty-Hunt proportions.

cally goes into the oil business. This is a legal way to escape confiscation of earnings."

Before readers rush out to invest their last hard-earned pennies in oil ventures, they should recognize that oil has made paupers as well as millionaires out of the venturesome. But whether luck is with you or against you, the tax laws are on your side. The effect of percentage depletion was neatly summed up by a Houston oil expert who was describing the tax joys of oil ventures to some would-be investors in Cleveland:

In [oil] exploration, the government permits you to deduct all gambling losses. An individual in the 90 percent tax bracket can consider Uncle Sam as his partner in up to 90 percent of all *losses*. [But] because of the 27½ percent depletion allowance, Uncle Sam takes a relatively modest share of the income of successful ventures. *If you are in the 90 percent tax bracket, you are risking only 10 cents out of a dollar spent on unsuccessful ventures.* As to *successful* ventures, [the average tax rate] to a 90-percent-bracket couple is about 65 percent. (Emphasis added)

It may be unpleasant to think of Uncle Sam being "taken" in a business deal, but the above description allows no other conclusion. After all, in a normal business arrangement, a person who puts up most of the money and takes most of the risk expects to get back his full share of the profits. Not kindly, generous Uncle Sam. He willingly ("helplessly" might be more accurate) puts up as much as 90 or 91 percent* of the "risk" money for drilling. If a "dry hole" results, Uncle Sam is left holding up to 91 percent of a very empty bag. If the result is a gusher, he must content himself, as the Houston oil expert so gracefully put it, with "a relatively modest" share of the proceeds, far less than he would receive from any other industry.

* Under pre-1964 tax rates.

In all, investors in oil and gas enjoy three separate, distinct and unique tax advantages. They may be summarized as follows:

		Oil Men	Others
ADVANTAGE	1	*Immediate* write-off of most capital costs.	*Gradual* write-off of most capital costs.
ADVANTAGE	2	*Double* deduction of initial investment.	*Single* deduction of initial investment.
ADVANTAGE	3	*Continuing* deductions for *no* investment.	*No* deductions beyond initial investment.

Follow through the simple steps of an oil investment and each of these advantages will be made clear: Suppose you invest $100,000 in drilling an oil well. Roughly $25,000 of this pays for the derrick, the pipe in the ground and other immovable material and equipment. The other $75,000, called "intangible drilling expense," goes for wages and salaries, fuel, machine and tool rental. Now this $100,000 is, in essence, the cost of developing an income-producing property (namely, the oil well), and is therefore, a "capital" cost. In any other industry, the entire $100,000 would be deducted gradually, over the "useful life" of the property. That is, if the well were deemed to have a "useful life"* of twenty years, the deductions would come to $5,000 a year; with a ten-year life, they would be $10,000 a year.

But if you are an oil man, such paltry deductions will not do. At least three quarters of your capital costs—the so-called "intangible drilling expenses"—may be deducted *immediately,* in the year you make the outlays. Thus, instead of a first-year deduction of $5,000 or $10,000, *you get a first-year deduction of*

---

* Treasury regulations offer guidelines on the "useful life" of various kinds of machinery, equipment, buildings, etc. For simplicity's sake, the illustrations here assume even, or "straight-line" depreciation.

$75,000 *or more,* (The other $25,000, of course, is permitted to be written off gradually, like the capital costs in other industries.)

True, this huge first-year deduction will mean foregoing later deductions. But this does not diminish your enthusiasm, for, as a sensible businessman, you know that a dollar in hand is worth far more than the expectation of a dollar at some future date.* Assuming you have $75,000 of non-oil income that can be helpfully offset by your $75,000 deduction† (and thus escape taxation), you have a splendid opportunity to use Uncle Sam's money to parlay your first well into still others. Thus, if you're smart, you'll follow in the footsteps of many an oil operator before you, and you'll take your tax-free $75,000 and "drill it up"—i.e., put it to work drilling more wells and generating still more depletion-sheltered income.

One student of the oil industry has said that the privilege of the immediate deduction of "intangible" expenses is a more powerful incentive to oil exploration than the depletion allowance. It is certainly generously used: in 1957, for example, corporations taking depletion deductions of $678 million also took $471 million of "intangible" deductions.

Let's move on. Year One has ended. You have your first well, and as Year Two begins, it starts pouring forth liquid gold, and thereafter, with pleasurable monotony, it produces a steady $100,000 worth a year.‡ With even more pleasurable monotony, you are entitled to keep $27,500 of this income—or half your net profit from the well, whichever is smaller—wholly unsullied by the hands of the tax collector. Herein lie Advantages Two and Three.

---

* Businessmen scrambled to take advantage of a vastly milder fast-deduction privilege made available during World War II and the Korean emergency, as a tax incentive to the building of war-related facilities.

† Of course, if you're the kind of independent, hand-to-mouth "wildcatter" for whom all these incentives were supposedly designed, chances are you don't have the $75,000 of income to offset, and the "intangible" deduction won't do you any good.

‡ The figure of $100,000 is used for simple illustrative purposes, although production controls in many states limit most wells to less than this.

Remember that your original $100,000 investment has already been taken care of *once*, through the $75,000 of "intangible" deductions you've already taken, plus the deductions scheduled for future years for the remaining $25,000. Now, for most investors this is deemed sufficient; but in the case of oil and gas investors, Congress apparently wanted to make *doubly* sure they get their initial investment back tax-free, for they provided the 27½ percent depletion allowance *over and above* the regular deductions to cover their original dollar input.

But even the double deduction does not seem, in Congress' eyes, to offer the proper compensation to oil and gas investors. The depletion allowance does not stop even after they have recovered their investment a second time. It goes on and on and on, just as long as the oil or gas well continues to produce. This can get to be extraordinarily generous: in the case of oil, for the years 1946 through 1949, the depletion allowance permitted deductions amounting to *nineteen times* what other industries may deduct. But sulphur puts oil to shame: in that same period, the depletion deductions for sulphur came to *two hundred times** the deductions permitted other industries.

Those are the basic tax advantages which the oil and gas industry find so congenial. But, as with most tax favors, there are one or two other subtle escape routes available to the well-counseled.

There is, for example, the capital gains route. When a top-bracket oil operator avails himself of the generous "intangible expense" deduction—and Mr. B (p. 19) did so to the tune of $6,600,000 in a four-year period—he is *saving* 91 cents on every deducted dollar (see Glossary under *Deduction*). But if he turns around and sells a well, or an interest in it, he pays only the special 25 percent capital gains tax rate on his profit. Clearly,

* This is because the cost of finding sulphur (usually a by-product of looking for oil) is extraordinarily low in relation to the later sulphur *income* on which the depletion deductions are based.

for every dollar on which he has *saved 91 cents* but *pays back only 25 cents,* he is ahead of the game *on taxes alone* by 66 cents. On this basis, Mr. B stood to make a "tax profit" of $4,356,000. In all, those who do avail themselves of this pleasant arrangement are making a $50 million tax profit. President Kennedy asked in 1963 that this one-sided arrangement be made a two-way street* but Congress rejected his proposal outright.

The Kennedy Administration also asked for a curb on another depletion practice which has been benefiting the oil industry to the tune of nearly $100 million a year. Remember that the law permits annual depletion deductions amounting to 27½ percent of gross oil income—but with a ceiling of 50 percent of the *net* (after-expenses) income from a given property. But under Treasury rules, this net-income ceiling can be considerably raised by either judicious or fortuitous timing of oil drilling.

Suppose an operator drilled in November or December of Year One. He would have large drilling expenses but no oil production in that year. This would put him in the happy position of applying his drilling deductions against *non*-oil income (and, in effect, enjoying that income tax-free). By the time his well began producing oil in Year Two, with his drilling expenses already out of the way, his "net (after-expense) income" from that oil property would be unusually high. Result: he would not bump up against the 50-percent-net-income ceiling, but would enjoy the full 27½ percent depletion allowance.

Meanwhile, his oil field neighbor, who happened to drill in January, and began producing oil in the same year, would not be nearly so well off. *His* drilling expenses would have to be applied against his oil income. This would bring the 50-percent-net-income ceiling down on him and deprive him of some of the depletion allowance enjoyed by the December driller next door.

The Kennedy Administration, arguing that the 50-percent-net-

---

* By providing that profits on a mineral sale that had previously enjoyed a full-rate deduction be taxed at that same full rate instead of at the favorable 25 percent capital gains rate.

income ceiling should logically apply *over the life of any oil property,* rather than to artificially separated years, wanted prior deductions against non-oil income to be carried over and figured into the net-income ceiling when any property began producing. The proposal got nowhere in Congress.

The Administration had better luck with its proposal to curb another practice for raising the net-income ceiling. A 1954 amendment to the depletion laws permitted an operator to raise the ceiling on a low-profit property by grouping it together, for tax purposes, with a high-profit property. But the tax bill passed by the House in 1963 clamped down on the "grouping" practice.

Another more obscure 1954 provision has been a boon to successful oil men, and remains quietly in the law today. Ordinarily, when business expenses or deductions result in a taxpayer showing a net *loss* on his tax return, he is entitled to carry that loss forward and use it to offset income or profits in future years. Prior to 1954, an oil operator was prohibited from carrying his tax losses forward to the extent the losses were due to his percentage depletion deductions. But a little-noticed provision crept into the mammoth 1954 over-all code revision, repealing this prohibition and allowing oil-deduction losses to be freely carried forward. At the time, one revenue agent in an oil state predicted that henceforth, many large oil operators would cease paying taxes entirely, year after year. He proved right. Look back at the record of Mr. B, on page 19. Not only did he manage to pay no taxes on $9,419,000 of income during the four-year period from 1958 to 1962; *at the end of that four years, he still had excess deductions (i.e., tax losses) of nearly $2,700,000 that he could carry forward to protect future years' income from taxation.* Thus, the total of his tax-free income, mainly due to his oil deductions, came to $12,100,000.

If the iron ore industry were to come before Congress and ask that its depletion rate be raised from 15 percent to 90 percent, or if the salt industry asked for a 120 percent rather than a 10 percent rate, they would probably be politely hooted out of the hearing room (if that can be done politely). But various mineral industries, helped immeasurably by the courts, have managed to achieve just this effect by successfully contending that the depletion allowance should be computed not on the value of the mineral as it emerges from the mine, but on its semi-finished- or finished-product value. For example, several iron ore companies computed their depletion on the basis of finished steel, and thus sought to increase their depletion allowance six-fold, for a possible tax saving of $5 million. The depletion on salt brine was computed on the value of chlorine and caustic soda, for a thirteen-fold increase in the depletion allowance and a $6,400,000 tax saving. Finished brick was used as the basis for the fire clay depletion allowance (tax saving: nearly $5 million), etc., etc. The Morton Salt Company even asked that its depletion allowance be computed on the basis of the price of salt in packaged form, but a court rejected the request.

Although later stretched to absurd lengths, the original basis for these processing allowances was reasonable. Some minerals are simply not salable as they emerge from a mine (e.g., coal must be broken up and washed) and the court cases revolved around the question of how much processing (including such intriguing processes as "nodulizing" and "sintering") was necessary to make a mineral commercially marketable. In 1960, a congressional measure and a simultaneous Supreme Court decision joined to bring the problem within reasonable bounds.

The percentage depletion privilege does not stop at the water's edge. American companies enjoy the full benefits of percentage depletion on their foreign oil operations. The domestic depletion allowance is often justified by the high-risk, high-cost character of American oil exploration. Yet, although in places such as Kuwait and Saudi Arabia, dry holes are rare and drilling costs are low (thanks to the fabulous oil reservoirs near the surface), foreign oil extraction enjoys the same 27½ percent depletion allowance as higher-risk, higher-cost domestic production.

This is of substantial comfort to American companies overseas. In 1955 and 1956, the Arabian-American Oil Company (Aramco) had depletion deductions amounting to $148 million and $152 million, respectively. This alone benefited the company by (and cost the U.S. Treasury) some $124 million for the two years. So great are the after-tax profits of Aramco that two of its corporate owners—Standard Oil of New Jersey and Socony Mobil—were able to recover their entire original investment in Aramco in a single year.

These overseas depletion privileges are vital to U.S. oil companies: three fourths of the after-tax earnings of Standard Oil of New Jersey in 1956 came from foreign oil activities. A year later, thirty-three major oil companies found that well over a third of their after-tax profits came from foreign operations.

A second tax pleasure enjoyed by American oil companies overseas has to do with royalty payments to foreign governments, disguised as "income tax" payments. The result is that beneficent old Uncle Sam ends up footing the entire bill for the companies' royalty payments. It works this way: suppose Aramco makes a $100 million payment to the government of Saudi Arabia. If this is considered a royalty payment, it is merely allowed as a deduction from Aramco's *income* in computing its U.S. taxes. At the pre-1964 52 percent corporation tax rate, Aramco is out of pocket $48 million, the remaining $52 million in effect being diverted from the United States Treasury to the government of Saudi Arabia. If, on the other hand, the $100 million is labeled a tax payment, *Aramco is permitted to reduce its U.S. tax payments by the full $100 million* (see Glossary, under *Tax Credit*). Uncle Sam ends up bearing the entire load, and Aramco is $48 million better off.

To Saudi Arabia, it couldn't matter less which way it gets its $100 million, whether in the form of "royalties" or "taxes." Whether or not it is done deliberately to help the U.S. companies operating there, it happens that "taxes" are far higher than "royalties." In 1955 and 1956, Aramco's "royalty" payments to Saudi Arabia were $78 and $80 million, respectively, while its "tax" payments were $193 and $200 million, respectively.

One strong supporter of the *domestic* depletion allowances, Senator Mike Monroney of Oklahoma, has strong reservations about the tax privileges enjoyed by overseas companies. The treatment of "royalties," he says, amounts to giving these companies a 55 percent depletion allowance—twice what the domestic companies get.

How did all of these preferences come to be written into the tax laws?

Although the term "depletion" was contained in the original 1913 income tax law,* depletion deductions were limited to the *original cost* of the property (the formula still applicable to non-mineral industries), or its value as of March 1, 1913.† Because this latter qualification was thought to discriminate against new versus pre-1913 discoveries, the law was changed in 1918 to permit an oil investor to base deductions either on original cost or on the "fair market value" of the well at the time of its discovery—a system known as "discovery depletion." But the calculation of this "fair value" proved uncertain and cumbersome and, in 1926, percentage depletion—for oil and gas only—was ushered into the tax law wearing the unarguable garb of "simplicity." (It is noteworthy that nearly thirty years later, many minerals were still operating under the supposedly unworkable "discovery depletion" formula.) The Treasury Department had the unkindness to suggest that if simplicity was the object, what could be simpler than to return to the "original

---

* Technically, there were two prior U.S. income tax laws: the first, enacted in 1861, was repealed in 1872. The second, enacted in 1894, was declared unconstitutional by the Supreme Court in 1895. The 1913 statute was, therefore, the first permanent income tax.

† This proviso was inserted in order to avoid taxing values that had accrued prior to the adoption of the Sixteenth Amendment.

cost" concept of the 1913 law? Apparently this argument did not appeal to Congress.

The very year percentage depletion was enacted, a Senate study revealed that "discovery depletion" contained some of the very same weaknesses for which the depletion allowance is criticized today. For example, although then, as now, the special tax treatment of oil and gas was justified on the basis of the high risks involved in oil exploration, the 1926 study showed that two thirds of the "discovery depletion" deductions were being taken in *proven* oil fields, where the risks were relatively small; that 60 percent of the deductions were benefiting "large operators" whose extensive drilling operations diminished their risks; and that deductions were also being taken by land owners who simply leased their lands for oil drillings and "[sat] idly by and [risked] nothing . . . not risked by every investor in real estate." Despite these revelations, Congress passed up the opportunity to cure the defects, and, instead, perpetuated them in the new and more generous "percentage depletion" provision.

Why the odd figure of 27½ percent? The more zealous defenders of the oil depletion allowance sometimes behave as if that 27½ percent was arrived at by heavenly decree, and that to reduce it to, say, 27¼ or (perish the thought) 27 percent, would cause the earth to tremble. The fact is, it was nothing but a negotiated compromise—between the 25 percent desired by the House members and the 30 percent in the Senate version of the 1926 measure. (An effort to write a 35 percent depletion allowance into the Senate bill lost by a one-vote margin.) Supporters of the percentage depletion provision acknowledged at the time that the figure was an "arbitrary" one.

The privilege of an immediate write-off for "intangible drilling" costs was first permitted in 1916—not by a law enacted by Congress, but by Internal Revenue regulations. Over the years, there has been considerable legal controversy over whether Internal Revenue had the power to grant this privilege. In 1945, one court held it did not, since these expenditures were in fact "capital outlays" (deductible only over a period of years) and no Internal Revenue regulation could magically transform them into "expenses" (which are immediately deductible). This decision sent a tremor through the oil industry (the shock was the greater since the heresy came from none other than the Fifth Circuit Court of Appeals, whose jurisdiction includes Texas). The tremor was quickly communicated to Congress, which promptly adopted a resolution affirming Internal Revenue's power to grant the more favorable treatment to the "intangible" expenses. In 1954, to end all doubt, Congress *directed* Internal Revenue, by statute, to issue such a ruling.

Over the years, under the principle of tax "equity" described in Chapter 15, percentage depletion has been extended to more than 85 specifically enumerated minerals, from A (Anorthosite) to Z (Zinc). So all-encompassing is the list of minerals, in fact, that Congress felt it necessary to specify that it did *not* mean to grant the depletion privilege to "soil, sod, dirt, turf, water or mosses" or to "minerals from sea water, the air or similar inexhaustible sources." Even this has not deterred some imaginative taxpayers from claiming percentage depletion on certain underground water and steam, nor did it prevent one federal district judge from upholding a depletion claim on underground water.

Oil and gas alone are favored with a 27½ percent depletion allowance. The rates for others are, variously, 23, 15, 10 and 5 percent—always subject to the 50 percent-of-net-income ceiling.

The use of the depletion allowance is increasingly in vogue. Total depletion deductions by corporations quadrupled in the decade 1946-56—from just under $800 million to over $3 billion.

What are the reasons for and against the depletion allowance? To become acquainted with them, one might eavesdrop on a hypothetical discussion between an Oil Man and a querulous Taxpayer who experiences some difficulty in understanding why he and others like him should be paying higher taxes in order to make up for the $2 billion-plus in tax preferences for oil, gas and other minerals—especially in view of what has been called a "world glut" of oil.

OIL MAN: When will everybody learn that oil is different from anything else? Every time you lift a barrel of oil out of the ground, there's one less barrel left, and there's not a thing you can do about it.

Suppose I own just one well, and I'm pumping it at a rate that will dry it up in ten years. Every year, my property gets smaller by ten percent. At the end of the ten years, it's disappeared, vanished, it doesn't exist—and I'm out of business.

You've heard oil called a "wasting asset"? Well, that's why.

TAXPAYER: But isn't *everything* a wasting asset? I mean, a machine doesn't last forever. And once it's worn out, it's just as useless as a worn-out oil well, and there's "not a thing you can do" (to use your words) to get it back. As far as its usefulness is concerned, it might just as well have "disappeared —vanished."

OIL MAN: Sure, but you know perfectly well that the tax laws let the machine owner "write off" or depreciate that machine, so that when it's worn out, he'll have the money to go out and buy a new one. That's basically what depletion is for the oil industry. It's supposed to give me the money to go out and find a new well to replace my worn-out well.

TAXPAYER: Now, just a minute. First you told me that when a well was used up, there wasn't a thing you could do about it. Now you're saying you need the depletion allowance to go out and look for a new well. What's the difference between that and going out and buying a new machine?

Besides, if we're going to start giving special tax treatment for "irreplaceable assets," why leave out Elizabeth Taylor and Mickey Mantle? You can go out and find yourself a new oil well. But what about them, when they grow old? All the money in the world won't buy them back their youth or their beauty. Why not give them a depletion allowance?

OIL MAN: Oh, come on now. You can't be serious.

TAXPAYER: Let's go back for a minute to the oil well-versus-machine example we were talking about. Let's say a tool making company buys a new lathe. Under *depreciation,* the toolmaker can never deduct more than the *original cost* of that lathe. But your *depletion* deductions go on as long as your well keeps producing—even though you may deduct 100 or 200 times your original cost. How come?

OIL MAN: Well, for one thing, the toolmaker can count on his lathe lasting a certain number of years. But I never know for sure how long my oil well is going to produce. It may give out next year. And then where am I?

Besides, I have no way of knowing how much it's going to cost to find new oil. I may hit five or ten or twenty dry holes before I strike a new well—and I might never hit a producing well.

TAXPAYER: But on both scores, the toolmaker is in essentially the same boat. For one thing, a new kind of automated lathe might suddenly come along and make his present machine as obsolete and useless as your suddenly-worn-out well. For another, he can't tell how much it's going to cost him to re-place his lathe—and even if it turns out to cost him twice as much, *he only gets to deduct his original cost.* I still don't see why you oil men should be special and get deductions for more dollars than you put in.

OIL MAN: Obviously you're not aware that our depletion deductions are less than our outlays. Why, in the late fifties, for instance, we were laying out $1.18 a barrel looking for new oil—but getting only 80 cents a barrel in depletion deductions.

TAXPAYER: But you're no worse off than any other industry. Nobody gets deductions equal to their *replacement* costs, which is what you keep talking about. Besides, you're leaving out half the picture. You get back your money *once* through your "intangible drilling" deductions, and then *again* through your depletion deductions. Why the *double* deduction when everyone else only gets one?

OIL MAN: There is no double deduction. You see, the depletion allowance is to compensate a man for the fact that his oil is disappearing and the intangible expenses you mention are to cover the cost of drilling and putting up a well and getting it into production once the oil pool has been found.

TAXPAYER: Well, the Supreme Court doesn't agree with you. It ruled that depletion is supposed to cover both and another court ruled that the "intangible" deduction is a "special favor."

OIL MAN: You know, you keep harping on this "special treatment" theme, but all depletion does is to put us on the same footing as everybody else. You see, when I find new oil, I'm creating *new* capital, and when I sell it, all I'm getting is a "return of capital." Other people don't pay taxes on that—why should we?

TAXPAYER: Well, it seems funny to me that when you tell your *stockholders* about your oil sales you list the proceeds as income and profits. But all of a sudden, when you're telling the *tax collector* about them, they are magically transformed into a "return of capital." Some companies even keep two sets of books—one for their stockholders, showing the same kind of "original cost" figures that all other industries use, and another for the government.

OIL MAN: But that's done—sometimes required—in many industries. Besides, you people always forget the terrific risks we run when we look for oil and the fantastic money it costs us. And it's getting more expensive all the—

TAXPAYER: Let me stop you right there. Surely you're not suggesting that oil is the only risk-taking business. As a matter of fact, from one point of view, oil is one of the safest. The figures on business failures in *Dun's Review* show that in every year from 1925 to 1954, oil had about the lowest rate of failures. In the mid-fifties, the failure rate per 10,000 businesses was 20 in food, 50 in apparel, 86 in construction, over 400 in retailing—*and only 4 in oil, gas and mining!*

OIL MAN: Now I've heard it all. Are you saying oil is a "safe" industry?

TAXPAYER: No, I'm not denying there are risks in oil, just as there are in every business. But if the oil industry is going to get a tax concession on the basis of its risks, then the only fair thing would be for the government to try to measure the exact amount of risk in *every* industry—in fact, every individual business—and give a tax concession to everybody to compensate for their risks.

You know, you oil men talk a lot about free enterprise. Why aren't you willing to rely on free enterprise to take care of the risk factor? Other industries assume that if risk is high, prices and returns on investment will reflect it. Why can't the oil industry stand on its own feet? How come it needs a government subsidy?

OIL MAN: What are you trying to do, make me mad or something? We oil men are individualists. We get no subsidy; we want no subsidy.

TAXPAYER: Frankly, I don't see what else you can call it when thirty-three oil companies saved a billion dollars in taxes in one year simply because they paid only half as much as other companies.

OIL MAN: I still can't seem to get you to realize the extent of the risk we take. In "wildcat" drilling, for instance, when you're exploring in a brand new field—eight out of nine tries turn out to be dry holes. It's true that drilling near proven oil pools, only one out of four is a dry hole. But where else— other than in wildcatting—do you get eight-to-one odds against you?

TAXPAYER: You admit there are different risks involved in different kinds of drilling. Yet why does everybody get the same depletion allowance—whether his risk is high, low, or even zero?

As a matter of fact, most of the depletion deductions don't go to the small wildcatters, who are really risking their financial necks. They go to the giant corporations who take much smaller risks.

OIL MAN: You'll have to prove that one to me.

TAXPAYER: All right. Government statistics show that in 1958 and 1959, out of every $100 in depletion deductions, about $70 went to the enormous companies that have assets of $100 million or more. Only the top 1/10 of 1 percent of American companies are that big—one in a thousand.

And about $97 out of every $100 went to companies with assets of a million dollars—that's still a pretty big company. And do you know how much the smallest companies got? *Thirty cents* out of every $100 of depletion deductions!

OIL MAN: All right, everybody. All together. Let's all hiss the giant corporation and weep for the little fellow. Touching, very touching—but I didn't hear one statistic that had anything to do with the *riskiness* of an oil investment.

TAXPAYER: On the contrary, my statistics were right to the point. In the first place, one of your most ardent senatorial supporters admits the big oil companies do very little wildcatting. They buy a lot of their new oil *from* wildcatters as proven wells—so there's no risk there.

Secondly, the drilling they do is fairly conservative, and highly successful. Take the five largest oil companies. In 1958, they hit 3,447 *productive* wells against only 868 dry holes. That's a four-to-one ratio. Even the *worst* record among the forty top oil companies was 105 successes to 96 dry holes—a far cry from an 8–to–1 odds you were talking about. Why, your own oil-industry witness told Congress that of *all* wells drilled, the successes are about two to one compared with the dry holes!

OIL MAN: But depletion isn't for risk alone. Everybody's capital —the big fellow's just the same as the little guy's—is disappearing as the oil gets pumped out. But since you're talking about risk, let's concentrate on the small wildcatter, the guy who's *really* taking the risks. If you cut down on the depletion allowance, he just won't go out looking for new oil. He'll sell out to the major oil companies.

TAXPAYER: Now maybe we're getting somewhere. If it's the small wildcatter who's taking the risks and needs the help, let's by all means give it to him. *But let's make sure the help really goes to him,* and not to a lot of people who take no risk and need no relief. The trouble with a tax deduction is that it's absolutely no good to the really small, hand-to-mouth wildcatter who doesn't have the outside income to offset against the deduction. Besides, why give a tax concession to a man who simply leases his land to an oil company, *risks nothing,* and then sits back and collects royalties? Or what if I buy an interest in a *proven* well? Where's my risk? And yet I may get more of a tax break than the wildcatter who risked his shirt.

OIL MAN: But even now, the oil industry is less profitable than a lot of other industries, even *after* taxes, which proves there's no gouging or profiteering. So if you cut down on the depletion allowance, first of all, oil and gas prices will rise sharply, and secondly, how are we going to attract the capital to go on drilling for new oil?

Besides, what if there's a war? What if we get caught like Europe after Suez—suddenly deprived of our foreign oil supplies, just by the whim of some dictator?*

TAXPAYER: Well, if we're going to give tax concessions to one industry because it's "war-essential," we ought to give it to all of them—airplane companies, electronics and missile companies—there'd be no end to it.

Secondly, if the object is to make sure we have plenty of oil

---

* The Taxpayer could, if he wished to indulge in peccadilloes, invoke the assurances proffered by one defender of the depletion allowance who proudly stated that even if we were entirely cut off from foreign oil during a war "the productive capacity of all the wells in America" would cover "our requirements for fuel."

here at home in case of a war, percentage depletion is just
180 degrees wrong.

OIL MAN: What do you mean?

TAXPAYER: Because percentage depletion doesn't give you a
single penny's benefit for *discovering* the oil. You only begin
to get the advantages *when you begin drawing the oil out of
the ground*—that is, simply using up the oil we might need in
a war.

Besides, if we need every drop of our oil for defense, why
do we limit the imports of foreign oil? Why not do just the
reverse: rely mainly on foreign oil now and conserve our
domestic supplies in case of a war?

OIL MAN: Oh, sure—and shut down the American oil industry!
Where do you think we'd get the skilled hands to start up our
industry again if war did break out?

TAXPAYER: First you tell me we need lots of domestic oil in
case of war, and then you say we should use up our oil here
at home to keep our industry going.

Besides, if, as you say, all this foreign oil is going to be cut
off from us in time of war, why give it *any* depletion allowance? What sense does it make to subsidize foreign oil, and
then deny ourselves the use of it by import quotas?

OIL MAN: You mean grant depletion on *domestic* oil but not on
American-owned foreign oil? Why, Congress would never
discriminate that way.

TAXPAYER: I beg your pardon, sir. Congress has done precisely
that. In the case of some thirty-five minerals, it has drawn a
clear distinction between the domestic and the foreign production. It could do the same with oil.

OIL MAN: I think we'd better wind this up. Let me make two
final points. First, the depletion allowance has become as
much a part of the oil industry as the rotary rig. You wouldn't
dream of depriving us of that important tool; don't deprive us
of depletion.

Second, the depletion allowance has worked. Since it's

been in effect, we've had fabulous discovery of oil, we have lower prices to the consumer on oil and gas—lower, in fact, than in 1926, when depletion began, despite huge cost increases since then. We have one of the greatest oil industries in the world. Why rock the boat? Why experiment with something you don't know will work? I say you can't argue with success.

TAXPAYER: Despite that last admonition, let me put in my final two cents.

Success? Yes. Discovery? Yes. But how much of it is due to the depletion allowance? After all, not a penny of depletion helps new *discoveries*. And most of it goes to people who are doing little or no *high-risk* exploration.

You say we should continue depletion because it's always been there (which it hasn't) and has become part of the industry. Well, child labor and the twelve-hour day were also once part of American industry, but we abolished them. Besides, the premises behind the original depletion program have now been turned upside down: whereas once there was a shortage of oil, now there's a glut. Whereas once depletion helped the *discoverer*, now it mainly benefits the *non*-discoverer.

Now if—and I emphasize the "if"—the oil industry (or any other mineral industry) needs special government help because of the risks of exploration, let's design a specific, tailor-made way of helping the real risk-taker, the explorer, the discoverer.

And let the help come directly out of the Treasury. Let Congress appropriate the funds every year, as they do with the farm program. But as long as the subsidy is embedded in the tax laws, the billions lost to the Treasury will be unseen, unquestioned, and uncounted—until it's too late. As it is now, for instance, there is no assurance that the tax savings from depletion will be used to find new oil or mineral deposits. A directly-appropriated subsidy could be channeled specifically to those who *do* explore. And, like the farm program, *it would bear an annual price tag.*

What's more, the program would automatically be reviewed and debated every year. There would be a chance to ask questions, such as: Does it make sense to give hidden tax windfalls to people who risk little or nothing—such as those who buy *proven* oil reserves and the land owners who let others take the risk but reap the tax benefits? Does it make sense to subsidize exploring for coal when we already know of 2,400 *years'* worth of coal in the ground (and nearly all of that discovered before 1913), and when the lack of demand for what we already have has made an invalid of the coal industry? Does it make sense to spend billions to stimulate the search for more oil, when we are deliberately curbing oil imports and deliberately holding Texas oil wells to less than 30 percent of production capacity?

I think the public deserves an airing of those questions.

While the Oil Man has begun showings signs of wear and tear, the inquisitive and persistent Taxpayer appears as fresh as when he started.

Having fathomed the Oil Man's arguments on behalf of percentage depletion, he longs to inquire how they apply to the eighty-five odd other minerals that now bask in the warmth of the depletion provisions.

He reflects on the "national defense" argument. But try as he may, his imagination does not perceive any connection between the defense needs of the nation and, say, flower pot clay or ornamental stone or table salt, all of which are accorded percentage depletion.

What about the high-risk argument? His mind drifts back to the beaches of his summer vacation, with their limitless stretches of rolling sand dunes, and he wonders what unusual risk is involved in the finding and removal of sand, another depletion-favored mineral.

And what of that troublesome "wasting asset" concept? An alarming thought overwhelms him as he reflects on Congress' decree that oyster shells and clam shells are an exhaustible and irreplaceable asset. Could it be that Congress has been secretly warned of an imminent end to the procreative faculties of the oyster and the clam?*

---

* Be not alarmed; as you will discover when you read Chapter 15, Congress, in granting depletion to oyster and clam shells, was simply rendering "equity."

3 /

Ah, To Be
Louis B. Mayer

On the surface, there seems nothing unusual about Section 1240 of the Internal Revenue Code of 1954—it looks just like any other provision of the tax law. It reads as follows (to aid in deciphering the legal terminology, a layman's translation is provided):

Section 1240	*Layman's Translation*
Amounts received from the assignment or release by an employee, after more than 20 years' employment, of all his rights to receive, after termination of his employment and for a period of not less than 5 years (or for a period ending with his death), a percentage of future profits or receipts of his employer shall be considered an amount received from the sale or exchange of a capital asset held for more than 6 months if—	*If* you've worked 20 years for one company . . . and *if* you have rights to future profits of the company for at least 5 years after you leave its employ . . . and *if* you sell those rights . . . the proceeds are taxed at the special 25 percent capital gains rate . . .

Section 1240	*Layman's Translation*
(1) such rights were included in the terms of the employment of such employee for not less than 12 years,	*provided* you've had those rights at least 12 years before you stop work . . .
(2) such rights were included in the terms of the employment of such employee before the date of enactment of this title, and	and *provided* those rights were in your contract before August 16, 1954 . . .
(3) the total of the amounts received for such assignment or release is received in one taxable year and after the termination of such employment.	and *provided* you sell your rights after you leave and all in a single year.

Even your tax lawyer (if you have one) would probably pass over the section as meaningless, on the assumption that no client of his could ever comply with all those "ifs" and "provideds."

But to the late Louis B. Mayer, former head of Metro-Goldwyn-Mayer studios in Hollywood, Section 1240 was far from meaningless. For him, it had a special meaning: it saved him roughly $2 million in taxes. He had no trouble meeting all the "ifs" and "provideds"—and for a very simple reason: Section 1240 was written with him specifically in mind, tailored to fit his own individual situation. It didn't mention him by name, but it might just as well have.

Section 1240 is but one of a number of sections of the tax laws—probably no one knows just how many there are—enacted specifically for the benefit of a particular taxpayer. As you can see, they name no names. They may have every appearance of a general law applicable to anyone whose circumstances are similar, but they are not.

Section 512 (b)(13), for example, applies only to persons who happened to die after August 16, 1945 and before January 1, 1957. It was carefully designed to benefit the estate of Charles

Merrill, late a partner in the celebrated brokerage firm of Merrill Lynch, Pierce, Fenner and Smith. Section 2055(b) (2) is of interest only to those over eighty years old when their husband or wife died—and stood to save $4 million in taxes for the estate of Mrs. Gerard Swope, wife of the former president of General Electric.

Section 26 of the Revenue Act of 1962, anonymously entitled, "Continuation of a Partnership Year for Surviving Partner in a Two-man Partnership Where One Dies" reached back fifteen years to overturn two court decisions and take care of a 1947 tax problem of Mr. Howard F. Knipp of Baltimore.

Another special statute was enacted in 1956 under the heading, "Certain Claims Against the United States." Nowhere in the congressional proceedings will you find any mention of the name of Leo Sanders, an Oklahoma City general contractor for whom the late Senator Robert Kerr of Oklahoma tailored the provision, or the several hundred thousand dollars in taxes and penalties it spared him, or the fact that the Tax Court had sharply censured Mr. Sanders for filing improper tax returns.

There is nothing unique about Congress granting legislative relief to designated individuals: hundreds of "private laws" entitled, "An Act for the Relief of John Doe" are enacted every year, granting individual exceptions to the immigration quotas, dealing with claims or other grievances against the government, or simply relieving specific hardships. But these measures do not wear the disguise of a supposedly general provision of law. Not only is "John Doe" named, but the amount of relief sought and the reasons for it are fully set forth in congressional proceedings for all to see and judge.

But there was no such disclosure in the case of the Charles E. Merrill amendment or the Swope bill or the Leo Sanders amendment—or the Louis B. Mayer amendment, which is namelessly headed, "Taxability to Employes of Termination Payments."

The background of the Mayer amendment has been described by Louis Eisenstein with special felicity:

> Mr. Mayer was about to retire from his eminent position as a contributor to American culture. He had faithfully served his employer for about 20 years; on retirement he was entitled to share in the future profits of his employer for about five years or until his death; and his contract of employment had so provided for about 12 years. Instead of assuming the risk of future operations, Mr. Mayer desired to depart with one large lump-sum payment. However, if he took the payment, relatively little would remain after taxes. The [Senate] Finance Committee was informed of his acute problem and proved to be a friend in need. It declared that an employee so unfortunately situated was in a peculiarly distressing situation. He was caught between the bleak prospect of an "unduly harsh" tax and the unpleasant alternative of leaving "his retirement income dependent upon the operation of the business."

Mr. Mayer's "plight" was brought to the attention of the Senate Finance Committee in the form of a proposed amendment offered by Mr. Mayer's lawyer, Ellsworth C. Alvord, appearing not in his capacity as a private attorney but as the official spokesman of the United States Chamber of Commerce. Anyone else in Mr. Mayer's position would have paid the regular tax rates (in this case, presumably 91 percent) on a termination settlement of this kind. But the amendment proposed by Mr. Alvord, presented as though enjoying official Chamber of Commerce blessing, sought to spare the movie executive this unpleasantness and permit him, instead, to pay the far more favorable 25 percent capital gains rate.

The Finance Committee adopted Mr. Alvord's proposal, bolstering its action with a phrase frequently invoked to allay the apprehensions of other senators and ease the passage of special provisions. "The revenue loss from this amendment," said the

Committee, "will be neligible." (It is doubtful that Mr. Mayer considered his $2 million tax saving "negligible.") As but one trivial provision tucked away in a major revenue-raising bill, the Mayer provision passed the Senate unnoticed, without opposition or debate.

Three years later, in 1954, in the process of completely overhauling the tax code, the House of Representatives unaccommodatingly omitted the Mayer provision, perhaps on the assumption that it had already served its purpose and had no further utility. The alert Mr. Alvord, however, was on hand to point out the omission to the Senate Finance Committee, which re-enacted the provision "in such a way as not to affect" the past Mayer, but also in such a way as to bar future Mayers from equal treatment (see clause (2) of the provision). There will, in short, be no poaching on the "Hollywood Rajah's" private preserve.

The story of the Mayer amendment has a postscript, for later, the provision returned loyally to the native state of its beneficiary. In 1953, California, in revising its own statutes, bodily lifted and inserted into the state income tax laws great sections of the federal tax code, including, perhaps unwittingly, Section 1240—a provision that had once greatly blessed one of the state's most renowned citizens, but which now can no longer benefit anyone, in or out of the Golden State.

The estate of Charles E. Merrill, of Merrill Lynch fame, is the beneficiary of another anonymous provision of the tax code—to wit, Section 512(b)(13). At his death on October 6, 1956, Mr. Merrill willed an interest in his firm to a charitable trust. Under the generally applicable law, the trust's share of the firm's income would be taxable. But, thanks to Section 512(b)(13), the general rule does not apply in the case of a partnership interest willed by "an individual who died after August 16, 1954* and before January 1, 1957." Any decedent other than Mr. Merrill, in order to obtain similar treatment, would have to have been

---

* The date of enactment of the 1954 Revenue Code.

endowed with special prescience, for Section 512(b)(13) did not become law until April 7, 1958—fifteen months *after* the provision's final cut-off date.

Many is the lawyer (or client), caught by the frailties of human foresight, who has wished that the past might be reopened and all the advantages of hindsight applied to decisions that went awry. Usually, the law is sternly intolerant of oversight. But on page 1075 of Volume 70 of the General Statutes of the United States, lies a statute (Public Law 1011, 84th Congress, 2nd Session) that made that wish a reality. PL 1011 made it possible to erase the effects of some unhappily unforesighted estate planning (or lack of it) and to save $4 million in taxes for the estate of Mary Hill Swope, wife of former General Electric president Gerard Swope.

Mrs. Swope died on October 28, 1955, leaving a sizable estate in trust and giving her husband power to dispose of it at his death, either to their children or to charity. From a tax viewpoint, there were two unfortunate aspects to Mrs. Swope's will. One was that it was written in such a way as to deprive Mrs. Swope of the privilege of leaving half her estate tax-free to her husband* (the will was written in 1947, before that privilege was part of the law), and apparently was unrevised in the subsequent eighteen years so as to take advantage of the 1948 provision. The other was that by the time of her death, Mr. Swope had already amply provided for their children, and wished her estate to go entirely to charity. Had anyone thought to accommodate Mrs. Swope's will to that fact, she could easily have bequeathed her estate directly to charity and paid no estate tax on it. As it was, though, as a result of these two unfortunate oversights, which neither foresight nor hindsight could now correct, her estate was liable for some $4 million in taxes.

At the behest of a bi-partisan pair of New York Congressmen —Democrat Eugene Keogh of Brooklyn and Republican Daniel

---

* The so-called estate tax "marital deduction." See p. 257.

Reed of Sheridan—Congress reopened the past and expunged
the consequences of unprescient decisions. The measure Messrs.
Keogh and Reed shepherded through* made, of course, no mention of Mr. or Mrs. Swope or the perfectly understandable human frailties the measure sought to remedy. Instead, it bestowed
a special power on husbands (and wives) who are over 80 at
the time of their spouse's death (Mr. Swope was one month
short of 83 when his wife died). If such a surviving spouse (no
one younger than 80 may qualify), within a year of his wife's
death, exercises the power under her will to transmit her property to charity, the law will treat this as if she had decided to
do this herself. Thus, the charitable gifts may be subtracted
from her taxable estate and not be subjected to tax.

Public Law 1011 remains in the tax code today, as Section
2055(b)(2), but Treasury officials are not aware of any other
80-year-old surviving spouses who have come along to take advantage of it.

The "Leo Sanders amendment," fully as anonymous as the
Mayer, Merrill or Swope provisions, is a testimonial to the
efficacy of the late Senator Robert S. Kerr of Oklahoma. Barely
four months elapsed between the Supreme Court's rejection of
Mr. Sanders' tax case and the enactment of a tailor-made provision, sponsored by the Senator from Oklahoma, reversing the
courts' verdicts.

Leo Sanders was a general contractor in Oklahoma City, who,
in 1949, received settlement from the government of $955,000
in connection with a World War II contract. Although the tax
law provides for such settlements to be taxed at the regular
income tax rates, at first, Sanders failed to include any of the
$955,000 on his income tax return.† Then, after government

---

* With the aid of the special "member's bill" procedure peculiar to the
Ways and Means Committee and described on pp. 282-283.

† He claimed a government attorney had told him there would be no
tax to pay on the settlement, which the lawyer denied.

prodding, he claimed the bulk of the settlement as a "capital gain," taxable at the special 25 percent tax rate. The government filed suit for $729,446 in tax deficiencies and $226,258 in delinquencies for failing to file proper tax returns (for three years, Sanders had filed blank returns). In 1955, the Tax Court* ruled against Sanders and sharply criticized him for his tax-filing practices which, the court found, were "due to willful neglect." The Supreme Court denied an appeal on February 27, 1956.

Precisely two months and one day later, a bill emerged from the Senate Finance Committee. Ostensibly, it has nothing to do with Mr. Sanders (its main title involved the transfer of patent rights), but tucked away in it was an extraneous section entitled, "Certain Claims Against the United States." In order to qualify under the section, these "certain claims" had to meet certain qualifications. They had to (1) arise "under a contract for the construction of installations of facilities for any branch of the Armed Services of the United States" (2) which "remained unpaid for more than 5 years" and (3) which were paid in the year 1949 (six years prior to the enactment of this provision)— no sooner, no later. For the happy taxpayer whose claim could meet all of these specifications, the maximum tax rate was 33 percent, instead of the 90 or 91 percent top rate that would otherwise have applied. In addition, the provision excused Sanders from the massive penalties for his failure to file proper tax returns, despite the Tax Court's findings that "all excuses [for improper filing] have been carefully considered and found inadequate upon analysis."

None of these circumstances was even hinted at in the congressional report accompanying the measure. The bill slipped easily through the Senate, without explanation or debate. There is, however, a suggestion that those appointed to reconcile the differences between the House and Senate versions of the bill were not entirely comfortable about the Sanders provision, for they took pains to make clear their "understanding" that the

* See Glossary.

provision was "not to be considered a precedent for future legislative action."

But Leo Sanders needed no "future legislative action." His
made-to-order provision—you won't find it in the tax code
itself, because it lies tucked away in Volume 70 of the General
Statutes of the United States—was quite sufficient to save him
a large part of the $955,000 the Tax Court had said he owed
the government.

Leo Sanders is not the only fortunate individual who has lost
in the courts of law, only to win later in the halls of Congress.
On June 12, 1952, the Tax Court had ruled against a Mr. L. R.
McKee, a wholesale and retail feed and grain dealer from
Muscatine, Iowa, for claimed deficiencies totaling more than
$190,000 for the years 1946, 1947 and 1948. By the time the case
came before the Court of Appeals in October, 1953, the pertinent section of the law had been changed—not just for the
future, but, under certain conditions, retroactive for seven years,
to include "taxable years beginning after December 31, 1945"—
just far enough back to relieve Mr. McKee of the effect of the
Tax Court's adverse ruling.

Section 1342 of the Internal Revenue Code is entitled, "Com-
putation of Tax Where Taxpayer Recovers Substantial Amount
Held by Another under Claim of Right."' Anyone can avail himself of this provision *if* he was involved in a patent infringement
suit and *if* he claimed a tax deduction for certain expenses in
connection with the suit, and *if* the deduction was later disallowed because the decision in the suit was found to have been
"induced by fraud or undue influence," and *if* the disallowed
deductions exceeded $3,000. It would be miraculous if this re-
markable array of specifications should fit more than a single
company. But, then, one shouldn't expect too much—it did, at
least, fit one: the Universal Oil Products Company, which had
been involved in a patent infringement suit in which the decision
was later found to have been fraudulent because the judge was

bribed, and certain of whose expense deductions in connection
with the suit were later disallowed.

Members of Congress at times show a tender solicitude
toward each others' needs. For example, although as a general
rule, cousins may not be claimed as dependents, Section 152 (a)
(10) of the tax law provides that a "descendant of a brother or
sister of the father or mother of the taxpayer" (i.e., a cousin)
may be claimed as a dependent if he or she first resides with the
taxpayer and then receives institutional care. One such cousin
belonged to Representative Jere Cooper of Tennessee, formerly
chairman of the tax-writing House Ways and Means Committee.

The section defining "head of household" is said to have been
carefully written so as not to bar the lower "head of household"
tax rates* to North Carolina's venerable Representative Robert
L. ("Muley") Doughton, Representative Cooper's predecessor
as Ways and Means' Chairman. At the time the "head of household" provisions were enacted, Representative Doughton was
a widower whose daughter was living with him. Consideration
was given to requiring that children and grandchildren living
with "heads of household" earn less than $600 per year, but this
would not have suited Representative Doughton's fancy, since
his daughter, at the time, was on his Congressional office payroll, and earning considerably more than $600 a year.

Private Law 490 of 1955 is namelessly entitled, "An Act To
Provide Tax Relief To a Charitable Foundation and the Contributors Thereto." A reading of the law itself discloses that the
principal "contributors thereto" are Mr. and Mrs. Clarence
Cannon of Elsberry, Missouri—the same Representative Clarence Cannon who presides powerfully over the House Appropriations Committee. Mr. Cannon's influence on Capitol Hill is
eloquently demonstrated in the dispatch with which the legislators acted on Private Law 490, which decreed that the Cannon
Foundation was indeed a tax-free institution, any doubts to the

---

* See p. 70.

contrary notwithstanding. A bill to this effect was introduced in
the House on Saturday, July 30, 1955. On Monday morning it
was referred to the House Judiciary Committee and, no more
than three minutes later, "approved" by that committee and,
simultaneously, passed by the House. The following day it received the Senate's blessing. Hours later, Congress adjourned
until the following January—but not without having resolved
the doubts that apparently had existed about the tax-exempt
status of the Cannon Foundation of Elsberry, Missouri.

Examine any wartime excess profits tax law and you will soon
find a number of provisions so narrowly drawn that they could
only apply to one company—or, perhaps, to a select few companies.

For example, Section 518 of the Revenue Act of 1951 provides
special relief for any taxpayer "engaged primarily in the newspaper publishing business" which in a certain limited time
period "consolidated its mechanical, circulation, advertising and
accounting operations" with those of another newspaper "in the
same area"—a circumstance that happened to fit two Fort
Wayne, Indiana, newspapers, the *Journal-Gazette* and the *Sen-
tinel*. Almost surely, no other newspapers in the country could
qualify.

Section 516 of that same law had its own peculiar restrictions.
All a company had to do to reap its advantages was: (1) to
have been in business prior to 1940; (2) to have assets as of a
certain date worth not more than ten million dollars; (3) to have
government contracts account for more than 70 percent of its
total income in 1942-45 but less than 20 percent in 1950; and
(4) to have profits in 1945-and-the-average-of-1948-and-1949
at least three times as great as average profits in 1946 and 1947.

The Owens-Corning Fiberglas Company was able to wedge
itself within the confines of those limitations, but could any
other?

The following year, excess profits relief was specifically

granted to the Budd Company of Philadelphia (maker of railroad cars), the Sangamo Electric Company of Springfield,
Illinois, and the Bridgeport Brass Company—and, possibly, a
few other independent brass fabricators—under circumstances
detailed on pages 292 to 293.*

The custom-made provisions mentioned so far are those for
which the beneficiaries have been identifiable. But there are
dozens of other statutes which seem clearly fashioned for a lone
taxpayer perhaps known only to himself, his attorney (or lobbyist) and the lawmaker who favored him by sponsoring his made-
to-order provision.

If you are interested in sleuthing these provisions yourself,
one telltale signal is a retroactive date, for chances are its purpose is to reach back and take care of a single taxpayer's *past*
difficulty, perhaps with the courts, perhaps with the Internal
Revenue Service. And don't confine your searches to the tax
code itself. Many of these custom-tailored provisions are, like
the Leo Sanders amendment, tucked away in the General Statutes. If, for example, you chanced to open Volume 70 of the
General Statutes you would find five tax measures in a row
(Public Laws 396 through 400), four of which have retroactive
provisions.

Even in the tax code itself, though, you will find provisions so
narrowly circumscribed that they seem clearly to have been
written with a single taxpayer in mind. For example, as a general rule, non-citizens of the United States do not qualify as
"dependents." But Section 152(b)(3)(A) of the Internal Revenue Code provides an exception to this rule, applicable to any
child of a taxpayer (1) "born to him, or legally adopted by him,
in the Philippine Islands"; (2) if that event occurred "prior to

---

* Some contend (with considerable reason) that specially-tailored excess
profits provisions of this sort result from the inherent awkwardness of the
excess profits tax itself—relying, as it does, on an arbitrary "base period"
that cannot accommodate the individual peculiarities of particular companies' growth patterns.

January 1, 1956"; (3) if the child was a resident of the Philippines; and (4) "if the taxpayer was a member of the Armed Forces of the United States at the time the child was born to him or legally adopted by him." The amendment, enacted on August 9, 1955, reached back eight years, and was effective as of 1947.

Ordinarily, you may not claim a charitable deduction for contributing to organizations engaged in electioneering. But, thanks to Section 29 of the Revenue Act of 1962, anyone was allowed to deduct contributions made *during 1962 only*—not before, not after—to organizations electioneering for or against state or local judicial reform proposals "with respect to which a referendum [occurred] during . . . 1962." Section 29 was specifically tailored to help the fund-raising efforts of the Chicago and Illinois Bar Associations in backing a judicial reform program voted on in November, 1962.

The beneficiaries of these special statutes are not always anonymous. In rare instances, they are actually named. Section 25 of the Revenue Act of 1962, for example, is entitled, "Pension Plan of Local Union Numbered 435, International Hod Carriers' Building and Common Laborers' Union of America," and grants tax exemption to that pension plan roughly a year earlier than would otherwise have been the case.

In other cases, while the bill itself may name no names, its object is openly acknowledged. When, in 1961, Congress debated a bill entitled, "Distributions of Stock Pursuant To Orders Enforcing Antitrust Laws," it was stated that the measure made a specific tax-law exception for the sale of nearly $3 billion worth of General Motors stock by owners of DuPont, following a federal court anti-trust order. A similar bill, before the Congress in 1962 and again in 1963, named no names, but its retroactive provisions were known to apply specifically to the court-ordered sale by the Hilton Hotel Corporation of certain of its properties. A minority report by Ways and Means Committee members opposed to the bill pointed out that the bill was broad enough, potentially, to excuse nineteen other companies from the tax consequences of their anti-monopoly offenses.

Nor was it any secret that a provision of the 1962 tax bill entitled, "Income Tax Treatment of Certain Losses Sustained in Converting from Street Railway to Bus Operations" applied exclusively to the Twin Cities Rapid Transit Company of Minneapolis-St. Paul, Minnesota. Senator Eugene McCarthy explained to the Senate that the company's management had made a too-rapid changeover from streetcars to buses "in order to complete [certain] fraudulent activities quickly, intentionally disregarding the income tax consequences"—incurring losses so large that they could not be fully tax-deducted in the required period of time. As a result, the company, now under new management, was left with over $5 million of losses for which it could get no tax advantages. The proponents of the provision argued that the new management of the transit company should not have to bear the consequences of fraudulent activity by their predecessors in which they took no part.

The Twin Cities provision was not new; it had been passed by Congress in 1961 as a separate bill, and had been vetoed by President Kennedy. Now, by tacking the same provision on to the omnibus 1962 tax bill, which the Kennedy Administration had been struggling to pass for the better part of two years, its sponsors had made the measure veto-proof.

Also enjoying a free ride as part of the 1962 bill was a previously-vetoed provision for the specific benefit of Howard F. Knipp of Baltimore, Maryland, but here there is an important difference from the Twin Cities case.

As a result of a special partnership arrangement and the death of Mr. Knipp's partner-uncle in 1946, Internal Revenue ruled that nearly two years' income was taxable to Mr. Knipp in the single year 1947, causing him to pay roughly $110,000 in additional taxes. After losing both in the Tax Court and the Appeals Court, Knipp's attorneys sought relief through a "private law," candidly entitled, "A Bill for the Relief of Howard F. Knipp." Congressional committee reports set forth all the circumstances of the case and, unlike in the Leo Sanders case, openly acknowledged that the measure would reverse court decisions. The Treasury Department opposed the measure as an "undesirable precedent" that would invite others to seek congressional reversal of adverse court decisions, and the private law was vetoed. Thus thwarted, Knipp's protagonists sought relief via the nameless "general law" route and finally succeeded in tacking on to the 1962 revenue act the "Knipp amendment" —retroactive fifteen years to take care of Mr. Knipp's 1947 tax problem.

The Knipp case, by illustrating the two means by which Congress can accommodate an individual taxpayer's problem (either by a "private law" or by a nameless "general" provision) illuminates the central question posed by these tailor-made measures: if Congress wishes to bestow a tax favor on Louis B. Mayer or Leo Sanders or Charles Merrill or Howard F. Knipp, why not come right out and say so?

If, as with the first Knipp bill, the Mayer, Sanders and Merrill provisions had set forth the reasons for requesting special relief, Congress, the public and the President, with his veto power, would have had a means of judging the measure on its merits, based on all the facts. Why mask these actions behind the thin disguise of a "general" law?

To the practical politician, this is a self-answering question. The Treasury Department and the President rarely perceive as clearly as does Congress why a lone taxpayer should be excepted from the laws and rules applicable to others. Thus most efforts to grant tax relief through the more candid "private law" route have, like the Knipp bill, succumbed to a presidential veto. Therefore, explains one Ways and Means Committee member, when he is appealed to by a taxpayer with a case he considers meritorious, he has no choice but to disguise his tailored pro-

vision as a general law, and attach it, if possible, to an unveto-
able measure. Besides, the anonymous-bill method avoids the
annoyance of having to explain why special relief should be
granted to a taxpayer such as Leo Sanders, who has availed
himself of all the regular channels of justice and whose case
has been found wanting by the courts.

Moreover, members of the tax-writing committees, observing
their congressional colleagues on other committees dispensing
subsidies, public works and politically lucrative appropriation
items, are understandably reluctant to have tax bills diverted
to the respective Judiciary Committees, where, under congressional rules, private relief bills of the Knipp variety are referred.

There is another defense of the "general law" method of dispensing single-taxpayer relief. When Taxpayer A, with a meritorious case, seeks relief, how, it is asked, can anyone know
that there aren't dozens of other Taxpayers B, C, D, and so on,
in the same predicament? To name Taxpayer A in a bill for his
exclusive relief would be to discriminate against B, C, D, and
all the others. But this argument collapses when applied to the
Sanders provision (six years retroactive) or the Merrill amendment (applicable only to those who died fifteen months *prior*
to its enactment). It is, moreover, a transparently thin defense
of such absurdly hedged-in provisions as the Mayer amendment.

Ironically, in many cases, the very narrowness of these statutes
results from the urgings of the Treasury Department itself,
which reasons that if special relief is to be granted at all, better
to protect the federal revenues by confining the relief to the
narrowest possible circumstances.

In opposing these made-to-order relief provisions, the Treasury usually finds itself a lonely Horatio at the bridge. The few
private groups, such as the labor unions, who might be disposed
to speak up against such provisions, have no way of knowing
(in time, at any rate) that Amendment A is for Louis B. Mayer
or Provision B is for Charles Merrill. Nor have busy newspaper-
men had any success in rooting out the identity of these amend-

ments as they are being enacted. Even the Treasury can't always detect the beneficiary, and Stanley Surrey, in citing the factors abetting such special measures, complained in 1955 that tax attorneys have been of little help in rooting out and identifying such provisions. So numerous and technical are these special clauses, says Surrey, that they present an "impenetrable curtain" to the mass media and to public understanding.

Besides, there is a certain contagion among legislators in the passing of these amendments, since none can, with equanimity, deny favors to his own constituents while less fastidious colleagues are enacting special provisions for theirs. In defending the Twin Cities amendment, for example, Minnesota's Senator Hubert Humphrey, one of the most vocal opponents of tax "loopholes," acknowledged that this was "special legislation." But, he said, "it is not unique."

Few senators are immune from the charge of having pushed a particular provision on behalf of a favored constituent. When, for example, Ohio's Senator Lausche protested the Twin Cities amendment, Senator Kerr turned on him savagely and accused him of having objected, at the behest of an Ohio constituent, to one aspect of a "loophole-closing" provision, a charge indignantly denied by Senator Lausche. In a gentler manner, Senator Eugene McCarthy reminded Illinois' Paul Douglas, principal objector to the Twin Cities amendment, that "we passed a bill for the Senator from Illinois" providing retroactive relief for a union pension fund."

If the portrait painted thus far in this chapter is that of a tax law riddled with individually-tailored provisions and of a Congress wholly pliant to the pressures or blandishments of special pleaders, it is an incomplete picture. Provisions of the Mayer variety make up a small part of the tax laws. And, although the pressures on the tax-writing committees of Congress are great (the greater, perhaps, because they have shown themselves willing to let down the bars at propitious times), they do turn down many requests for special favors. Even among those they sponsor, few are finally enacted.

One knowledgable critic of tax preferences, Professor Walter Blum of the University of Chicago, is restrained in his criticism of the tailor-made tax provision. Because so few taxpayers are involved, he says, these measures do not complicate the tax system "to any appreciable extent" or lend themselves to "spawning new preferential provisions by suggesting analagous situations."

Nevertheless, the question remains whether raw political power or close acquaintanceship with a member of Congress (or a tax lobbyist) satisfactorily qualifies a citizen for favorable tax treatment not generally available to other taxpayers. It has been observed that "popular imagination holds taxes to be as ruthless in the certainty of their incidence as is death." If that is true, then popular imagination is not familiar with the efficacy of lobbyists or the ways of legislators.

When he was a professor of law at Columbia University, William L. Cary, now chairman of the Securities and Exchange Commission, devoted an entire article to special tax provisions, inspired in considerable measure by the "casual remark" of one Washington lawyer, who asked, "What is the point of litigating a tax case when we can have the statute amended for the same outlay of time and money?"

Cary poses this question:

> Can relief be scattered sporadically among a few individuals—whose only common characteristic is access to Congress—without making a mockery of the revenue laws? For every person who successfully argues [before Congress] that he is discriminated against, there are thousands of others, inarticulate or ineffective, who are suffering the same fate in silence.

4 /
Your Wife May
Be Worth a Million

Just this one morning, make an exception. Lower your break-fast-time newspaper and take a look at your wife. How much do you think she's worth? Oh, *of course* she's the priceless gem without which your life would be an utter void. But try, for a moment, to be wholly unsentimental. Put out of your mind the delicious aroma of those pancakes she is cooking for you (or, at the other extreme, that toast she is burning). Try to forget that her hair is in curlers and her face is greasy. Make, in short, a coldly practical dollars-and-cents calculation of just what she is worth to you in hard cash. The results may surprise you.

If you are a young executive with a $10,000-a-year salary, the little woman is an asset worth precisely $11,818.25. If you are a junior vice president, with a salary of $25,000 per year, the image of your wife is likely to be more dazzling, for she is the equivalent of $131,931.75. If you have reached the $75,000 level, you should experience a certain humility, for you are in the presence of a million-dollar asset.

If you are a corporation president drawing a salary of $100,-000, you may feel an impulse to go out and buy your spouse an expensive present, upon discovering that her cash value to you is $1,891,875. If you are able to so arrange your life as to have an annual taxable income of $445,777.78, your joy and wonder attain peak levels, your helpmate having attained the lustrous value of $6,996,994.00.

As you move up the income scale from there, however, a strange phenomenon occurs. Your wife begins to lose some of her monetary allure. When your annual income reaches $1,000,-000 the worth of your life companion has slipped to a mere $2,766,153.75. From there on, her value drops rapidly, and extreme care should be taken to prevent your annual income from exceeding $1,399,555.55 per annum, for above that point, your spouse becomes worthless (in a monetary sense, at least).

The experience of having a worthless wife is not, however, reserved to those in the over-$1,399,555.55 income group. On the contrary, it is shared by every married man with an annual income of less than $2,889—hardly the most exclusive "club" since, according to government statistics, about seven million belong.

Moreover, to the fifteen million married men with incomes of less than $5,000, the lady of the house represents a tax saving of only 73 cents a week, which a surly husband might say makes her worthless.

All of this comes to pass by virtue of a fiction written into the tax laws in 1948. In most American homes, of course, if there is only one breadwinner, it is the husband. The weekly paycheck is made out in his name. Nevertheless, the tax laws permit the husband, in making out his tax return, to make believe that half of the paycheck has been earned by the little wife. This is commonly known as filing a "joint return."

This is a highly expensive fiction: it costs the United States

Treasury $5 billion annually. Its bounties, moreover, are dispensed with singular unevenness. When it was enacted, 97 percent of its benefits went to the top 5 percent of the taxpayers. On the other hand, nearly four-fifths of the married couples of the nation were entirely denied its benefactions. So lopsided are its effects that Married Couple A, with 20 times the income of Married Couple B, can enjoy 319 times as much tax benefit.

A hypothetical illustration will demonstrate how the application of this fiction makes marriage financially as well as spiritually rewarding. Picture a promising young executive, Jeremy Hornblower, who at this point in his budding career earns just under $12,000 and has taxable income of $10,000.

It is his wedding day: at noon he is to become conjugally joined with a delectable southern maiden, Sue Alice Beauregard. But until noon he remains a bachelor, obligated to Uncle Sam for an annual $2,650—$1,100 on the first $5,000 of his income and $1,640 on the second $5,000 (since the tax rates rise as income increases).

At 12:17, the minister ties the knot, and at that instant Jeremy's annual tax bill drops to $2,200. Why? Because, as of 12:18 P.M., the government suddenly permits him to make believe that half of the $10,000* is earned by the former Miss Beauregard. As far as the government is concerned, his $10,000 income is now divided into two separate but equal parcels, labeled "His" and "Hers." The taxes on "His" half are $1,100; the taxes on "Hers" also $1,100—for a total tax of $2,200, $440 less than his tax as a bachelor.

Clearly, then, his new bride is not only an ornamental but a monetarily valuable asset. How valuable? Well, at his salary level, 38 cents out of every *added* dollar of income goes to the government. Hence, in order to enjoy an additional $440 of after-tax "keeping money," he would have to earn $709.68 more. He would get precisely that amount of added income if sud-

---

* Simplicity compels disregarding the extra $600 exemption that comes with the bridal "package."

denly a rich aunt were to deposit in his savings account $17,742, drawing 4 percent interest.

Thus, days later, basking on the beach at Waikiki, our honeymooning bridegroom can take a satisfied glance at that $17,742 asset lying by his side (for that is her equivalent cash value). If he closes his eyes and indulges in Walter Mitty dreams of ascending the corporate promotion ladder, she becomes monetarily even more alluring. When his taxable income reaches $25,000, he calculates, Sue Alice will mean added "keeping money" of $2,920 each year. At the 59 percent bracket into which he will have ascended, this will require $7,121.95 of before-tax income—the equivalent of an annual 4 percent return on a $178,048.75 deposit in his savings account.

His calculations assume that she does not earn a penny of her own, and, since the advantages of income-splitting are greatest when the wife's income is zero, if she wishes to keep her cash value at a maximum, she must at all costs avoid remunerative activity.

The following table will give male readers an opportunity to gain a true appreciation of the value of the wife they so often take for granted.

Annual income of husband	Cash value of wife*
$5,000	$ 1,218.00
$7,500	4,714.25
$10,000	11,818.25
$25,000	131,931.75
$100,000	1,891,875.00
$250,000	6,296,666.75
$445,777.77	6,996,994.50
$1,000,000	2,766,153.75
$1,399,555.55 and over	0

* This is the amount of cash which, drawing 4 percent interest, would net a husband the same increase in *after-tax* dollars he receives, thanks to marital income-splitting.

This information should be used with the utmost discretion and selectivity. Clearly, it should at all costs be concealed from one's wife who, upon learning her true cash value, will quickly become insufferable and begin making unreasonable demands on the family budget.

It can, however, be usefully referred to by the husband whose pique at his wife's proverbial tardiness (or, more likely, his infatuation with another woman) leads him to consider severing the conjugal knot. A quick glance at the table would readily convince him that he cannot afford *not* to be married.

Ludwig S. Hellborn, a research economist with the General Motors Corporation who originated many of the concepts described above, terms the income-splitting feature of the U. S. tax laws "Uncle Sam's Dowry"—quite different from the private dowry customary in many parts of Europe.* There, the size of the dowry varies with the wealth of the bride's father rather than that of the bridegroom. To the romanticists of Europe, therefore, the most satisfying event is the marriage of the worthy pauper to the millionaire's daughter, whereas in America, the dowry reaches its maximum when Cinderella marries a Rockefeller. In Europe, moreover, the dowry is a one-time gift. But kindly, magnanimous Uncle Sam renews the dowry annually, in even more generous amounts as the husband's affluence grows.

These lighter aspects of income-splitting are not likely to be appreciated by struggling young marrieds at the lowest end of the economic scale, who are virtually or wholly excluded from the joys and benefits of this tax feature. Nor is there likely to be great amusement among the single people who are obliged to support, say, aged and ailing relatives, but for whom the tax laws do not show the mercy proferred to *all* middle and upper-income married couples, no matter how small their obligations.

The fiction of income-splitting became part of the United

---

* West Germany and France also provide a governmental dowry since their tax laws provide for income-splitting.

States tax laws in 1948, largely because of a distinction between the property laws of the various states. Eight states,*
taking their laws from Spain or France rather than from England, treated half the income and property of the husband as
if legally belonging to the wife. Hence, before 1948, the married citizens of those eight states enjoyed all the federal
tax advantages accruing to the hypothetical Jeremy Hornblower
when he took his bride—a pleasure denied the citizens of the
other forty states. For low income taxpayers, the difference
was small ($26 a year for those with $4,000 incomes), but for
the well-to-do (those with $500,000 income), living in one of the
favored eight states meant $25,180 a year more spending
money.

To close the gap, various state legislatures began enacting
"community property" laws of their own—Oklahoma in 1945
(to prevent an exodus of wealthy oil men to the community-
property comfort of neighboring Texas); Oregon, Michigan,
Nebraska and Pennsylvania in 1947. Other states were im-
patient to pass similar laws. The pressure was on Congress to
act.

Politics was a factor, too. The Republican Eightieth Congress
was pledged to a tax cut, but President Truman had successfully vetoed two GOP tax bills. Income-splitting seemed a
hopeful way of breaking the impasse: it enjoyed the support
of some in the Truman Administration, and it offered those
primarily interested in bestowing tax relief on the middle- and
upper-income groups a way of doing so under the respectable
guise of "reform."

And so Congress proceeded to act, but with great illogic.
It ended one discrimination but created another. The very
distinction that had been considered so unfair to the married
citizens of forty states was picked up bodily and imposed upon
the *single* people of *all* the states.

The results are shown in the following table:

---

* Louisiana, Texas, Idaho, Washington, Arizona, Colorado, Nevada and
New Mexico.

To those with incomes of:	*Matrimony brings this tax bliss:*	
	AMOUNT	PERCENT
$5,000	$ 38	4.7
$7,500	132	7.4
$10,000	312	14.9
$20,000	1,504	25.5
$50,000	5,792	25.4
$250,000	22,668	12.7*
$500,000	25,180	6.6
$1,000,000	14,384	1.8

* The advantages of income-splitting taper off because of an upper limit on the tax, which can be no higher than 87 percent of taxable income in any year.

There is a tinge of political irony to the events of 1948. Clearly, income-splitting, which by-passes the poor and bestows lavish favors on the wealthy, does violence to the principle of "ability to pay"* historically embraced by the Democratic Party. Yet the congressional Democrats of the day, far from denying this offspring, proudly claimed paternity, boasting they had impelled the Republicans "toward consideration of equity and the elimination of discrimination in the tax system."

Apparently the lawmakers of 1948 considered the equity of income-splitting self-evident, for committee reports at the time omitted the customary justification of the new provision. Some have since sought to rationalize it on two principal grounds. First, they contend, it is both unfair and socially undesirable that two people should pay more taxes when married than they would pay on the same total income if they were earning it as single persons. Imagine, for example, Sophie and Ray, each leading separate and desolate lives, each with $5,000 of taxable income, each paying $1,100 of taxes (or $2,200 between

* See Glossary.

them). Were it not for income-splitting, love and matrimony would increase their combined tax bill on their newly-combined $10,000 income to $2,640. Surely (say the defenders of income-splitting) we do not wish thus to discourage marriage and encourage unconventional activity, such as concubinage, cohabitation and other unmentionables.

But, counter the critics of income-splitting, if husband and wife pool their incomes (as most compatible couples do) and share as one, why should they not be taxed as one? Besides, they say, if the institution of marriage is so frail as to depend on the slender reed of a tax incentive, how does one explain the popularity of matrimony among those with incomes of less than $2,889—who do not share in the blessings of income-splitting?

The second main defense of income-splitting, invoking economic reasons, holds that, contrary to the maxim, two *cannot* live as cheaply as one, and hence deserve to be taxed more gently than one. But logic deals this argument a fatal blow. For if the purpose of this tax concession is to help married couples make financial ends meet, *why are those with the lowest incomes either wholly or virtually excluded from its benefits— while, at the same time, couples with $100,000 of income (hardly on the brink of starvation) are blessed with $12,108 of added spending money?* (Even for childless couples with incomes as high as $5,800 and two-children families with incomes less than $7,100, income-splitting means a tax saving of only $65 a year, or less than $1.25 a week.)

The "economic" defense founders on another shoal. The most expensive part of marriage is the rearing of children; yet income-splitting bestows the same advantages to childless couples as to those with ten children. To be sure, each new offspring brings the tax savings of an added $600 exemption, but consider how this compares with the benefit to the American male (taxable income, $20,000) when he quits the state of bachelorhood.

	His tax bill is:	So that next step saved him:
As a blissful bachelor	$7,260	—
As an even more blissful bridegroom	$5,076	$2,184
As the proud father of one	$4,872	$ 204
As the even prouder father of two	$4,668	$ 204

If the gentleman in question is fortunate enough to have a taxable income of $50,000, the statistics are even more striking:

	Tax	Saving
Bachelor	$26,820	—
Bridegroom	$19,946	$6,874
Father of one	$19,592	$ 354
Father of two	$19,238	$ 354

Moreover, is it *always* true, as income-splitting assumes, that single people are better able to pay taxes than married persons? What if they must take care of aged (and perhaps ailing) parents? What if they suddenly find themselves responsible for the care of children, in the wake of a bereavement or divorce? Their burdens may well be far heavier than, say, a couple without children; yet the original 1948 income-splitting provision denied them the tender treatment accorded married couples.

In 1951, Congress acknowledged this logical defect of the 1948 provision and granted *one-half* the benefits of income-splitting to so-called "heads of household": unmarried persons obliged to support children, grandchildren or other dependent relatives actually living with them, or dependent parents, wherever they may live. But this modification suffers the same basic defect of the 1948 provision: those with the lowest incomes, on whom the burdens of dependency press the hardest, are excluded from its benefits. In 1960 there were just over a million heads of household, *roughly one-fourth of whom gained nothing from semi-income-splitting*. Moreover, although the responsibilities of a head-of-household can easily be greater than those of a married couple, they still receive only *half* the tax concession accorded the married.

In 1954, an effort by the House of Representatives to place heads-of-household on a par with married couples and to ease the living-in requirement for dependents was defeated by the Senate. As if to show they were not wholly devoid of compassion, however, Senators did grant to widows and widowers a two-year extension of their income-splitting privileges after the demise of their spouses.

There is a general belief, even among those who feel that income-splitting is illogic and injustice personified, that nothing can be done to undo the deed without reverting to the chaos of the pre-1948 situation, with the community property states once again enjoying a favored tax position over the other states.

Such is not the case, and the solution is remarkably simple: permit income-splitting, but abolish its benefits.

That is, for those wishing to file joint returns, the intervals between tax brackets would be made *half* as large as for single people (if revenue considerations dictated raising the taxes of the married to the level of the unmarried—which would raise $5 billion of revenue) or twice as large for single people (if the decision was to lower *their* taxes to the happier level of married couples). Either method would be a satisfactory way of ending the unwarranted discrimination against those who for their own private reasons are either unwilling or unable to join in the institution of matrimony.

If all the happy consequences described above can spring from a mere *two*-way splitting of income—between husband

and wife—think of the added joy that can flow from a three-, four-, or five-way division. $100,000 of taxable income in the hands of Father alone, for example, would mean a tax of $67,320. The filing of a joint return with Mother brings the tax down to $53,640. If Junior can somehow be brought into the picture, in a three-way split, the tax becomes $45,980. Include Sister in a four-way split and the tax is reduced to $40,600—only three-fifths of a single man's tax.

But can this be done? Few things are too difficult for the mind whose ingenuity is stimulated by the possibility of a 40 percent tax saving—for self or for client.

One solution, popular some years ago but somewhat more difficult to employ effectively today, is the family partnership, an intimate arrangement in which infants are sometimes born into the world as full business partners in a thriving enterprise.

Take the actual case, for example, of Paysoff Tinkoff, a New York accountant who operated his firm as a partnership. For a time the enterprise consisted of himself and his wife, with the partnership income divided equally between them, thus giving them the benefits of marital income-splitting. On November 11, 1929, an infant son, Paysoff Tinkoff, Jr., was born to them, and on that very day, the partnership agreement was amended to include the diapered infant. Thereafter, the partnership income was divided *three* ways equally, among father, mother and son. Yet, as a court later found, neither mother nor son "ever contributed any capital or services to the business . . ." (The judges were unkind enough to point out that Mrs. Tinkoff was not "a lawyer, accountant, bookkeeper or stenographer" and had "never worked in an office.")

Vintage readers will recall Stanback Headache Powders ("Snap Back With Stanback"). These powders, together with the less celebrated Stanback Liver Fixers, were the product of a company owned by two Stanback brothers, Thomas and Fred. Each brother had a wife and two minor children who were duly made full partners in the business, although the brothers retained full control and management.

Although the courts were unkind to both these arrangements, and ruled them invalid for tax purposes, apparently other family partnerships were faring better, for between 1939 and 1948, the number of partnership tax returns more than trebled, and in 1947, nearly a third of them indicated that the partnership included the wife or child of one of the partners.

The court cases that resulted from this proliferation of family partnerships were sometimes illuminating. In one case, the eager and forward-looking parents caused all the necessary partnership legal documents to be drawn up during the wife's pregnancy, leaving only the name and sex of the prospective new partner to be filled in. Thus, once the infant was safely in the world, the papers could be promptly filed and not an hour would be lost in the quest for greater splitting of the family income.

During another court case, involving a partnership made up of a husband, wife and four children, aged 7, 5, 2 and three months, the partner-wife was asked:

Q. Now, do you participate in the management of the business of the La Salle Livestock Company?
A. Well, I have been producing partners.
Q. Beg pardon?
A. I have been too busy producing partners so far.

Up until 1951, the law, as interpreted by the courts, permitted family partnerships to be invalidated, for tax purposes, unless "the parties, in good faith *and acting with a business purpose*,"* intended to join together in the present conduct of the enterprise. But in 1951 the "business purpose" test was dispensed with in cases where a bona fide and outright gift of a partnership interest had been made—even if the gift was to an infant

---

* Emphasis added.

child who had no intention or capacity to engage in "the present conduct of the enterprise." If a father were to give his son stocks or bonds, it was argued, the income from them would certainly be taxed to the son and not to the father. Why not apply the same principles of ownership to a part interest in the family business? Senatorial defenders of the 1951 provision were careful to point to its supposed safeguards designed to prevent a father from artificially shifting partnership income away from himself and his own high tax brackets and into the hands of less heavily taxed family members.* These senators failed, however, to explain why the 1951 provision should be made retroactive all the way back to 1939, the effect of which was peremptorily to decide a great many pending government challenges of family partnership arrangements against the government and in the taxpayers' favor.

Tax experts who have probed the details of many a family partnership insist that the 1951 formula is not as effective a bulwark against tax avoidance as its protagonists claimed. In an ordinary arm's-length business partnership, the incentives are all against the artificial shifting of partnership income, since each partner will insist on his proper share. Not so in a family partnership, where the dividing up of the business income is not done by arm's length negotiation (especially where one of the partners is an infant) and where the father has every incentive to allocate as much income as he can to his lightly-taxed offspring.

This is not mere theory, as actual court cases show. Take the case of the Uneeda Doll Company, a highly profitable venture (profits $327,350.97 one year) in which a paltry $15,000 capital contribution (made on his behalf by his father) won a 15 percent interest for a minor son. This $15,000 contribution netted the son a 300 percent return, which the government termed "inordinate," arguing that it was really the firm's trade name, good will and know-how that accounted for the profits. The

---

* Described in Appendix note.

court agreed in principle but said it had no power to re-allocate the profits and the arrangement was permitted to stand.

Another case involved a highly reputable West Coast construction company engaged in building highly complex multi-million dollar bridges, office buildings and stadiums. A family partnership was formed and a 6 percent share given, in trust, to the son of one of the partners, in return for a mere $20,000 given by his father. By contrast, the adult partners received *no* share of the profits for the $80,000 of capital *they* put up. The government argued that the firm's success rested on its reputation, business contacts, bank credit and know-how—all built up by the adult partners, and that a $20,000 capital input could only play the most miniscule role. Yet the court held that since a bona fide gift had been made, the arrangement could not be challenged.

Those most familiar with such court cases feel this way: family partnerships are, after all, supposedly business arrangements. Why shouldn't they be subjected to a "business purpose" test? Would the Uneeda Doll Company, with over $300,000 in annual profits, sell a 15 percent interest to an outsider for only $15,000? Would the partners in a major construction firm ordinarily accept no profit share for their $80,000 capital contribution, and then give up a 6 percent share for $20,000? If not, why shouldn't such arrangements be subject to challenge as a mere tax avoidance device?

A second income-splitting device is known as the multiple corporation, an arrangement by which a business conducts its operations through a large number of separate corporations (it has gone as high as 734) rather than as a single large corporation. The tax savings are substantial ($5,500 for each separate corporation) so that the benefits to a 734-corporation business could exceed $4,000,000 a year. The Treasury Department has cited two actual examples where the savings have exceeded a million dollars annually, and several where the tax

benefits run into several hundred thousand dollars (e.g. a
finance business split into 137 corporations for an annual tax
saving of $433,000; a retail chain with 142 corporations saving
$619,000 a year, and so on).

The savings result from the way the corporation tax is set
up: the first $25,000 of a corporation's earnings are taxed at
30 percent; everything above that at 52 percent. Thus, each
separate corporation avoids that extra 22 percent tax on $25,000
—for a $5,500 saving.*

To take advantage of this, new corporations may be spawned
without limit, provided a legitimate business purpose can be
demonstrated. Occasionally, though, the proliferation has been
carried out somewhat ungracefully, and the courts have
frowned. One construction company, for example, created no
less than eighty-eight separate corporations, none having either
employees or payroll, with all books and records maintained by a
single parent corporation. Finding names for the eighty-eight corporate offspring, however, apparently proved troublesome. The
owners started off by using the wife's middle name (Tyree)
as the basis for naming seventeen of the corporations and the
husband's middle name (Leith) for an additional sixteen.
Thereafter, a Latin note crept in: forty corporations were given
the names of Spanish numerals (Treinta Cinco, Inc., Cuarento
Uno, Inc., and so on) running from Uno to Cuarento Uno, Inc.
—but with Ocho, Inc. curiously left out. Another construction
company formed sixteen separate corporations imaginatively
and alphabetically named as follows: Adlon, Barca, Carab,
Dolan, Efton, Fonte, Grail, Hajon, Ilgar, Johan, Kiltor, Misap,
Nadre, Oland and Pewante. The court, however, gave no credit
for originality of names and ruled that the sixteen must be
taxed as one. The makers of the famous Revell plastic models
for children met the same fate when they created fifteen separate

---

* Under the tax measure passed by the House in 1963, the rate on the
first $25,000 would become 22 percent, beginning in 1965, and the rate on
profits over $25,000 would be an additional 26 percent. Under such rates,
the saving for each new corporation would be $6,500 instead of $5,500.

corporations for each of their product lines, bearing names such as PT Boat Molds, Inc., Hot Rod Molds, Inc., 307 Carrier Molds, Inc., and so forth.

By 1963, the unwarranted use of multiple corporations had come to cost the Treasury an estimated $120 million annually, prompting the House of Representatives, in 1963, to approve curbs on this practice (related corporations subject to 80 percent or more common ownership or control will be taxed as one, insofar as the lower taxation of the first $25,000 of profits is concerned or pay a penalty tax).

"Trusts" are yet another means of splitting up income into smaller, less heavily taxed bundles, although they clearly serve useful non-tax purposes as well (e.g., a parent wishing to give some stocks or bonds to a child too young to manage his own affairs or make immediate use of the income might place them "in trust," with trustees appointed to care for the property until such time as it passes to the child outright).

The income-splitting and tax-saving possibilities spring from the fact that a trust can be taxed as if it were a separate person.

To illustrate, picture a hypothetical wealthy family, the van Meers—father in the 75 percent bracket, son in the 62 percent bracket (thanks to the generosity of his grandfather)— with a tax problem many readers might almost envy: Mr. van Meer has some stocks producing a yearly income of $5,000, but he doesn't want the added income to be taxed at his 75 percent rate or his son's 62 percent rate. Solution: he gives the stock to a newly created trust, which is taxed as if it were a separate person. Result: since the trust's income is only $5,000,* its top tax rate is only 26 percent.

If the creation of a *single* trust can be thus helpful, then surely the establishment of a *large number* of trusts can bring

---

* This leaves aside, for simplicity's sake, the $100 exemption and possible deductions for administrative expenses enjoyed by all trusts.

even happier results by splitting income into even smaller parcels. If Mr. van Meer's bothersome stock holdings produced $50,000 of income instead of $5,000, there would be little point in putting them into a single trust, for its top bracket rate would be 75 percent, the same as Mr. van Meer's and higher than his son's. Solution: create *ten* trusts, each receiving $5,000 of income. Result: each trust would have a top bracket rate of 26 percent. Sensible? Very. Legal? Yes, provided Mr. van Meer exercises a modicum of care and sophistication, and stays within the bounds of reason. He should avoid the inelegance displayed by a Dr. Boyce who, on a single day, using identically mimeographed forms, established no less than ninety identical trusts to hold only $17,000 worth of stocks and bonds. A court found this a "preposterous" maneuver, whose sole purpose was to have each trust fall within the $100 exemption, and thus escape taxation entirely. "Straining reason and credulity," the court said, "it ought to be struck down forthwith." It was.

Comparatively speaking, Dr. Boyce was playing for penny-ante stakes. In a 1937 message to Congress, President Roosevelt noted that "one thrifty taxpayer [had] formed 64 trusts for the benefit of four members of his immediate family and thereby claimed to have saved them over $485,000 in one year in taxes." The Stranahan family, principal owners of the Champion Spark Plug Company, saved a total of $701,227.48 over a three-year period, by creating over thirty trusts.

Multiple trusts are still a favorably regarded tax avoidance device. Recently, two members of the New York bar acknowledged in a technical journal that "minimizing of income taxes" is "an important reason for using multiple trusts," even prompting their use by grantors "who would otherwise have created a single trust or made an outright gift."

As these attorneys noted, beyond their income-splitting usefulness, multiple trusts can also be exploited to circumvent what tax lawyers call the "throwback rule."

To press the van Meer family back into illustrative service, the throwback rule provides that any income over $2,000 that might build up in the van Meer trust and be distributed to son Henry before five years have passed must be taxed to son Henry (at his 62 percent rate) instead of to the trust at its lower rate. But to Mr. van Meer, blessed with ample wealth and a clever tax attorney, the throwback rule presents no insurmountable obstacles. If he wishes son Henry to receive $10,000 a year, he simply creates five trusts, each of which pays $2,000 to Henry, and thus stays within the limits of the throwback rule. Of course, if he desires that Henry be more generously financed and receive $50,000 a year, he might set up ten trusts, spaced a year apart, each of which would spend five years building up the desired amount of income, hold it for the requisite five years, and then take its annual turn in disgorging the accumulated income to the fortunate lad.

Congress was once on the brink of tightening up the law on multiple trusts, but fell short of taking the final steps. A bill (developed by dint of the voluntary services of private tax attorneys at Congress' request) passed the House of Representatives in 1960, and was approved by the Senate Finance Committee, but the Senate's Democratic leaders, said to look upon the measure with disfavor, never brought it before the Senate. The bill died and has not been revived since.

Dan Throop Smith, top tax adviser to the Eisenhower Administration, feels that even the 1960 reform measure did not "get to the heart" of the problem. The only effective way of eliminating tax avoidance through the use of trusts, he says, is to ignore trusts, for tax purposes, and tax their income to the creator of the trust or to the beneficiary, depending on the terms of the trust and the completeness of the gift. This, he says, would "wipe out completely" the tax advantages of multiple trusts, multigeneration trusts (see pp. 259-260) and single trusts accumulating income, without impairing the usefulness of trusts for non-tax purposes.

The use of trusts has risen dramatically, nearly doubling in number and more than doubling in income* between 1949 and 1958, although, since trusts serve non-tax needs, this increase should not be presumed entirely tax-inspired. Because of the complexity of trust arrangements, it is difficult for Internal Revenue to determine how much revenue is lost through the manipulation of trusts. But the House of Representatives and the Senate Finance Committee indicated, by their 1960 approval of a reform measure, that a tightening up of trust taxation is needed.

It is manifestly clear that income-splitting can be a source of considerable tax joy for the well-advised taxpayer. There are even greater pleasures to be derived, however, in the quest for the magical "capital gain"—the holy grail of tax avoidance— as you will discover in the next chapter.

---

* From $925 million to nearly $2.5 *billion*.

5 /

The Great
Capital Gains Trial[*]

(The scene is a packed U.S. courtroom. The occasion: the trial of People v. The Capital Gains Tax. *The jurors—(twelve regulars and four alternates)—have been chosen, and the opposing lawyers are scheduled to make their opening statements. The noise in the courtroom subsides as the Judge enters.)*

CLERK: Oyez, oyez, oyez! All persons having business before this honorable court are admonished to draw near and give their attention, for the court is now sitting. God save the United States and this honorable court.

JUDGE: Be seated, please. The jury having been duly selected,

---

* The capital gains tax has here been placed on hypothetical trial simply as a means of simplifying and dramatizing the arguments, pro and con. Readers who happen to be trial attorneys are asked to indulge the obvious deviations from regular courtroom procedure, especially the freedom accorded the jury to question counsel and to debate issues in open court. At the conclusion of the trial, the author appears, thinly disguised as the Foreman of the Jury.

we may now proceed with the case of *People v. The Capital
Gains Tax.*

This case is, of course, most unusual. The Defendant, the
Capital Gains Tax, stands accused of two contradictory offenses. On the one hand, the People contend that because the
tax is so *low*, it is guilty of injecting unfairness and complexity
into the American tax system. On the other, the Investors, in
a separate brief, maintain that because the tax is so *high*, it is
hampering the free flow of American capital. Apparently, the
Defendant can do no right.

Counsel for the People, you may proceed with your opening statement.

PEOPLE'S COUNSEL: Thank you, your honor.

Ladies and gentlemen of the jury, his honor, with his usual
succinctness, has ably stated the People's case. Our charge is
two-fold: first, that the Defendant, the Capital Gains Tax, is
perhaps the greatest source of unfairness in the American tax
system; and second, that it is the most significant single cause
of tax complexity.

To understand these charges, picture, if you will, a dam in
a river—high water behind it, low water in front. As you know,
the high water exerts steady pressure against the dam as it
seeks the level of the lower water.

Our tax system is not unlike that. On the high side of the
tax dam lies what the tax laws call "Ordinary Income"—the
wages and salaries all of us earn, as well as any interest or
dividends we might receive. This Ordinary Income is subject
to the regular income tax rates that run as high as 91 percent.

On the low side of the dam are so-called "Capital Gains"
—the profit you make when you sell a share of stock or, say,
a piece of land, for more than you paid for it. The profits on
property you've owned six months or more don't come under
the regular tax rates. They get a special rate that is never
more than 25 percent*—far less, obviously, than the top in-

---

* It can be less. See Glossary.

come tax rate of 91 percent. The tax bill passed by the House of Representatives in 1963 provides an even lower rate—21 percent—on most property you've held more than two years.

The pressure on the dam results from the difference between the rates. Everybody in the upper brackets would naturally like to pay less taxes—and they're constantly badgering Congress and the courts to have this or that kind of income classified—and taxed—as a "capital gain." After years of pressure, the dam has deteriorated quite a bit so that today the distinction between so-called "ordinary income" and "capital gains" sometimes doesn't make much sense.

In order to illustrate this point to you ladies and gentlemen of the jury, I have prepared signs describing certain ordinary income and capital gains situations, which I have placed side by side on easels in front of you, for easy comparison.

Ordinary Income Situation No. 1	*Capital Gains Situation No. 1*
You are a novelist.	You are an inventor.
You have written a widely-acclaimed, best-selling novel.	You have invented a new pretzel bender.
You have just sold your novel to the movies for $300,000.	You have just sold your invention to a pretzel company for $300,000.
You pay a tax of $223,640.	You pay a tax of $75,000.
You get to keep $76,360.	You get to keep $225,000.

FOREMAN OF THE JURY: You mean to say, Counsel, that the inventor gets to keep nearly three times what the novelist keeps?

PEOPLE'S COUNSEL: That's right.

FOREMAN OF THE JURY: But why? What's the difference between them? They've both used their brains to create something of value. Why should one pay three times as much tax as the other?

PEOPLE'S COUNSEL: Because Congress says so.

FOREMAN OF THE JURY: What do you mean?

PEOPLE'S COUNSEL: In 1950 Congress simply decreed, in effect, that the proceeds of an invention can be classified as capital gains, whereas the proceeds from a "literary, musical or artistic composition" must be classified as ordinary income.

FOREMAN OF THE JURY: It doesn't make sense. Did Congress give any reason for all this?

PEOPLE'S COUNSEL: They just said it was desirable to "foster" the work of inventors. Let's look at the second pair of signs.

Ordinary Income Situation No. 2 *(pre-1964)*	*Capital Gains Situation No. 2* *(pre-1964)*
You are a businessman, in the 75% tax bracket.	You are a businessman, in the 75% tax bracket.
You own an interest in *iron* mines.	You own an interest in *coal* mines.
You receive $20,000 of iron ore royalties.	You receive $20,000 of coal royalties.
You pay tax of $15,000.	You pay tax of $5,000.
You get to keep $5,000.	You get to keep $15,000.

ENGINEER JURYMAN: I don't understand. Isn't a dollar of iron ore royalty exactly the same as a dollar of coal royalty?

PEOPLE'S COUNSEL: That's what the iron ore people kept telling Congress. Congress gave capital gains treatment to coal royalties, they said, why not iron ore? So in 1963, the House voted to give iron ore royalties the special rate, too—even though it admitted there was no real "capital gain" involved.

ENGINEER JURYMAN: But why was Congress so generous to coal royalties in the first place?

PEOPLE'S COUNSEL: The coal royalty owners claimed they were in a bind because their contracts forgot to take into account the rising price of coal. Congress concluded this was a hardship situation and simply decreed that coal royalties should be taxed as capital gains—even though there clearly isn't any "capital asset" involved, and even though other kinds of royalties are taxed as ordinary income.

ENGINEER JURYMAN: It's a kind of "legislative alchemy," isn't it? You take a dollar that comes from a coal royalty or selling an invention: one day it's ordinary income and then, Presto! Congress transforms it into a capital gain. It's the same dollar, from the same source, earned in the same manner—but it's suddenly taxed differently!

JUDGE: Counsel, may we proceed to the next signs, please?

Ordinary Income Situation No. 3	*Capital Gains Situation No. 3*
You are an apple farmer, with a top tax rate of 50%.	You are a Christmas tree farmer, with a top tax rate of 50%.
You make a $4,000 profit on the apples you have grown.	You make a $4,000 profit on the Christmas trees you've raised.
You pay a tax of $2,000.	You pay a tax of $1,000.
You get to keep $2,000.	You get to keep $3,000.

LABOR-LEADER JURYMAN: Christmas trees! You mean there's something special in the tax law for Christmas trees?

PEOPLE'S COUNSEL: I quote, sir, from Section 631(a) of the Internal Revenue Code which states that the capital gains treatment for timber specifically extends to "evergreen trees which are more than 6 years old at the time severed from the roots and are sold for ornamental purposes." In plain English, this means Christmas trees.

LABOR-LEADER JURYMAN: But why? Why Christmas trees?

PEOPLE'S COUNSEL: Well, when Congress gave capital gains treatment to certain tree sales—another case of legislative alchemy, by the way—Christmas trees were ruled ineligible. When there were complaints of discrimination, Congress wrote Christmas trees into the law.

The next pair of signs illustrate a far more basic point:

Ordinary Income Situation No. 4	*Capital Gains Situation No. 4*
You are a lawyer.	You are a corporation vice-president.
Your top income tax bracket is 62%.	Your top income tax bracket is 62%.
By working extra-long hours on a big case, you earn an extra $30,000.	For your extra-hours work and superlative job performance, your company has given you the right to buy company stock at a favored price. You buy the stock and later sell it for a $30,000 profit.
On your added $30,000, you pay a tax of $19,380.	On your added $30,000, you pay a tax of $7,500.
You get to keep $10,620.	You get to keep $22,500.

LAWYER JURYMAN:* Counsel, that one really hits home with me. No matter how hard I work, or how big a practice I build up, everything I earn from my practice is ordinary income, and Uncle Sam ends up with most of it.

LABOR-LEADER JURYMAN: What's wrong with that? Your fees are no different from my weekly paycheck. It's all ordinary income, isn't it?

LAWYER JURYMAN: That's right, and if the rule applied to everybody, I wouldn't kick. But these stock options† are nothing but salary bonuses—and what gets me is seeing some of my own clients getting twice the income I do, but paying a lot less in taxes—just because they happen to work for a corporation. I read about one lawyer who quit Wall Street and went to work as general counsel of Ford, and it wasn't long before he had nearly half a million dollars worth of these stock options. He certainly couldn't have done that on Wall Street.

ENGINEER JURYMAN: Nearly everybody on this jury is in the

---

* The presence of a lawyer on the jury is a literary license, since ordinarily attorneys may not serve as jurors.

† Discussed more fully on pp. 181-190.

same boat. All we have to sell is our services—and the more successful we are, the rougher our taxes are.

PEOPLE'S COUNSEL: You gentlemen have made my point for me. Why, I hope you will all ask yourselves, should people be taxed differently on their earnings just because of their profession?

Next pair of signs, please.

Ordinary Income Situation No. 5	*Capital Gains Situation No. 5*
You are a junior executive, single, with a taxable income of $14,000.	You are a junior tycoon, single, with a taxable income of $200,000.
Your hard work has earned you a $1,000 raise in your yearly salary.	Your broker has sold one of your stocks for a $1,000 profit.
Your top income tax bracket is 47%; your extra $1,000 of salary is taxed at 47%.	Your top income tax bracket is 91% but your $1,000 stock profit is taxed at 25%.
On your added $1,000 you pay a tax of $470.	On your added $1,000 you pay a tax of $250.
You get to keep $530.	You get to keep $750.

LABOR-LEADER JURYMAN: How can that be? Why this junior tycoon, or whatever you call him, has—let's see—about fourteen times as much income as this junior executive, but he pays about half as much tax on his extra $1,000.

PEOPLE'S COUNSEL: Absolutely correct.

LABOR-LEADER JURYMAN: But our tax system is supposed to be based on "ability to pay"—with people with bigger incomes paying *higher* taxes, not lower.

PEOPLE'S COUNSEL: Sir, you are perspicacious, discerning, and astute. As you have perceived, the capital gains tax and the principle of "ability of pay" have nothing whatever to do with each other. In fact, the junior tycoon might have had *fifty or a hundred* times the income of the junior executive and still paid less taxes on the extra thousand.

LABOR-LEADER JURYMAN: You know, I've always read about this capital gains tax, but I don't think I've ever met anybody who's been able to use it.

PEOPLE'S COUNSEL: That's not surprising, when you consider that if this jury happened to be a typical cross-section of American taxpayers, chances are that only *one* of you would have listed a capital gain on your tax return.

DOCTOR JURYMAN: One out of sixteen? That's only about 6 percent, Counsel.

PEOPLE'S COUNSEL: That's correct, sir. Out of sixty-one million tax returns filed in 1960, less than four million listed any capital gains.

But that's only part of the story. Even among the lucky four million, the gains were heavily bunched in the upper brackets —so much so that of the four million, the top 2/10 of 1 percent get more than a third of all of the capital gains. This chart will show you what I mean.

Those with incomes of:	*Comprise only this % of all taxpayers:*	*But get this % of all capital gains:*
$200,000 and over	96/10,000 of 1%	16%
$100,000 and over	4/100 of 1%	24%
$50,000 and over	2/10 of 1%	35%
$10,000 and over	8.7%	69%

JUDGE: Counsel, may we move on to your next signs, please?

Ordinary Income Situation No. 6	*Capital Gains Situation No. 6*
You are a businessman in the 75% tax bracket.	You are a businessman in the 75% tax bracket.
You buy a 20-acre tract in the suburbs.	You buy a 20-acre tract in the suburbs.
Being a go-getter, you subdivide your property and build houses on it.	You do nothing with your land; you just let it sit.

Ordinary Income Situation No. 6	*Capital Gains Situation No. 6*
You sell the lots and houses and make a $100,000 profit.	You sell the land and make a $50,000 profit.
Your tax is more than three-fourths of your profit ($81,000).*	Your tax is just one-fourth of your profit ($12,500).
You get to keep $19,000.	You get to keep $37,500.

ENGINEER JURYMAN: Let me be sure I understand, Counsel. Do you mean the "go-getter," as you put it, who does something with his land, makes twice the profit—and yet ends up with half as much take-home money?

PEOPLE'S COUNSEL: That's correct.

ENGINEER JURYMAN: But doesn't that amount to penalizing initiative and rewarding inaction?

PEOPLE'S COUNSEL: That's the way it seems to work out—although I'm sure Congress didn't intend such a result. Nonetheless, more than two pages of the tax law are devoted to warning taxpayers how little they must do with a piece of land if they want to be sure of getting the special capital gains tax rate.

Let's move on.

Ordinary Income Situation No. 7	*Capital Gains Situation No. 7*
You are a baseball player.	You are a drug store manager.
For 10 years you have been working your way up through the minor and major leagues.	For 10 years you have owned 50 acres of unused land, left you by your father.
You have just been voted Most Valuable Player in your league.	A company has just decided to build a huge factory right next to your property.
You sign a contract for $100,000 for the next season.	You sell your land to a developer for a $100,000 profit.

---

* The added $100,000, on top of your regular income, throws you into the 81 percent bracket.

Ordinary Income Situation No. 7	*Capital Gains Situation No. 7*
You will pay a tax of $45,576.	You pay a tax of $25,000.
You'll get to keep $54,424.	You get to keep $75,000.
P.S. The following year, due to a serious injury, you are forced to retire, and your income drops back to $8,000.	P.S. The following year, your income is back down to your $8,000 salary.

LABOR-LEADER JURYMAN: How do you like that? This drug store fellow gets $100,000 dumped in his lap—doesn't lift a finger to earn it—but pays about half as much tax as that guy who worked his heart out for that MVP award.

DOCTOR JURYMAN: Counsel, would you explain to us the significance of the P.S. at the bottom of each poster? I know you put it there for a purpose.

PEOPLE'S COUNSEL: Gladly, sir. As I know Defense Counsel will explain,* one of the main reasons behind the special capital gains rate is the so-called "bunched"-income problem. That is, a person like the drug store manager, suddenly getting $100,000 in one year, will pay more taxes than another person *getting the same amount of money,* but spread evenly over, say, ten years. You'll be hearing more about the pros and cons of this later. My point here is that the "bunched"-income problem is not unique to capital gains. Movie stars, athletes, writers, composers share it, too, but they don't get any special 25 percent rate on their income.

JUDGE: Counsel, you seem to have stunned the jury into rare silence. Proceed with your next illustration.

Ordinary Income Situation No. 8	*Capital Gains Situation No. 8*
You are a single lady, supporting your aged aunt.	You are a single lady, supporting your aged aunt.
Your taxable income is $6,000.	Your taxable income is $200,000.

---

* See p. 97.

Ordinary Income Situation No. 8	*Capital Gains Situation No. 8*
On May 1 you buy a share of Alleghany Stovepipe, for $40.	On May 1 you buy a share of Alleghany Stovepipe, for $40.
5 months and 29 days later—October 29—you sell the stock for $60 in order to meet an insurance premium payment.	Six months and one day later—November 2—you sell your stock for $60.
Your profit on the sale of the stock is taxed at your regular income tax rate of 30%.	Your profit on the sale of the stock is taxed at the special capital gain rate of 25%.

HOUSEWIFE JURYWOMAN: Why, that's perfectly outrageous! Why should that poor lady with the $6,000 income pay a higher tax than the other lady with more than thirty times as much income?

PEOPLE'S COUNSEL: Because, madam, the $6,000 lady is a "speculator" while the $200,000 lady is an "investor."

HOUSEWIFE: What do you mean, "speculator"?

PEOPLE'S COUNSEL: She sold her stock in less than six months —and that makes her a speculator, at least as far as the tax law is concerned.

HOUSEWIFE: How ridiculous! She sold that stock to keep her insurance from lapsing. She's no speculator.

PEOPLE'S COUNSEL: This, strangely enough, is one point on which the People and the Investors agree. We both feel it's ridiculous to distinguish speculators from investors by an artificial time cut-off. But there has always been a holding period requirement in the law. At first it was two years, but now it's been shortened to six months.*

I have one final—and crucial—point to make.

Up until now, you may have gotten the impression that the only way a person could cash in a capital gain was by paying a 25 percent capital gains tax. But that's not the case. *It can be done without paying any tax at all.*

---

* In 1963, President Kennedy proposed lengthening the holding period to one year, but Congress would have none of it.

DOCTOR JURYMAN: How can that be, Counsel?

PEOPLE'S COUNSEL: Because all the capital gains on property you hold when you die *escape tax entirely*. Suppose your grandfather gave you some General Motors stock. At the time he bought it and gave it to you, it was only worth $5,000, but over the years, what with stock splits and a rising stock market, it's come to be worth $105,000. Now if you sell it for that during your lifetime, you have a capital gain of $100,000 and you'd pay a $25,000 tax. *But if you leave that stock to your wife in your will, she can sell it for $105,000 and pay no capital gains tax at all.*

LABOR-LEADER JURYMAN: How come? The stock only cost $5,000. Why isn't the gain taxed?

PEOPLE'S COUNSEL: Because the law makes believe that after you die the "cost" of the stock is its value at your death. That is, according to the law, your wife's "cost" of the GM stock you leave her is $105,000, she sells it for $105,000—so there's no gain, and, of course, no tax.

LABOR-LEADER JURYMAN: You mean to say there's zero tax on all the gains that pass at death?

PEOPLE'S COUNSEL: That's a good way to put it.

LAWYER JURYMAN: That's not quite fair, though, Counsel. The $100,000 doesn't really pass tax-free, since there's an estate, or death, tax to pay on it.

PEOPLE'S COUNSEL: Not necessarily. $50,000 of it can pass tax-free to your wife automatically, and there's a $60,000 estate tax exemption, so there need not be any death tax.* But even if there were, there's still an enormous advantage to leaving capital gain property over leaving cash. Suppose all you can leave your wife is the cash you've managed to build up from your take-home pay. You've already paid an income tax on it —*and you pay a death tax besides.* Your neighbor, who leaves the General Motors stock, only pays the death tax, so he's way ahead.

---

* See Chapter 14.

LAWYER JURYMAN: But, Counsel, is it really as important as you make it out to be? After all, most of the gains must be left by just a few rich people, so the number of dollars that escape tax at death must be pretty small.

PEOPLE'S COUNSEL: Sir, I think you are in for a major surprise. Not one person I have ever asked about this has come any-where near guessing the right answer. The fact is, though, that *from $12 billion to $13 billion escapes tax at death every year.*

By failing to tax these billions, the government is passing up *nearly $3 billion a year of revenue.*

ENGINEER JURYMAN: And how much revenue are we losing by not taxing capital gains the same as other income?

PEOPLE'S COUNSEL: Something over $2 billion. One tax expert figured out that if you taxed capital gains on a par with other income, you could afford to take the top tax rate down from 91 percent to 50 percent, and take two percentage points off of each tax rate below 50 percent—and still not lose any revenue. That top 50 percent rate ought to please all the people who moan about Uncle Sam being their "majority partner."

LABOR-LEADER JURYMAN: Yes, but what a sop to the rich—taking the top rate down to 50 percent.

PEOPLE'S COUNSEL: That's the way it looks at first glance—but let me ask you this: did you know that taxpayers with incomes of over $5 million pay taxes, on the average, of less than 25 percent?

LABOR-LEADER JURYMAN: That's impossible. Twenty-five per-cent—that's only a little more than the lowest-bracket rate. How can that be?

PEOPLE'S COUNSEL: Well, 70 percent of their incomes is taxed at the special 25 percent capital gains tax. That is, their aver-age income is just under $9 million, but over $6 million of this is capital gains, and so it escapes the regular income rates. So you see, lowering the top rate to 50 percent, along with end-ing the special capital gains rate should certainly not be looked on as a "sop to the rich." This chart I've prepared will show you how important capital gains are to the wealthy—and how little the lowly share in this tax favor:

	Percent of this income group having any capital gains	*Percent of this group's income that comes from capital gains*
Under $5,000	86%	2%
$10–25,000	4%	4%
$50–100,000	18%	18%
$1,000,000 and over	58%	64%

JUDGE: Counsel, you told the jury, initially, that you had a two-fold indictment against the Capital Gains Tax, but you haven't covered the second part of your charge.

PEOPLE'S COUNSEL: Your honor and members of the jury, a justified complaint is frequently leveled at our tax laws and regulations that they are so complex as to be virtually incomprehensible—sometimes even to the experts. The People maintain that the special capital gains tax rate is the principal culprit—and we cite, as our authority, Mr. Stanley S. Surrey, top tax advisor to the Kennedy Administration and former Harvard law professor, who has said that capital gains are "the subject singly responsible for the largest amount of complexity" in the American tax laws.

The explanation for this lies in the image of the dam I cited earlier, with the high water pressing against it, seeking the lower level of the water below. Taxpayers on the high side of our two-level tax system exert a similar pressure as they seek the lower-level capital gains tax below the dam. They press upon the Treasury, Internal Revenue, the Congress and the courts in a never-ending battle to create new and more ingenious ways by which "ordinary income" can be alchemized into capital gains. They devise schemes with intriguing names like "collapsible corporations" and "corporation spin-offs."

Where does the complexity come in? Well, as an example,

Congress' effort to prevent tax avoidance through the "collapsibles" ended up adding 3,000 words to the tax law itself, and the Treasury added 5,600 words to its own tax regulations —and even with that, "collapsibles" can still be put to great advantage in the real estate field.* "Spin-offs"† were slightly easier to control—it only took 1,000 words in the law and 4,000 words of added regulations to curb them.

Those, of course, are only two of the capital gains contrivances in the law. There are personal holding companies and stock options, real estate "tax shelters" and cattle raising,‡ timber and lump-sum pension settlements, and many others. Government officials estimate that roughly half of all tax cases in the courts involve the capital gains field.

Members of the jury, it would be difficult to measure or describe to you the effort, talent and ingenuity devoted to "working the capital gains angle." What a shame this talent isn't being channeled into minimizing costs and prices and maximizing profits.

President Kennedy asked Congress to undo some of the legislative alchemy it has performed in the past, and to end capital gains treatment for such things as cattle, timber, stock options, coal royalties and some others. Fine—but these are merely attacks on the symptoms, rather than the cause, which is our two-level tax system. (In fact, the *lower* capital gains tax in the 1963 tax bill passed by the House would *increase* the pressures for special capital gains treatment.) Even if Congress had closed up all the capital gains "loopholes" suggested by the President, new ones would, in time, spring up to take their place. For as long as the two-level system exists, these pressures will persist. Close up this major avenue of escape, and the pressures may not vanish, but they will subside substantially.

I submit, members of the jury, that we should put an end

---

* See pp. 150-151.
† See Glossary.
‡ Described in more detail on pp. 131-137, 181-190, 143-161, and 139-141 respectively.

to the preferred status that capital gains enjoy in our tax laws. We should tax all income at uniform rates, whether the income be from wages or the sale of stock, from novels or inventions. And we should end the zero tax on gains passing at death. These changes should, of course, be accompanied by a system of income-averaging* that would mitigate or solve the "bunched"-income problem.

If we take these steps, we can—and *must*—drastically lower the top tax rates, down to a 50 percent maximum.

I ask you, members of the jury, to envisage the dramatic benefits that would flow from such a reform.

It would make our tax system fairer: everyone would be taxed according to the same rate schedule, and according to his ability to pay.

It would restore sensible values to our society: no longer would the work of *money* be vastly favored over the work of *people*.

It would put an end to much of the pressure for special tax treatment, and would liberate much of the energy and talent now devoted to tax avoidance.

Finally, no more than 50 cents of any dollar would be taken by the tax collector.

I submit, your honor and members of the jury, that the abolition of the special capital gains tax rate is the single greatest tax reform this nation could undertake.

JUDGE: Counsel for the defense, you may proceed with your opening statement.

DEFENSE COUNSEL: Your honor, I am aghast at the radical proposal made by People's Counsel, which would, of course, shake the very foundations of our enterprise system. This country has had a separate capital gains rate ever since 1921, and so far as I know, Congress has never, in all those years, seriously questioned the principle of a separate rate.

---

* See Glossary.

JUDGE: Would you tell the jury what prompted Congress to enact the separate rate in 1921?

DEFENSE COUNSEL: Two considerations, your honor, which remain the principal reasons behind the special capital gains rate today.

The first is the manifest unfairness of taxing, *in a single* year, all the gains that may have accrued over a number of years, in, say, a share of stock or a piece of land. Clearly, to do so would push a taxpayer into an artifically high tax bracket. For instance, take a man who buys a piece of land, holds it for twenty years and sells it for a $100,000 profit. Now if this were to be taxed as if the gain had occurred evenly over the twenty years he held the property, this would mean just $5,000 of added income a year, which would probably affect his tax bracket very little. But if the entire $100,000 were taxed in the year he sells the land, he would suddenly be catapulted into the 75 percent or 89 percent bracket (depending on whether he's married or single), and the government would take most of his profit. As long as the tax rates get stiffer as a person's income goes up, this so-called "bunching" effect is going to be unfair.

JUDGE: What was the second main reason for the capital gains tax, Counsel?

DEFENSE COUNSEL: Congress felt that having to pay a tax on the sale of stocks and other properties was tending to make people hold on to them instead of selling them, and that capital was becoming too "frozen."

There is, members of the jury, a crucial difference between capital gains and ordinary income. Most of the income you receive—salaries, wages, interest, dividends and the like— involves no *choice* on your part. The income is paid to you, you're taxed on it, and that's that.

But with capital gains, you do have a choice. You can either sell a particular stock or bond or piece of land, and pay a capital gains tax, or you can hold on to the property and pay no tax. It's this element of *choice* that creates a tax barrier to selling property—and it's this that justifies special tax treatment of capital gains. It's important to lower that barrier and make capital more mobile.

JUDGE: Perhaps, Counsel, a numerical example would illustrate what you mean by a "barrier.'"

DEFENSE COUNSEL: Well, suppose you have a share of stock you bought for $20. It's now selling for $100 and paying you a $3 dividend. Your broker suggests you sell. If you do, of course, you'll pay a $20 capital gains tax and have only $80 left to reinvest in a new security.

Now that may make you pretty reluctant to sell. Say, for instance, you're mainly interested in maintaining the $3 dividend you've been getting. If that's the case, you ought to turn down your broker's suggestion unless he can find you a stock with a 3.75 percent return—considerably higher than the 3 percent return your old stock paid. Remember, after paying the $20 tax, you'll only have $80 to put into a new stock and it takes a 3.75 percent return for an $80 stock to pay a $3 dividend.

On the other hand, if you're more interested in preserving your $100 of *capital*, it won't pay you to sell unless you can find a stock you're pretty sure will go up from $80 to $100 in the reasonably near future. At best, you'll be trading the *chance* that your new stock will go up, for the *certainty* of having to pay the $20 tax and having only $80 to reinvest.

So you see, the capital gains tax gives you every incentive to stay "locked in" to your existing investments, instead of switching to new ones. Of course, raising the tax, as People's Counsel proposes, would only intensify the locked-in effect.

So if People's Counsel, with his tender regard for the Treasury, is trying to increase revenues by raising the capital gains rate, he's going about it the wrong way, because raising the rate will simply make people hold on to their stocks instead of selling and paying the tax, and the Treasury will raise less, not more, through the capital gains tax.

ENGINEER JURYMAN: Let me make sure of one point. You don't contend, do you, that the tax deters *new* capital from coming into the market? After all, a person pays no tax when he makes a new investment.

DEFENSE COUNSEL: That's correct.

ENGINEER JURYMAN: So your point is not that the tax "starves" industry from getting the volume of capital it needs, but merely that it deters people from switching the money they've already put into the market from one particular investment to another.

DEFENSE COUNSEL: Right again.

ENGINEER JURYMAN: Well, I don't understand what's so "bad" about people holding on to the stocks they have and what's so "good" about their switching from one stock to another.

DEFENSE COUNSEL: Well, "switching," as you call it, is the way capital finds its way out of the staid old conservative blue-chip stocks and into the pioneering, venturesome new companies. It's an essential ingredient to a dynamic and forward-moving economy.

Your honor, that is the essence of the two main arguments the Defense will offer.

People's Counsel, do you wish to rebut the points made by the Defense?

PEOPLE'S COUNSEL: Thank you, your honor. I shall try to take them up point by point.

First, Defense argues that we should not change the preferential capital gains rate because it has been in the law since 1921. But must we accept the notion that just because a provision has been in the tax laws for years, it is *ipso facto* virtuous, just and immutable? If so, we might as well end this trial and give up all thought of tax reform.

Besides, the special capital gains rate does not enjoy the

historical sanctity with which my adversary seeks to endow it. On the contrary, my supposedly "radical" proposal is, in reality, the soul of conservatism. It simply calls for reverting to what the Founding Fathers of our tax system wrote into the original 1913 income tax law. In fact, this "radical" plan of mine prevailed for a full nine years for individual taxpayers, and for nearly thirty years for corporations. Yet the country survived quite nicely.

DEFENSE COUNSEL: Ah, yes, but the 1913 law had a top tax rate of 7 percent. You can't compare that with the 91 percent rates we have today.

PEOPLE'S COUNSEL: True, but during the first nine years, the tax rates went as high as 77 percent—nearly as high as we have today.

DEFENSE COUNSEL: And soon after that, Congress saw the error of its original decision, and established a 12½ percent rate for individual taxpayer's capital gains.

PEOPLE'S COUNSEL: But for the most specious reasons. Take, first, the so-called "bunched"-income reason—as exquisite an exercise in illogic as the mind of man could invent. Now, I readily admit there *is* a "bunched"-income *problem* with capital gains. But as a *solution*, a flat preferential tax rate is the acme of absurdity.

First of all, the six-months' holding period makes a mockery of Defense's "bunched"-income argument. Suppose a man sells a stock for a profit after holding it just six months and a day. His gain all took place in one year and he is taxed in the same year. He has no "bunched"-income problem—yet he gets the same delicious 25 percent rate as the man who held his stock for twenty years.

ENGINEER JURYMAN: And what about corporations? I don't see why the "bunched"-income argument applies to them, since no matter how "bunched" their income is, its always taxed at their flat 52 percent rate. Why do *they* need a special rate?

PEOPLE'S COUNSEL: As to that, sir, I am as baffled as you. Now, if the capital gains rate were *really* what it is supposed to be— a device for averaging out the "ordinary income" rates— you'd expect it to go up and down as the regular income tax rates rise and fall. But it hasn't. For instance, in 1950, the income tax rates went up some 10 to 20 percent, to finance the Korean war, but the increase in the capital gains rate only amounted to about 4 percent.

ENGINEER JURYMAN: It would seem to me, Counsel, that to the extent there is a hardship from "bunched" income, it would be different in every case, depending on a person's income and tax bracket, the length of time he's held the property, the amount of the gain, and so on. How can a single flat rate, such as we have now, be an accurate and fair answer to the "bunched"-income problem in every case?

PEOPLE'S COUNSEL: It can't—and as a matter of fact, the present capital gains tax rate is so low that it more than offsets any "bunched"-income hardship and really gives most taxpayers a big windfall tax break. For example, take a person with a $25,000 taxable income who suddenly realizes a $50,000 capital gain on a stock he's held for twenty years. Taxing the entire $50,000 to him in the year he sells the stock makes him pay nearly 58 percent of it in taxes. If, however, you tax him as if he'd received the $50,000 evenly over the twenty years he owned the stock, he'd only have to pay 43 percent of it in taxes —but that would remove the "bunched"-income problem. But the existing capital gains tax goes far beyond that. Instead of paying 43 percent (which would be fair), he only has to pay 25 percent. In other words, he gets nearly *twice* the concession that equity requires. And, of course, the wealthier he is, the greater his windfall tax break, as the table in front of you clearly shows.

PEOPLE'S COUNSEL: Turning now to Defense Counsel's second argument—the so-called "locked-in" argument—my adversary has the right charge, but the wrong culprit. The existing system

THE "BUNCHED"-INCOME PROBLEM AND TWO SOLUTIONS
(Comparison of tax that has to be paid)

Income Level	Problem	Two Solutions	
	INCOME "BUNCHED"*	INCOME "UNBUNCHED"†	FLAT 25%‡ CAPITAL GAINS RATE
On a gain of $50,000			
$5,000	44.6%	22.0%	16.9%‡
$25,000	57.6	43.0	25.0
$100,000	77.4	75.0	25.0
$500,000	91.0	91.0	25.0
On a gain of $100,000			
$5,000	56.4%	23.6%	22.3%
$25,000	65.3	44.6	25.0
$100,000	81.0	75.0	25.0
$500,000	91.0	91.0	25.0

* Entire gain taxed all in one year.

† Gain spread evenly over 20 years (on the assumption the property has been held for that period)—i.e., tax is computed as if ½₀ of the gain had been taxed in each of 20 years.

‡ The rate can be lower than 25%, since a person is entitled to choose between having his gain taxed at 25% (the maximum), or at *half* his regular top-bracket rate. If this latter is less than 50%, it pays to choose the second method.

does have a locked-in effect, but the preferred capital gains tax rate is not to blame—in fact, it produces an opposite or anti-locked-in effect. No, the real culprit is the failure to tax capital gains at death.

FOREMAN OF THE JURY: Counsel, you covered too much ground in one breath. Could you explain *why* the failure to tax gains at death creates a locked-in effect?

PEOPLE'S COUNSEL: Because, as Defense Counsel has explained, the deterrent to selling comes from a person asking himself, "Shall I sell and pay a tax or hold on and pay no tax?"

But he's able to pose the question in this way only because if he holds on long enough—namely, until he dies—he will indeed "pay no tax." So of course there's an incentive to hold on rather than sell.

But if the rules were changed, and gains were taxed at death, as President Kennedy proposed in 1963, then a person would pose the question differently: "Shall I sell and pay the tax now or hold on *and pay the tax later?*" Either way, the tax would have to be paid; it would just be a matter of timing, so the incentive to hold on would be much less.

FOREMAN OF THE JURY: And why do you say that the existing capital gains tax encourages "switching"—an "anti-locked-in" effect, I think you called it?

PEOPLE'S COUNSEL: Well, put yourself in the shoes of a person in the 75 percent tax bracket. You have two choices: you can leave your money in AT&T stock, which fluctuates very little in price but pays a nice, steady dividend, on which you keep only 25 cents out of every dollar. Or you can sell your AT&T and put your money in a stock that stands a good chance of doubling in price in the next three years, *with you keeping 75 cents out of every dollar of profit, instead of 25 cents.* Which would you do? Wouldn't you be tempted to sell the AT&T and go for the stock profit?

ENGINEER JURYMAN: Your argument sounds logical in theory. But does it work out in actual practice?

PEOPLE'S COUNSEL: Three professors of the Harvard Business School made a nationwide survey of the habits and behavior of actual investors, and their findings were summarized as follows:

> Quite contrary to the indictment, the facts established by cross examination of investors show that it is precisely in drawing funds into new ventures and unseasoned securities that the capital gains tax at present rates exerts its strongest influences.

Actually, as far as over-all stock sales and purchases are concerned, *non*-tax reasons seem to be much more powerful than tax considerations. Take the years 1922 through 1933, for example. During that time, both the income tax and the capital gains tax rates were consistently at fairly low levels so that the supposed tax impediments my adversary has conjured up were at a minimum. Yet those years included both the fattest and the leanest in history in the volume of capital gains. The point is that economic conditions and market judgments are far more important than the level of taxes.

Also, a large proportion of stock buying and selling is done by colleges, pension funds, foundations, and insurance companies that are wholly or partially tax-exempt. For them, of course, taxes *couldn't* be a factor.

DOCTOR JURYMAN: Counsel, I am quite persuaded by what you say about the *present* tax system, but frankly I am concerned about what would happen to the economy if we were to tax capital gains the same as ordinary income—at rates as high as 50 or 65 percent.

For instance, you yourself have admitted that the present special capital gains rate has powerfully attracted investment into so-called venture or pioneering companies, where the risk is high and dividends may be years away. Where are those companies going to get capital under your proposal?

PEOPLE'S COUNSEL: Sir, Defense Counsel has sought to characterize the People's proposal as radical. Actually, it is based on the old-fashioned, laissez-faire, free enterprise principle that a free market is the best regulator, sifter and adjuster of economic forces.

The People believe that investors, given a free choice and free competition among companies for capital, will make sound decisions. Worthwhile ventures will get all the money they need. Since when did we need to subsidize risk-taking in America? After all, men invest—or even gamble—their personal energies and talents, even though they are taxed at the regular income tax rates. Is money so much more precious than a man's own talent that its risks must be coddled?

Besides, stock issues play a relatively unimportant role in meeting corporations' capital needs. In 1962, for example, they furnished less than 4 percent of total corporate funds. Corporations get most of their capital either by borrowing or by plowing back their depreciation reserves and their profits.

My plan would also offer more liberal tax treatment of investment *losses* than is now allowed, which would provide considerable inducement to risk investment by top-bracket taxpayers.

JUDGE: I'm afraid we may be turning this trial into a seminar on economics. If neither side has anything further to submit to the jury at this time, this trial will stand adjourned for the day.

JUDGE: Mr. Foreman, has the jury concluded its deliberations?
FOREMAN OF THE JURY: Yes, your honor, and we are prepared to render our conclusions.

We start from a simple proposition: a dollar is a dollar, no matter how it was earned or where it came from. It will buy just as much in groceries, or shoes, mink coats or Cadillacs, whether it was made from a sale of stock or a sale of the sweat of a man's brow or the fruits of his brain. It will pay taxes just as well, too. The voice of Equity, therefore, calls clearly and eloquently for taxing *uniformly* "all income, *from whatever source derived*"—to use the words of the tax law itself.

The voices of Practicality and Simplicity speak, too. The voice of Practicality tells us that the pre-1964 top income tax rates of 90 and 91 percent not only stifled initiative, but also stimulated tax avoidance. Because such rates were intolerable, means were found to avoid them and very few were actually paying those rates. Much the same is true of the 70 percent rate approved by the House of Representatives in 1963. Taxing capital gains on a par with ordinary income, however, would not only make it possible but, in our opinion, essential to do away with useless top rates, and bring the maximum rate down to 50 percent. That way, as People's counsel put it, Uncle Sam would no longer be anyone's majority partner—either in business or in every-day life.

At the same time, the voice of Simplicity tells us, a major avenue of tax avoidance would be closed. The incessant pressure for special tax treatment would be enormously lessened. Energies now devoted to minimizing taxes could be more constructively dedicated to minimizing costs and prices and maximizing profits, as People's Counsel put it.

We note the apprehension felt by many that the equal taxation of capital gains and ordinary income will dry up the wellsprings of capital and greatly reduce American risk-taking. But this viewpoint supposes the American economy to be so frail as to require a subsidy for risk-taking. We do not share such a view, and even if we felt a subsidy were required, we would certainly choose a device less clumsy and ill-directed than a blanket tax preference to *all* investment, safe as well as risky.

We have faith in the free enterprise system. We believe the free play of the market is the best regulator of economic forces—that investors, operating freely amid a free and open competition for capital, will produce the soundest economic and investment decisions. Institutions and investors will adjust themselves. Values will find a new—and sounder—level. As long as there are reasonable investment opportunities in America, there will be investors and capital to take advantage of them, with or without a tax subsidy. But if no such opportunities exist, no amount of tax preference will lure investors into the market.

We are well aware, your honor, that what we propose would be a sharp departure from the past. But we are persuaded by People's Counsel when he says that this would be "the single greatest tax reform this nation could undertake." And as Justice Brandeis once said, "If we would guide by the light of reason, we must let our minds be bold."

The light of reason tells us that we can have a far simpler and far fairer tax system. The question is whether our minds are bold enough to make this a reality.

6 /

Living High at the Taxpayers' Expense

Tom Rowland's intercom buzzer interrupted his study of an advertising layout for his ad agency's biggest would-be new client. "Yes, Rita?"

"George Hopkins is on extension seventy for you, from Cleveland, Mr. Rowland."

Tom quickly pressed the lighted button on his telephone. "George, how the hell are you? You must be a mind reader. I was just this minute looking over some layouts for that big promotion we've been talking about and it's really exciting."

"Hi, Tom. Guess we're on the same wave length. I'm calling you about coming to New York to talk over that campaign, and I want to map out my schedule. How would a week from Monday be for you?"

As Tom flipped through his calendar, he found a date that had long been circled in red. A thought struck him. "Say, George, I've got a hell of an idea. Why don't you step up your

schedule a few days and come in next Thursday for the big
heavyweight title fight in the Garden? I know a guy who can
get us ringside seats. Bring your wife along, and we could go
out for dinner beforehand, go to the fight and do the town
afterward—really make a night of it."

"Well, I suppose I could rearrange things and get there Thursday. But that's some expensive evening you're talking about,
my friend. The papers here say ringside seats are going for a
hundred dollars."

"Don't give it a thought. What the hell, it's deductible.
Uncle Sam will be paying seventy-five percent of the bill.*
What time can you get here?"

"Let's see—I suppose I could be in your office by four o'clock
or so."

"Any chance you could make it earlier? If we're going to
charge those fight tickets to Uncle Sam, we have to get in a
'substantial' business discussion beforehand. And with what
I have in mind for that evening, we're going to be in no shape
to have one the next day."

"Well, there's a flight that gets in at eleven-thirty."

"Perfect. Tell you what. We'll meet you and your wife at one
o'clock at the Pavillon—it's the best restaurant in town—and
then we'll come over to the office afterward."

"It's a date, Tom. See you next Thursday."

"Great, George. See you then."

Tom Rowland buzzed his secretary. "Rita, first get me my
esteemed partner on the phone, and then my wife. And call
my ticket broker and have him get six tickets to the fight next
Thursday, the best he can get, and get a table for six at Pavillon, one o'clock, and a table for six at the Four Seasons, seven-
thirty, the same at the Copa for midnight and . . . well, we'll
ad lib after that."

As he waited to talk to his partner, Tom let himself indulge
in some pleasurable thoughts about the following Thursday.
What an evening—with Uncle Sam, old true-blue Uncle Sam,

---

* Tom Rowland is in the 75 percent tax bracket.

picking up three-quarters of every check. We might spend a thousand bucks, all told, what with the six fight tickets—Lord, what a beating Uncle is going to take on this one. And what a break that George Hopkins is bringing his wife. "Why, Mr. Revenue Agent, George Hopkins as much as told me his wife would be *very* uncomfortable if she were the only lady that evening, so my partner and I just *had* to bring our wives. We couldn't displease a big potential client, now could we, Mr. Agent?"

The buzzer interrupted his dialogue with the Revenue Agent. "Thanks, Rita—don't forget, tell that ticket broker the best seats in the house. Money no object . . . Hello, Hank? Listen, I just had *the* greatest idea of the year . . ."

If Tom and Hank—both 75-percent-bracket taxpayers—did manage to spend $1,000 on their projected jamboree (and at New York prices, with a little stamina and perseverance they should have had no trouble), *their* out of pocket costs would come to only $250. The rest of the taxpayers of the United States would pay for the other $750.

And all of this is strictly within the law, even the new and stricter expense-account law enacted in 1962. Although the new measure is more stringent than prior law (the fictional incident just described is pale compared with pre-1962 expense account deductions—both claimed *and allowed*), it still answers in the affirmative the core question posed by business entertainment deductions. As succinctly stated by J. S. Seidman, a prominent New York accountant:

> The important question is whether it [entertainment] is a way of life that gives those indulging in it the right to require taxpayers *not* participating to pick up a share of the tax . . . *A deduction for one taxpayer means that every other taxpayer has to pony up that much more,* since the revenues to run the Government must be met. (Emphasis added)

Revenue officials estimate that only one taxpayer out of ten enjoys the benefits of travel and entertainment deductions. The question Mr. Seidman is posing is, Why should the other nine-tenths pay any part of the tab for the sheer entertainment of the favored 10 percent?

The expense-account problem is ancient. During the last half-century of the Roman Republic, traveling Roman senators enjoyed what was known as *"Legatio Libera,"* by which they could charge their traveling expenses against the people they visited. In time, the privilege was so much abused that the legitimately chargeable expenses were limited to bare necessities such as "beds and bedding, hay and fodder, firewood and salt."

The first legal strictures on U.S. business deductions, contained in the original 1913 income tax law, were by no means so severe. They permitted the deduction of "the necessary expenses actually paid in carrying on any business." In 1918, this phrase was changed to permit "all ordinary and necessary" expenses, a phrase that remains in the law today.

The vagueness of the words "ordinary and necessary" allowed revenue agents and the courts wide latitude in their interpretations, which, over the years, has produced some intriguing results. For example:

A mortuary claimed $77,740 of "ordinary and necessary" business expenses over a three-year period for the maintenance of a guest cottage and personal residence for the owner-mortician, as well as a yacht "used to entertain visiting morticians, clergymen and for the meetings of employers." Internal Revenue allowed $52,000 of the claim.

A manufacturer deducted $464,818 for the operation of resort facilities on a tropical island, complete with fishing cruisers and a company-owned airplane to transport fortunate customers to and from the tropical paradise. Revenue officials permitted a deduction of $357,609.

Another firm was allowed tax deductions of $111,804 for the maintenance of a yacht, $116,440 for ranch and hunting lodge expenses, $126,249 spent in the night club owned by one of the firm's principal stockholders, plus "other entertainment" expenses amounting to $119,647. A "beverage manufacturer" was allowed to deduct every penny spent for entertaining choice customers and their wives at the Kentucky Derby.

Even these extravaganzas are pallid in comparison to devices used in the 1930's, when wealthy taxpayers formed special corporations for such unbusinesslike facilities as yachts, racing stables and country estates. One ingenious lady caused her personal holding company, which owned her country estate, to hire her husband at a comfortable salary to manage the place, thus keeping him in pocket money and enjoying a tax deduction for doing so.

Expense-account living has not always been so novelesque. More commonplace have been the business deductions for theater tickets and high-priced dinners for favored customers; the conventions held at plush resorts, or even on shipboard (frowned on by Internal Revenue); the generous expense accounts given corporate executives in lieu of a heavily-taxed high salary; the deduction of country club dues as well as the expenses of weddings, debuts and other social occasions where customers and business contacts are among the invited guests; the tight little group of business friends who take turns charging the daily luncheon check to their respective firms (one New York executive boasted, "I haven't paid for my lunch in thirty-one years").

Business gifts have been generously bestowed on choice customers and business contacts, and fully deducted for tax purposes. Firms responding to a university survey told of such tax-supported expressions of gratitude as a trip to Jamaica, a Cadillac, $3,500 worth of stock. Corporate liquor purchases alone have been estimated at $1 billion annually, total business giving of all kinds at more than $2 billion.

Many companies have built into their pay scales liberal and non-taxable expense allowances in place of heavily-taxed high salaries as a device for attracting and holding executive talent. *U.S. News and World Report* tells, for example, of the bachelor president of one small corporation in an Eastern city receiving a salary of $25,000 on which he paid $8,300 in taxes. He was entirely content with this comparatively modest remuneration, since his company paid his apartment rent and entertaining expenses, his club dues and expenses, and an occasional trip abroad "to study business methods overseas and improve his firm's competitive position." He was thus able to enjoy the equivalent of a $98,000 salary, on which the income taxes would be $62,600, nearly four times what he actually paid.

An Eastern steel company executive tells of an erstwhile company practice, since discontinued, of sending company officers and their wives to the resort town of White Sulphur Springs, West Virginia, for a three-day "medical checkup." "The clinic was always careful to schedule tests so they wouldn't cut out a golf game," this executive says.

The expense-account-in-lieu-of-salary has also been useful at lower corporate echelons. One large oil company, for example, permitted its top salesman to claim expenses of $700 to $900 per week, compared with a $125 allowance for more average salesmen. This practice may, under the law, be disallowed by a Revenue Agent—*if* he can spot it.

If Internal Revenue has at times seemed to allow extraneous and extravagant business deductions, courts, whose rulings IRS must follow, must bear a share of the blame. In the Sanitary Farms Dairy case, for example, the court ruled that the entire $16,443 spent for a six-month African safari by the dairy owner and his wife were an "ordinary and necessary" (hence deductible) business expense, since the later showing of their movies and hunting trophies produced good publicity and advertising for the dairy.

In another case, the Tax Court permitted actress Olivia de Havilland to deduct the cost of a $775 oil painting she gave to her theatrical agent, a $920 silver coffee set she gave her dialogue director and a gold necklace and clips (cost: $810) she bestowed upon her dress designer. A brewing company was allowed a full deduction of the costs of operating a cabin cruiser because the brewery was located in a slum area and nothing would do, the company president testified, but to hold sales meetings and entertain customers on shipboard. The courts permitted a racing handicapper to deduct all of his expenses incurred in entertaining racing officials, track owners, horsemen and turf writers aboard his personal yacht, in part because the court found that his business was "highly competitive."

One district judge of unusual moral sensitivity ruled that an employee could take his wife to a convention at the company's tax-deductible expense because, among other reasons, her presence "assures a higher tone of the meeting and eliminates occasional misconduct problems that attend such meetings when they are stag affairs." A higher court, apparently unpersuaded by this reasoning, reversed the decision, ruling that the expenses of this vacation-like convention really constituted compensation, and hence taxable income for him.

This court case illuminated what tax officials say has been a frequent company outlook toward conventions. The gathering in question, solely for the employees of one insurance company, was held at Fort Monroe, Virginia, located near Williamsburg and the Yorktown battlefield. This fact was not lost on the sponsoring company, whose vice president wrote to the manager of the hotel expressing interest in the hotel's "proximity to Williamsburg and other famous historical places," and candidly stating:

While we hold two business sessions during our four-day convention, business is secondary. The main object is to give our people a good time. Specifically, I would be interested in knowing the fishing accommodations . . .

The actual schedule of the convention bore out the prediction that official duties would not be excessively onerous:

Wednesday, May 16:

1:30 P.M.	Arrival
1:30-5:00	Renewing old acquaintances and making new acquaintances
6:30	Company dinner and Water Show

Thursday, May 17:

7-9:30 A.M.	Breakfast
10:00	Meeting (2½ hours)
Afternoon	No planned activity (Ed. Note: The court said the taxpayer involved in this case played golf.)
8:30 P.M.	Movie

Friday, May 18:

7-8:30 A.M.	Breakfast
9:00	Tour of Williamsburg and Jamestown
8:30 P.M.	Bingo

Saturday, May 19:

7-9:30 A.M.	Breakfast
10:00	Meeting (2½ hours)
Afternoon	Boat trip
7:00 P.M.	President's Banquet and Ball

While a federal district court approved company deductions for this "convention," a higher court said it amounted to a company-paid vacation, with most of the expenses taxable to the employees.

Another court looked disapprovingly on an extraordinary display of ingenuity by a tax lawyer-accountant who purchased a yacht from which he flew a red, white and blue pennant bearing the numerals "1040." In reply to the inevitable inquiries about the pennant, the lawyer-accountant would divulge that the numerals stood for the Form 1040 federal tax return, in whose preparation he happened to be expert. "Further opportunities to discuss business arose from these replies," the court was told. "Often these discussions concerned taxes." Nevertheless, the court held, the expenses of maintaining the yacht could not be considered "ordinary and necessary."

During the late fifties, lurid news accounts of tax-supported yachts and hunting lodges stirred a movement toward expense account reform. In 1960, the Senate voted strict expense account curbs (far more severe, in fact, than the Senate was willing to support two years later) but the House would not agree, and Congress contented itself with directing the Internal Revenue Service to make a further study of the problem.

This study laid the groundwork for the Kennedy tax message to Congress of April, 1961. "The slogan—'It's deductible'— should pass from our scene," the President told Congress. Expense account reform, he said, is a "matter of national concern, affecting . . . our sense of fairness, our respect for the tax system [and] our moral and business practices as well." He asked that virtually *all* business entertainment be made non-deductible.

Under the Kennedy proposal, which would have netted an estimated quarter of a billion dollars in added annual revenues, the government would no longer pick up any part of the tab for theaters, night clubs, football games, yachts or hunting lodges, for gifts above $10 per recipient or for travel expenses over $30 per day. Only the quiet business lunch or dinner would still be deductible.

Congress, however, found the Kennedy formula "harsh," and enacted rules which, while less stringent than the President proposed, will bring in an estimated $100 million of added annual revenue (two-fifths of what the President had hoped) and will probably eliminate the more spectacular abuses.

For example, under the new expense account law (effective January 1, 1963), expenses for facilities such as yachts, hunting lodges and tropical resorts will be wholly disallowed as a deduction unless they are used more than half the time for business entertaining—and then only the business share will be deductible. Those who operate such facilities will, of course, have to keep careful records to prove that 51 percent or more of the use was for business; but *The New York Times,* in an angry editorial, commented this is "unlikely to prove too onerous a burden to the owners of yachts." The same rule will apply to country club dues (more than half the use of the club must be demonstrably for business purposes) and to company-furnished automobiles.

If businesses wish to bestow Cadillacs or trips to Jamaica on their favorite customers, or if actresses choose to shower gold and silver on their professional associates, the new law will not prohibit them from doing so, but will not lend tax support to their generosity beyond $25 per recipient per year.

One of the more controversial features of the 1962 law involves the business-mixed-with-pleasure trips. Heretofore, a businessman might journey to Europe (or Florida) for a business conference, follow it with a pleasant vacation, and deduct the entire cost of his transportation as a business expense. But, under the new law, where a business-plus-pleasure trip lasts more than a week, and where the pleasure component is greater than 25 percent, only a partial deduction of the transportation costs will be allowed. This was a particularly painful blow to resort areas such as Miami, where the climate and the facilities are peculiarly suited to an easy intermingling of business and relaxation. In 1963, Florida's Senator George Smathers spearheaded a drive to repeal this feature of the 1962 law. Subsequently, Internal Revenue regulations all but achieved Senator Smathers' objective by exempting from the travel-expense allocation rule all employees who do not have "substantial control over the arranging of the business trip"—i.e. (in effect), everybody but the boss. Even the boss can skirt the allocation rule by establishing that the vacation element of the trip was not a "major consideration."

As to entertainment activities (night clubs, theaters, sporting events, and so on), the new law contains a general rule with a significant exception. *The general rule* is that for business entertainment to be deductible, there must be some "possibility of conducting business affairs," and there must not be "substantial distractions." This would rule out night clubs, theaters and sporting events, but in general, restaurants will exude a sufficiently businesslike atmosphere to satisfy the new law. Large cocktail parties might run afoul of the "substantial distraction" rule, but a dinner party at home with three "business prospect" guests and seven "social" guests will probably be 30 percent deductible.

The significant exception to this general rule involves entertainment "directly preceding or following a substantial and bona fide business discussion." In such cases, the distractions may be of any magnitude and the atmosphere need not be conducive to anything other than sheer pleasure. Thus, the expenses of dinner, theater and a night club following an afternoon business discussion (or preceding a meeting the next morning) may be in part tax supported. (It was this rule that our hypothetical Tom Rowland was relying on in arranging his tax-supported night-on-the-town at the outset of this chapter.) Some skeptics foresee this major exception resulting in the strategic scheduling of "substantial and bona fide business discussions," at such select times as the eve of the Rose Bowl game, or the Kentucky Derby—or even the day of a heavyweight title fight.

Although Congress was not clear about the extent to which wives may be included in an evening's tax-deductible entertainment, Internal Revenue has interpreted the law to give a businessman wide latitude on including his wife while in his home town. Taking her on business trips at Uncle Sam's partial expense is far harder to achieve.

One important Kennedy reform proposal was adopted by the Congress: the requiring of more detailed documentation to support an expense account claim, so that taxpayers will have to tell Uncle Sam much more about the who-what-where-when-and-why of their night-clubbing and theater-going if they want it to be deductible.

Heretofore, the government has been handicapped by a court ruling involving the famous Broadway musical composer, George M. Cohan. Under the so-called "Cohan rule," the government has had to permit a reasonable expense-account allowance even if, as in Mr. Cohan's case, there are no vouchers or detailed records to back it up, but only general evidence that expenses were incurred. This has prompted many taxpayers to list on their tax returns only a rough approximation of their expenses, on the theory that the worst that can happen is a partial disallowance of their claim. Even then, by artful inflation or padding of the original "estimate," the taxpayer might well end up where he hoped to in the first place.

The new law will give the government far greater power to disallow expense claims that are not backed up by vouchers and other records showing the amount, nature and business connection of the outlay. Some feel this in itself will eliminate much of the corner-cutting and padding in the expense account field, since vague records can cover a multitude of petty transgressions. One trade association newsletter told its members that it was the new record-keeping requirements that would "make the wife's presence (on a business trip) more costly than heretofore" since "presumably, in the past, the expenses for the wife were often deducted because her presence was not so readily identified."

Not only will the new record-keeping rules be helpful to revenue agents; they may also ease a sore problem for the accountants who prepare tax returns for other taxpayers, and who have frequently found themselves in an unavoidable conflict of interest. On the one hand, they must pledge the government to exercise "due diligence" in the preparation of accurate tax returns. On the other, they are being paid to minimize their clients' tax bills, and if they are reticent about accepting an unsupported expense-account "estimate," they run the risk that the client will seek a more co-operative accountant. One group of young Washington accountants, the firm of Bobys, Switkes, Noble and Brotman, grew tired of watching most of their clients, as well as themselves, paying taxes with scrupulous honesty while a few of their accounts "seemed to feel they could make their own expense account rules." Even before the repeal of the "Cohan rule," these accountants voluntarily wrote their clientele warning that henceforth all expense claims would have to be "supported by canceled checks, vouchers or other substantiating documents," and that the firm would not "participate in the 'sport'" of deliberate expense account padding. The letter provoked a few responses: "Are you out of your minds?" or "I know you have to write a letter like that, but you really don't mean it." But soon thereafter their own stiff rules were embodied in the new tax law applicable to all accountants and taxpayers.

No one should infer from the fictional illustration at the outset of this chapter that the practices and attitudes of Tom Rowland are typical of American businessmen. Most either are not inclined or cannot afford to splurge in that manner, even if Uncle Sam is footing part of the bill.

Nevertheless, the supposition that expense account living, on a less spectacular scale, has become an integral part of "the American way of life" was substantiated by the cries of anguish and protest against the Kennedy expense account proposal emanating both from those who furnish and those who enjoy tax-supported entertainment.

Manhattan theater-district restaurateur Vincent Sardi blackly predicted that mid-town Manhattan would become a "distressed area" and that the live theater would be "virtually eliminated"—a pessimistic view not shared by another theater expert, who told Congress the tighter rules will "prove a wonderful boon" to the theater by bringing ticket prices back within the reach of the non-expense-account public. Representatives of the hotel and restaurant industries foresaw poorer service, reduction in hotel maintenance and repairs, wholesale hotel and motel failures and the loss of hundreds of thousands of jobs.

"Entertainment," the spokesman for the National Restaurant Association told the House Ways and Means Committee, "is a fundamental part of sales promotion," to such an extent that unless the tax laws are modified to make it "easier to do business that way, the business may not be done." Detroit Congressman Thaddeus Machrowicz's comment: "I do not think that is a very complimentary thing to say about our way of doing business in the United States."

But even if entertainment is an integral part of sales promotion, why must it so often take place in the highest price restaurants? Vincent Sardi proferred an explanation: in the expensive restaurants there isn't "the pressure for rapid turnover of seats," and "a businessman closing a big deal doesn't want to be rushed."

To some, the Kennedy proposals seem to smack of un-Americanism. "Entertainment allowances for tax purposes are as American as apple pie," proclaimed sixteen New York City Congressmen. An industrialist seemed to regard these deductions as a sacred right. To curb expense account entertaining, he told Congress, would be a "confiscation of . . . property," involving a "fundamental issue of property rights of free men and institutions."

Another defender of expense account deductions contends that the best judge of the business benefit to be derived from any entertainment outlay is the "competent and conscientious financial officer within each company." Cost-conscious accountants in competitive industries with thin profit margins can be relied on, he says, to curb lavish expense-account practices. A *Wall Street Journal* survey in late 1962 indicated that many companies are applying their own crack-down on expense-account allowances.

Others argue that entertainment is just one of the many legitimate methods a business might use to counter its competitors and is really akin to advertising or promotion, which is deductible; hence, they maintain, it is unreasonable to draw a distinction between the two. Florida's Senator George Smathers has injected an egalitarian note into the defense of entertainment deductions: unless entertainment receives tax support, he says, a tycoon, with independent income of his own, may be able to entertain more easily and thus enjoy an unfair advantage over his small and struggling competitor.

Some Congressmen pointed out, in support of business entertaining, that the government furnishes entertainment expenses to its overseas diplomats. Thus, they argued (in effect), when it comes to good-will entertaining, what is good for the country is good for General Motors.

One congressional witness opposed the Kennedy proposal for a flat dollar ceiling on travel expenses on the undemocratic and ungallant premise that "the expense of feeding a president of a bank would normally be higher than the expense of feeding a secretary who purchases office supplies." His view, if not his reasoning, prevailed, for Congress set no dollar ceiling on travel outlays in the 1962 law.

Others felt it unjust to penalize everyone and eliminate all entertainment deductions because of isolated fringe abuses by a few. Accountant J. S. Seidman countered this. "The abuse may be by some," he told Congress. "The effect of the abuse is on all. Laws come into existence . . . from just such background. That is the history of the Child Labor Law, the Work-

men's Compensation Law, the creation of the Securities and
Exchange Commission."

Advocates of tighter expense-account rules see many noxious
effects of tax-supported prodigality. Revenue officials, for example, cite the demoralizing effect on taxpayers who have no
expense account privileges of their own, but who must envi-
ously watch their neighbors not only enjoy but boast about
charging their pleasant living to Uncle Sam. One moderate-
income taxpayer, embarrassed by the extent to which he was
entertained by his next-door neighbor, was told, "Don't give it
a thought. Uncle Sam's paying for it." This response did not entirely relieve his embarrassment, however. "The catch comes," he
says, "when we try to reciprocate. I have no big expense account. When we entertain this man in return, it comes out of
our own pockets. We simply can't afford to entertain as lavishly
as he does."

A top revenue official, whose scrupulous records show his
car costs him $600 per year to operate, says of his neighbor,
whose car is company-owned, "He's getting $600 more a year
than I am and not paying a dime of taxes on it." One tax
accountant told Congress that such overt inequalities tempt
a taxpayer to "feel he is entitled to his own deductibilities and
gimmicks."

As to the "moral and business practices" to which President
Kennedy referred, Vincent Sardi told Congress, for example,
that expressing gratitude to a favorite client or customer by
giving him $10 outright "is not only in bad taste; it is prac-
tically illegal in many cases. However, you can send him tickets
to a theater or invite him to a dinner. This is good taste and
it is considered a moral way of showing gratefulness."

Some tax-supported business gifts are used to gain special
favors not available to the general public, such as "finding
space on 'sold out' planes or trains or in 'completely filled'
hotels."

Travel and entertainment ("T&E") deductions have been at the root of most of the bribery cases involving Internal Revenue agents (among whom venality is rare) because the T&E rules have been flexible and the agent's final ruling is highly negotiable. Says one IRS authority: "It's almost impossible to review an agent's judgment on T&E matters. A man may claim $10,000 and the agent says $1,000 and they settle on $7,000 with the agent getting a kickback of $1,000 on the side."

Internal Revenue Commissioner Caplin is concerned about the economic effects of the T&E deductions. "They get built into the price of a product," he says. "We've gotten lazy and used to padding the price of our products this way. But we are now going to have to compete with the European Common Market and we had better start tightening up."

Business received one of its severest lectures on the evils of expense-account entertaining from one of its own leading spokesmen, Clarence Randall. Objecting to the use of business entertainment as a sales tool, he said, "In the long run, the product must sell itself. It takes on no added value from exposure to neon lights nor is it likely that its special virtues can be explained more clearly at two in the morning than at two in the afternoon . . . The only relationship between seller and buyer that will endure . . . is one which rests solidly upon mutual satisfaction. No such lasting commercial partnership can be purchased with champagne."

Mr. Randall also sees international implications in lavish expense-account living. Businessmen, he says, "seldom pause to speculate on what image of the American economy their conduct creates in the minds of men from the new countries who come to study our way of life."

Mr. Randall sums up his view of expense-account living this way:

The unseen partner in all this largesse . . . the man who rides the afterdeck of the company yacht, co-pilots the duck hunters' plane, sits by while the caviar is spooned out and the crêpes suzettes are sizzling, the man who splits the check at the night spot and hands the big bill to the head-waiter, is none other than Uncle Sam . . . But who are the silent underwriters of this frenetic spending? You and I, the general taxpayers; it is we who make up to the U.S. Treasury the revenue lost through expense account deductions.

In view of this array of objections to tax-supported enter-tainment, will the Kennedy quiet-business-meal-only view ever prevail? Clearly, the Eighty-seventh Congress did not share that philosophy, for the 1962 law gave specific legislative sanc-tion to three-fifths of the deductible entertaining the President had hoped to bar, and subsequent Internal Revenue regula-tions are, in some respects, even more liberal than the law itself (*The New York Times* called the regulations a "craven retreat in an obvious attempt to give offense to no one").

Most Washington observers feel that Congress, having acted on the problem, will be ill-disposed to bring it up again for many years, and that even then, the outlook for further tighten-ing is distinctly dim. So golden is the egg, most believe, that the expense-account goose is not likely to perish easily or soon.

7 /

How "Show Biz"
Wards Off the Tax Collector

IT'S NOW "NO BIZ LIKE SOME OTHER BIZ" TO ESCAPE THAT BIG TAX RAP

CAPITAL GAINS TAX SAVING GETS INCREASING GLAD EYE FROM DISC NAMES

BERGEN NO DUMMY ON CAPITAL GAINS

"LOOK, MA, I'M A CORPORATION"—SOLE WAY TO STARS' RICHES

These headlines, in the unmistakable style of *Variety*, the newspaper of show business, tell of the entertainment world's preoccupation with warding off the tax collector. For at least four decades, the cream of "show biz" and the Internal Revenue Service have frequently found themselves eyeball to eyeball— often in the courtroom, and often with several hundred thousand dollars of tax savings at stake.

Show business luminaries have endeavored to shield their

prodigious incomes from the severity of the top-bracket tax rates in two principal ways. Some have sought to wrap their talents into a corporate package, to take advantage of the 52 percent corporate tax rate. Far more alluring, however—and more elusive—is the capital gain, with its special 25 percent tax rate. The capital gain has, in fact, become a sort of status symbol in some segments of show business.

The best-publicized, if not the most spectacular, of the capital gains transactions was that of comedian Jack Benny, who wrapped his top-rated radio show into a corporate "package" and sold it to the Columbia Broadcasting System for the tidy sum of $2,260,000. Nine days later, the Jack Benny show switched from NBC to CBS.

When Benny reported his own $1,356,000 profit on the transaction as a capital gain, taxed at the favorable 25 per cent rate, he ran head-on into Internal Revenue. The government contended that since the Jack Benny show was clearly unsalable without Benny, the price paid by CBS was really, in effect, a payment for Benny's personal services and therefore taxable at the regular income tax rates. But the Tax Court ruled in Benny's favor, saying his services were technically not part of the corporation and that his personal contract was with the sponsor, not NBC, and an $800,000 tax saving was his. But there was an extra dividend: *Variety* reported that the show's Hooper (audience) rating had jumped because of "the comedian's NBC-CBS capital gains switch."

This was not the first such "capital gains switch." A few months earlier, CBS had paid $2,000,000 to Freeman F. Gosden and Charles J. Correll—better known as "Amos 'n' Andy"—for all the rights to their popular radio show which, like the Benny program, soon began appearing on CBS. Said *Variety*: "This affects all radio stars and may be a forerunner for other top-notchers of like standard."

To some extent it was: on July 26, 1950, for example, Groucho Marx and producer John Guedel sold their partnership interests in the show, "You Bet Your Life" (starring Groucho Marx and produced by John Guedel) to NBC for a million dollars. The Tax Court overruled the government's claim that three-fourths of the million was attributable to the talents and services of Marx and Guedel, and clinched a tax saving in the hundreds of thousands of dollars. The law has since been changed, however, so that anyone with a "You Bet Your Life" deal should not bet his life on getting capital gains treatment.

No doubt, fans of Fred Astaire, Ginger Rogers and Irving Berlin could not have cared less how Mr. Berlin was paid for his songs from the movie "Top Hat," such as "Cheek to Cheek," "The Picolino," and "Isn't This A Lovely Day?"—i.e., whether in the form of capital gains or ordinary income. But this was a matter of considerable import to Mr. Berlin, who reported the sale of the tunes to RKO Pictures as a capital gain, but was overruled by the Tax Court.

Actor Fred MacMurray had better luck. He and producer-director Leslie Fenton bought a movie script entitled "Pardon My Past," and sold it for a $100,000 profit to Columbia Pictures, which produced the film—starring Fred MacMurray (salary $125,000) and produced and directed by Leslie Fenton (for a $50,000 salary). The Tax Court held that because MacMurray and Fenton were not in the business of buying and selling movie scripts—even though in this case the transaction did further their respective careers—they could claim a capital gain on their profit from "Pardon My Past." Film director Anatole Litvak received a similar favorable ruling on a profitable sale of story rights on "Sorry, Wrong Number," a suspense film he later directed.

Capital gains deals of this sort are apt to be limited to two —possibly three—to a customer, since if repeated too often they might be classed as "regular trade or business" and not entitled to capital gains treatment. Even this can be circumvented, though, by assigning some deals to one's wife.

Is the life story of a deceased celebrity a "capital asset"?

Mrs. Glenn Miller contended it was and reported, as a capital gain, the $409,336.34 she received in connection with the filming of "The Glenn Miller Story." A federal court disagreed. "Apparently," the court said, noting Mrs. Miller's profitable transaction, "'the good that men do,' if sufficiently publicized, does live after them." Nevertheless, the court concluded, all that is salable is not necessarily "property." For example, said the court, "if one is dishonest, one can sell his vote; but we would suppose that no one would seriously contend that the subject matter of such sale is 'property,' as that word is ordinarily understood."

Another court had a harder time ruling on actor Jose Ferrer's sale of certain rights in connection with the movie "Moulin Rouge," in which Ferrer portrayed the stunted artist Toulouse-Lautrec. "The difficulty Mr. Ferrer must have had in fitting himself into the shape of the artist," wrote Circuit Judge Henry Friendly, "can hardly have been greater than ours in determining whether the transaction here at issue fits the rubric of [a capital gain]." The court's conclusion: part did and part did not fit the rubric.

At one point, reports *Variety*, Edgar Bergen contemplated selling Charlie McCarthy and Mortimer Snerd as "capital assets," intending to "demonstrate that he's selling a property rather than a personality" by having another ventriloquist portray the two characters in his stead during the first two radio shows of the season.

There is pathos in the capital-gains efforts of one Alvin York, better known as the World War I hero "Sergeant York," who received $150,000 from Jesse Lasky for the filming of his life story, reported it as a capital gain and paid his taxes accordingly. Internal Revenue, however, ruled that the $150,000 was subject to regular income tax rates and assessed him $85,000 in added taxes. But York had long since spent the money, and when, in 1961, Internal Revenue finally agreed to settle the case for $25,000, the amount had to be raised by public donations. York, 73 and bedridden, had exactly $2.20 in the bank.

The movie "Sergeant York" made millions. In contrast to Alvin York's $150,000, Lasky's share of the profits rose to $822,000. He sold his interest in them for $805,000 and claimed the proceeds as a capital gain, paying about $200,000 in taxes. But Internal Revenue, backed up by the Tax Court, ruled against him, and Lasky had to pay an additional $450,000 in taxes.

Another ex-soldier by the name of Dwight D. Eisenhower fared far better than Alvin York. When he sold his rights to *Crusade in Europe* for a lump sum of $635,000, he obtained a ruling from Internal Revenue that because he was not a professional author, the sale could be treated as a capital gain. (Kathleen Winsor had more difficulty in claiming capital gains on the sale of her *Forever Amber,* but the Tax Court gallantly came to her rescue, ruling that she was no writer, in a professional sense, but had written the book "primarily because she enjoyed the research and writing which went into its composition . . .")

In the wake of the much-publicized Eisenhower ruling, and at President Truman's behest, Congress, in 1950, proceeded to slam the capital gains door in the face of artists, composers and authors. In what came to be known as "the Eisenhower Amendment," the law specifically precludes the fruits of their creativity —be they amateur or professional—from the favored 25 percent capital gains rate.*

President Truman, ironically, later found himself the victim of his own proposal, for when in 1953 he sold his memoirs to *Life* magazine for a reported $600,000, he was barred from capital gains treatment. However, he too obtained a ruling from

---

* Inventors, by contrast, are virtually assured capital gains treatment whether they are amateurs or professionals. They are even accorded the unique privilege of not having to hold their invention for the customary six months, and in some cases they can even license their invention and still get capital gains treatment on the royalty income.

the Treasury permitting him to spread the payments over five years, for a considerable tax saving.

Despite the "Eisenhower amendment," do not despair entirely for the successful and well-counseled Hollywood-Broadway author. The minds of the tax alchemists have not been idle, and formulas have been found to transform into capital gains the earnings not only of authors but of actors, directors and producers as well.

Generally, this is achieved by channeling income of these notables through specially-created corporations. Even if no capital gains advantage materializes, there is a distinct tax saving, since the first $25,000 of a corporation's income is taxed at only 30 percent, the rest at 52 percent—far lower than the individual rates that rose, until 1964, as high as 91 percent.

In 1955, *Variety* reported a surprisingly rapid swing by top stars toward the formation of their own movie corporations, to give these stars, as *Variety* put it, "a crack at capital gains." At that time, actor Kirk Douglas had already produced six pictures through his own corporations, Frank Sinatra five, Robert Mitchum five, Joan Crawford six, Henry Fonda six.

The wrapping of talent into a corporate envelope is a venerable tax-saving device. On August 16, 1920, for example, not a star, but a corporation was born.

Its name: Cecil B. de Mille Productions, Inc.

Its sole asset: the talents of Hollywood producer-director Cecil B. de Mille.

Its sole stockholders: de Mille, members of his family and his attorney.

This is the way its operations were later described by the Commissioner of Internal Revenue:

De Mille, the individual, went to work for de Mille, the corporation, at a salary far less than he knew he could command as a director . . . the corporation then sold de

Mille's services to producing companies. The difference between [his] salary from his own corporation and his actual earnings as a motion picture director was put into the corporation.

Not surprisingly, de Mille Productions, Inc. thrived. During the Hollywood heydays of 1924 to 1929, its income totaled $6,500,000—all taxed at the corporate rate rather than at de Mille's top-bracket individual rate. His tax saving: more than $1,200,000.

The courts upheld de Mille's private-corporation arrangement, as well as those of the late Charles Laughton and of Fontaine Fox, cartoonist-creator of "Toonerville Trolley," "Aunt Eppie Hogg" and "The Terrible-Tempered Mr. Bang." In 1937, though, the Treasury Department invoked the de Mille case to impress Congress with the enormous tax savings enjoyed by wealthy people, both in and outside of the entertainment world, through "personal holding companies." These offered a variety of conveniences: yachts, city residences and country estates were put into privately-owned corporations and rented at nominal costs to their owners; the racing stables of the wealthy were tossed in, too, and their losses tax-deducted. Other assets— stocks, bonds and real estate—were placed in specially created corporations. E. W. Scripps, no movie magnate but a founder of the Scripps-Howard newspaper chain, established the E. W. Scripps Company, which in 1934 saved Mr. Scripps some $449,-000 in taxes. That same year Paul Block, also a newspaper publisher, formed Consolidated Publishers and saved roughly $585,000. Former Treasury Secretary Andrew Mellon was a major owner in two holding companies—the Addason Tobacco Corporation and the Penn Tobacco Corporation, neither of which had anything to do with tobacco.

The revelation of these tax-saving activities of Messrs. de Mille, Scripps, Mellon and others prompted Congress in 1937 to clamp down on private corporations via a prohibitive penalty tax* on the undistributed profits of any corporation classed as a "personal holding company."

Despite the penalty tax, however, the privately-owned corporation remains a valuable shelter for the well-counseled and well-heeled show-business celebrity—and other top-bracket taxpayers as well. As one tax advisory service puts it: "No corporation need pay the personal holding company tax if it is familiar with the [pertinent] provisions" of the tax law.†

Up until 1964 the principal provision to keep in mind was that if more than 20 percent of a corporation's income is derived from any source (e.g., manufacturing profits) *other than* corporate dividends, interest, royalties and so-called personal service contracts, then the company avoids being classed as a personal holding company and also avoids the penalty tax. (The bill passed by the House in 1963 changed the 20 percent requirement to 40 percent.)

To see how this worked, consider the actual case of Actor T,‡ who also doubled as president of Corporation T (an unsurprising honor since he happened to be Corporation T's sole stockholder). As with Cecil B. de Mille, his corporation vastly underpaid him—his salary amounted to less than 30 percent of what his talents would ordinarily command—but he bore this indignity stoically since, again as with de Mille, his corporation sold his services at a profit for an amount commensurate with his talent. But this profit was "personal service income" which, if left undiluted, would subject his company to the 85 percent penalty tax—clearly an intolerable situation.

What to do? Buy a side business, advised T's tax lawyer. Buy a bowling alley, for instance. "But," Actor T might have said,

---

* Currently 75 percent on the first $2,000, 85 percent on everything over $2,000.

† An observation eloquently confirmed by the statistic that in 1958-59, a total of only $559,000 in penalty taxes were paid in the entire United States, although slightly more revenue might have been picked up in later revenue-agent audits.

‡ Cited in a special Treasury Department study of personal holding companies and therefore, by law, nameless.

"bowling alleys can be risky. What if it doesn't make enough profit to meet the 20 percent test?" Profits don't matter, the tax lawyer might respond. The law says it doesn't need to make a dime. The gross income is what counts—in effect, its total sales.

So Corporation T bought a bowling alley, and, lo and behold, ceased to be a personal holding company. This was a matter of considerable joy to Actor T, for if all of his acting salary had been paid directly to him, his personal taxes for 1958, 1959 and 1960 would have been $253,000 instead of $75,000—a 70 percent difference.

In 1955, *Variety* told again of a spate of new star-owned corporations with "side businesses," designed "to beat the federal income tax rap on 'personal service' earnings." Singer Tony Martin, through Tony Martin Enterprises, Inc., was licensing manufacturing rights on "items like pajamas and male perfumes" and, according to *Variety,* "stands to make about $250,000 this year." Groucho Marx set up Endorso, Ltd., "for peddling a 'TV Quiz game'," later to become a " 'You Bet Your Life' puzzler." George Burns and Gracie Allen "have licensed a furniture manufacturer to produce cushioned goods under their name." Early birds in setting up their own corporations, says *Variety,* were Bing Crosby and Gene Autry. Others following the corporate trend: Jackie Gleason, Ralph Edwards, Lucille Ball and Desi Arnaz, and Donald O'Connor.

It is also possible for top-name TV stars to provide corporate shelter for their salary income by "packaging" their own TV show—complete with guest stars, music, script, sets, and so forth —and selling the "package" at a profit, through their own corporation, to a network or sponsor. Among the luminaries who who have done this: Lucille Ball, Sid Caesar, George Gobel, Perry Como and Jackie Gleason.

The stars contend this is no tax avoidance device, since these "packaging" corporations are legitimate risk-taking companies earning a normal business profit. But others ask: Who would be interested in buying the "Jackie Gleason Show" without Gleason or the "Perry Como Show" without Como? Answer: no one. Conclusion: part or all of the profit on the sale of the "package" really amounts to—and should be taxed as—a salary payment for Gleason's or Como's services. Treasury regulations, however, permit an easy escape from the personal holding company tax. A "packaging" corporation merely has had to pay normal salaries to the director, producer and guest stars.

Prior to 1964, a company could wriggle out of the personal holding company category by having sufficient (50 percent or more) rental income. Again, this didn't need to be a *net* profit; a *gross* rent would do in meeting the 50 percent test. Thus, a top-bracket taxpayer might borrow from his favorite bank the money to enable his privately-owned corporation to buy a building. The corporation would then rent the building *in toto* to a professional rental-management outfit for just enough to pay back the bank loan, plus interest and taxes. Although the corporation wouldn't make a dime on the deal, a great deal of "rental income" would be flowing helpfully through it, serving to keep it out of the personal holding company class.

A nautical variation on the same theme has been known to operate as follows: A broker happens to know that A has a private yacht for rent, that C wishes to rent such a yacht, and that B has a private corporation badly in need of "rental income" to skirt the holding company tax. In a twinkling the broker arranges all: A rents his yacht to B's corporation, which immediately sub-leases it to C (clearing enough profit, of course, to pay the enterprising broker his fee). Everyone is now happy: A's yacht is rented and C is basking in the Mediterranean sun, his rental fee passing usefully through B's corporation.

Until 1964, the rental-income "escape hatch" was particularly helpful in the entertainment industry. When a star filmed a television series, the later broadcast proceeds were all considered film "rental" when they came in to the star's personal corporation. The 1963 measure passed by the House tightened the law on this.

One privately-owned corporation succeeded in cutting its
owner's taxes from an estimated $539,000 to roughly $90,000—
an 83 percent cut—by reporting *gross* oil income of over a
million dollars—although the actual *net* oil income, after sub-
tracting royalty payments, interest and depletion allowances,
came to only $17,000. If the 1963 bill becomes law, however, only
the net $17,000 will now be usable to skirt the holding company
classification. Rental income used for that purpose will likewise
be reduced by depreciation, interest and taxes, and thus will no
longer be as useful. Side businesses, such as bowling alleys,
will be harder pressed to fulfill their present function, since they
will have to account for at least 41 (rather than the present 21)
percent of the company's total income.

Well, you may say, here is a Gleason or a Bing Crosby or a
Lucille Ball with money piling up in their personal corporations
—but they can't use it to buy a second swimming pool or a third
Cadillac or a sixth mink coat. What good is the money lying
around in a stuffy old corporation?

The answer is, plenty. Imagine for a moment you are Actor T,
the president and sole stockholder of your own private corporation. Consider the choices open to you.

If you run short of cash for that swimming pool or Cadillac
you want, you can always pay yourself a higher salary (after all,
who deserves it more than you?) or declare yourself a dividend.
You'll have to pay an income tax on it, but the point is, the
money is always available when you want it.

If your cash is holding out all right, you would do far better
to leave the money in the corporation and invest it in other
stocks. Why better? Because on the dividends it receives from
other corporations, your company will pay no more than a 7.8
percent tax,* and chances are this is about one-tenth the tax
you would pay if the dividends were coming in to you person-

---

* This remarkably low tax rate results from the fact that corporations
are excused from paying any tax on 85 percent of all the dividends they
receive from other corporations. The 52 percent corporation tax, therefore,
only applies to the remaining 15 percent. 52 percent of 15 is 7.8.

ally. Besides, as president and sole stockholder of your company, you have as much freedom in deciding which stocks to buy as you would if you owned the money outright.

Now imagine the years have gone by. Not only have you been a great box-office drawing card, but you have invested brilliantly. Your company is worth three times what it once was.

You are confronted, now, with two extraordinarily pleasant choices: either you can liquidate your corporation, paying only a 25 percent capital gains tax on the increase in your company's worth; or, better still, you can simply let the company go on growing in value, and leave it to your family at your death. That way no one *ever* pays any taxes on its increased value (see p. 92).

They used to be called "Hollywood corporations." Now they're called "collapsible corporations." One lawyer claims to have thought them up while dining with Rosalind Russell at Antoine's Restaurant in New Orleans. Whatever their label or origin, they can be extremely useful in transmuting heavily taxed ordinary income into more gently taxed capital gains.

A case involving actor Pat O'Brien illustrates how a "collapsible corporation" works:

On June 30, 1943, O'Brien formed an all-Irish alliance with one Phil Ryan to form the Terneen Corporation, whose sole mission in life was to produce "Secret Command," starring none other than Pat O'Brien and produced by (who else?) Phil Ryan. O'Brien put up $6,250 for a half-interest in Terneen; for acting in the film he accepted a paltry $25,000, far less than he would ordinarily command as a first-rank star. This deficiency was more than made up for, however, when, in 1944, with the picture completed, the board of directors liquidated Terneen, at which time their rights to "Secret Command" were valued at $150,000. O'Brien's $68,750 profit brought his total intake on the film to more than $93,000—closer to his accustomed pay. But this was far better than receiving this amount in straight salary, for, thanks to Terneen, Inc., two-thirds of the $93,000 avoided

O'Brien's top-bracket rates and, instead enjoyed the far milder 25 percent capital gains rate.

In 1950, Congress restricted the use of "collapsible corporations" by requiring, generally, that a firm could not be collapsed for three years—by which time most movies have exhausted the bulk of their earning power. Still highly useful in the real estate industry,* they may also come in handy on the sale of television rerun rights on movies or TV shows more than three years old. Moreover, partnerships (as distinct from corporations) are not subject to the three-year rule and can sometimes be usefully "collapsed" for a capital gain advantage, especially in connection with Broadway theatre productions.

Switzerland has many charms, not the least of which, for top-bracket entertainers and other taxpayers, at least, is its favorable tax climate (maximum rate: 15 to 20 percent). In the beautiful town of Vevey, for example, stands the home of actor William Holden and his wife. The Holden home is not far from that of Charlie Chaplin, who left the United States owing roughly $700,000 in taxes.

A Treasury Department study of Americans who shielded their incomes from U.S. taxes by living and working abroad lists an "actor" and "housewife" who *each* reported $1,099,791 of income in Switzerland in 1960. Also cited are a "producer-director" reporting $332,142 of income in Switzerland in 1959 and 1960; a "cartoonist" reporting $110,315; and an actress, who apparently preferred the tax climate of Venezuela, reporting $996,200 of income in a single year, all of it exempt from U.S. taxes.

Entertainers make up only a small proportion of the list of those who, in 1959 and 1960, lived abroad and avoided U.S. taxes on their sizeable incomes. An "executive" reported $1,422,-230 of income in Brazil; another "executive" living in Japan had

---

* One realtor's highly successful exploitation of this is described on p. 150.

$557,873 of income out of Internal Revenue's reach; lawyers, bankers, insurance agents, a cotton merchant and a "gambling operator" also appear on this list.

All this, though, is a thing of the past. In 1962, Congress set a $35,000 limit on the amount of any U.S. citizen's overseas income that could escape United States income taxes.

Here is a problem for all those who have been through fourth-grade arithmetic:

A television star in 1960 had $30,000 of expenses and $16,000 of income from an investment in a cattle-raising farm. Did he make money or lose money, and how much?

What's the answer, class? You say he *lost* $14,000?
Terribly sorry, but you're all wrong. He *made* $8,700.
Evidently, you went astray because you were using the wrong arithmetic book. *Cowboy Arithmetic* explains the whole thing. *"The raising of livestock,"* it says on page 95, *"gets an income tax treatment in which even the basic principles differ from that afforded most other forms of American business . . . The overwhelming majority of the differences are most favorable."*

These "differences" offer great aid and comfort to the television star in the arithmetic problem above (an actual person whose name the Treasury Department may not reveal, but who has an income of $400,000 yearly and is in the 89 percent tax bracket). Using "cowboy arithmetic," you discover that his supposed $30,-000 of expenses (which are deductible at his 89 percent rate) shrinks to only $3,300, out-of-pocket. His $16,000 of receipts,

---

* This volume, published by the Interstate Printers and Publishers, Inc., of Danville, Illinois, takes pains, however, to disabuse readers that these tax provisions represent a "tax loophole" or "tax gimmick." This is "definitely not the case," says the book. "The special provisions were purposefully put into the law, after long study . . . to encourage private individuals to take over a program that would otherwise have to be handled directly by the government."

on the other hand, are taxable at the favorable 25 percent capital gains rate—so he gets to keep $12,000.

The contrast between regular and "cowboy" arithmetic may be more clearly seen by the following comparison:

	Regular Arithmetic (before taxes)	*Tax Treatment*	*"Cowboy Arithmetic"* (after taxes)
Outflow	$30,000	Deductible at 89% rate	$ 3,300
Inflow	$16,000	Taxable at 25% rate	$12,000
ENDS UP	$14,000 *behind*		$ 8,700 *ahead*

Tax experts who are also clever at mathematics have calculated that in his tax bracket, for every $100 this TV star puts in, he can actually lose $85.34—*and still come out even after taxes.* If he simply gets back his original $100, the rate of return on his out-of-pocket investment is 582 percent!*

But you don't have to be in an 89 percent bracket to do handsomely in cattle investments. An investment prospectus by Briarcliff Farms, a cattle-raising farm in upstate New York, showed how a 69-percent-bracket taxpayer can actually end up *ahead,* after taxes, by $64,367 in five years—even though an untutored eye, looking at this taxpayer's outlays to and receipts from Briarcliff would be convinced there was a cash *deficit* of $94,750.† Such an investor would achieve this happy result *without risking a penny of his own,* since every penny he put into Briarcliff Farms he would otherwise have had to pay to Uncle Sam anyway. As it is, patient, generous Uncle loses $159,117 in this whole transaction.

It is little wonder, then, that top-bracket notables in the entertainment world, such as Alfred Hitchcock—and other

---

* Description of how this is accomplished may be found in the Appendix.
† Explanation also in Appendix.

wealthy people outside of show business—have developed a
special fondness for brood cows. One musician-conductor with
an annual income of nearly $300,000 reported tax deductions on
his cattle investment of nearly $130,000 in 1959 and 1960, saving
him over $100,000 in taxes. And one manufacturer of chain link
fence, whose income in 1958, 1959 and 1960 totaled nearly
$9,300,000, was saved nearly $500,000 in taxes as a result of his
cattle investments.

The tax joys of being a "gentleman cowboy" are breathlessly
depicted in a pamphlet headed, in ersatz-Western lingo, "How
to Round up a Tax-Sheltered Second Fortune by Investing in
Cattle." The "secret to success," confides the pamphlet, lies in
"the population explosion" which is "giving cattlemen a built-in
market advantage—*Americans love steak smothered in onions.*
And, cattle owners get *preferential tax treatment.*" (Emphasis
not added.)

TV and movie stars—and corporate executives—are quickly
assured that they do not have to be tall in the saddle or quick on
the draw, or even know anything about cattle, in order to be
"gentlemen cowboys." Everything will be taken care of: heifers
will be bought, grazing leases arranged, even bulls supplied.
Then, says the pamphlet, the investor can just sit back and let
nature take its course." Lest this allusion be cloudy, the pamphlet
embroiders it: "Bulls+Cows=Calves."

The Kennedy Administration asked Congress to change the
law to prevent non-farmers from taking large cattle deductions
against their top-bracket non-farm income while paying only
the 25 percent capital gains rate on the fruit of their investment.
But Congress took no action—largely, some said, because of
the supposed difficulty of fairly differentiating between farmers
and non-farmers.

The tax consciousness of show business celebrities is entirely
understandable, for in the past the tax system has shown little
mercy to those such as entertainers and top professional

athletes, whose incomes ride a roller-coaster, hitting the peak but once and only briefly. Compare a $75,000-a-year executive to an actor, both making $750,000 in a ten-year period, but with $600,000 of the actor's income bunched into a three-year period, and you are likely to find the actor paying far more total taxes than the executive, even though their total incomes were the same. In 1963 the House responded to the pleas of entertainers and adopted a system that would permit people with uneven incomes, in computing their taxes, to smooth out the peaks and valleys.

Show business celebrities are disadvantaged in another curious way: their very prominence attracts a spotlight to any tax device they may employ, and the resulting publicity sometimes prompts Congress to clamp down on practices that might well remain untouched if employed by mere uncelebrated millionaires.

Moreover, not every star can or does make use of the tax-saving devices described in this chapter, and many of them pay prodigious taxes. As actor Kirk Douglas puts it, "You hear of actors getting tremendous salaries . . . But we're also great customers of Uncle Sam."

8 /

How To Get Rich Quick
in Real Estate—
With Uncle Sam's Help

In 1960, the following events occurred:

—Eight New York real estate corporations amassed a total of $18,766,200 in cash available for distribution to their shareholders. They paid not one penny of income tax.

—When this $18,766,200 was distributed, few of their shareholders paid even a penny of income tax on it.

—Despite this cash accumulation of nearly $19 million, these eight companies were able to report to Internal Revenue *losses,* for tax purposes, totaling $3,186,269.

—One of these companies alone, the Kratter Realty Corporation, had available cash of $5,160,372, distributed virtually all of this to its shareholders—and yet paid no tax. In fact, it reported a *loss,* for tax purposes, of $1,762,240. Few, if any of their shareholders paid any income tax on the more than $5 million distributed to them by the Kratter Corporation.*

---

* Some of these shareholders may have had to pay a tax at a later date, but if so, it was not at their regular income tax rates, but at the favorable 25 percent capital gains rate.

All of this may sound odd, since somehow profits are losses, and losses highly profitable. But it really happened.

How? Why?

A flight of fancy into the future—based on techniques and tax rates* *actually* used in the fiftes and early sixties—will suggest the *How*.

At 7:07 A.M. of January 2, 1966, the wrecker's ball struck the first blow at a tired red brick office building in a choice big-city location. Two years later to the day—January 2, 1968—the glistening $5 million Providential Building was ready for occupancy, a major part of its office space already rented.

The Providential Building proved aptly named, for in the ensuing years, it was to bring sparkling financial rewards to its succession of owners.

The first was Allen Ogilvie, who owed his considerable and dramatically-built fortune to his shrewd real estate investments and his avid attention to his tax lawyer's advice.

The Providential Building did handsomely by Allen Ogilvie, netting him nearly $200,000 cash a year. More important, however, were the $250,000 of depreciation tax deductions during the building's first year. These enabled him to keep, tax-free, not only the $200,000, but $50,000 of other cash income. Tax savings to the 81-percent-bracket Ogilvie: nearly $200,000 the first year, nearly a million dollars in the first five years he owned the building.

In the fall of 1975, Allen Ogilvie received an important caller: an agent representing Consolidated Cash Register offered to buy the Providential Building for the company's headquarter offices. By now Ogilvie had taken tax deductions of nearly $1,700,000, so the value of the building on his books was only $3,300,000. Yet the agent was offering $5 million for the building—precisely its original cost.

---

* If the new rates of the 1963 tax bill become law, the numbers will be different, but the principles will be essentially the same.

Two considerations brought Allen Ogilvie to a quick accept-
ance of the offer: first, he would make a big "tax profit" on the
deal. The tax deductions he had taken had *saved* him 81 cents
on every dollar; but the tax he'd have to pay on his "book profit"
would only be 25 cents on the dollar. Thus, his lawyer informed
him by telephone, he would end up precisely $942,422.78 ahead
on taxes alone! (See p. 149.)

Second, and even more clinching: he had by now skimmed
the cream off the tax deductions allowed him for the Providential Building. From now on they would decline sharply. It was
time to sell and find a new building where the depreciation deductions would be nearer the proportions to which he had
become accustomed. By the time the Providential deal was
signed, he had found just the building: the $10 million Fortuity
Building, on which the first-year tax deductions would permit
him to enjoy $435,000 of tax-free income—the equivalent, his
lawyer told him, of $2,175,000 of *taxable* income.

The president of Consolidated Cash Register was also pleased
with his purchase. Not only did he have a handsome new headquarters building; but he could start the depreciation cycle on
the building all over again, not on the basis of Allen Ogilvie's
old $3,300,000 "book value," but on the basis of the $5 million
Consolidated had paid. Result: over a million dollars of tax-
free income for his company over the next five years.

In 1984, a new era began for the Providential Building. It was
prefaced in the summer of 1983, when a new real estate tycoon,
Oliver Cransdale, offered the almost unbelievable price of $7
million for the building. Since Consolidated, in its turn, had by
then taken the bulk of *its* allowable tax deductions, a sale
seemed propitious, but Consolidated's president, Gordon
Johnson, was reluctant to risk losing his headquarters office
space.

"No strain," Cransdale told him. "Sell me the building and I'll
lease it right back to you, or as much of it as you want. It'll be

just like owning the building, and of course your rent payments will be tax-deductible, so Uncle Sam will pay half of them for you."

"Sounds ideal," said Johnson. "But tell me. I'm curious: Why are you willing to pay $7,000,000 for a sixteen-year-old building?"

"Taxes, my dear fellow, taxes," replied the enterprising Cransdale. "Sure, I'm taking a risk paying you $7,000,000—but the more I pay the bigger the deductions I can take, and in my situation, with a big cash income, it's worth the risk."

He pulled his chair closer to Johnson's desk and adopted a confidential tone. "If I pull off this deal," he said with a wink, "I'll have income of over half a million this year—and I won't pay a thin dime of taxes. How's that?"

"Extraordinary" was the only word that came to Johnson's mind.

And so, in the spring of 1984, the new owner of the Providential Building eagerly grasped the depreciation wheel and gave it another spin—not based on the $1,700,000 "book value" remaining after the combined Ogilvie-Consolidated Cash Register deductions, but on the new $7 million purchase price. Thus, the first year's depreciation deductions meant $437,500 of tax-free income to Oliver Cransdale.

But he was still not completely satisfied. In another of his ventures, he had sunk $750,000 into a piece of land on which he could take no depreciation deductions (land being non-depreciable)—clearly an intolerable situation. But, as is so often true in tax laws, inventive minds had the solution to his problem: sell the land, lease it right back, and take tax deductions on the rental payments to the new owners.* Thus, the government would, in effect, be paying a lion's share of the ground rental, and what had previously been non-deductible was transformed into a tax-deductible asset.

---

* This was precisely the technique used in the $6½ million sale of Yankee Stadium by Topping and Webb in 1953.

As 1992 approached, the Providential Building's tax allures once again began to wane. It was time to sell again. Now let's see, pondered Cransdale. Which one of my high-bracket friends might be in the market for a good tax shelter . . .?

To most ordinary mortals, the word "shelter" connotes a means of protecting humans from the elements. But to a high-bracket taxpayer blessed with a good tax adviser, the word "shelter" is usually joined with the word "tax," and both are frequently, though not exclusively, associated with real estate. Point to a large fortune built up since World War II and you may well find some handsome real estate tax shelters standing in the background.

The apparent anomalies cited at the outset of this chapter were made possible by such "shelters." Other illustrations are available. To the Statler Hotel Corporation, for example, in a period of five years, "shelters" have meant the amassing, *wholly tax-free*, of $13,023,931 in cash available for distribution to its shareholders.

Fortune magazine has described a prototype real estate situation involving a Manhattan skyscraper, wherein a happy investor was able, on a $2,500,000 cash investment, to emerge after only five years with an after-tax—repeat, *after-tax*—profit of $3,300,000, the equivalent, for a 75-percent-bracket taxpayer, of $13,200,000 of *before*-tax income, or, for a 90 percent taxpayer, of $33 million of pre-tax income.

The prospectuses of several New York real estate corporations tell of large amounts of cash available for distribution to stockholders paradoxically coupled with net losses, reported to the government for tax purposes. Examples:

—Transcontinental Investing Corporation's prospectus showed $2,447,000 "net cash available" in 1960, yet reported a loss, for tax purposes, of $1,042,800. Its depreciation deductions came to $4,522,800.

—The Tenney Corporation showed "net cash available" of

$1,579,000, with a tax loss of $12,000. Depreciation deductions came to $1,645,000.

—Moody's Bank and Finance Manual for 1962, which gives dividend and profit figures for many real estate corporations, shows that the Futterman Corporation, in 1960, distributed $1,429,036 to shareholders, but reported a tax loss of $430,-920.

In all, eleven new corporate prospectuses surveyed by the Treasury Department showed net cash available for distribution totaling $26,672,804, of which only $936,425—3.5 percent—was taxable. Nearly 97 percent of these corporate profits, therefore, were tax-free.*

Brochures, prospectuses and pamphlets avidly and vividly describe the tax advantages of investing in real estate, with titles such as, "How To Make A Killing In Real Estate," "Seven Real Estate Situations With 100 Times The Usual Profit Potential," and "Canadian Real Estate Offers Tax Bonanzas to U.S. Investors."

What accounts for the tax advantages of real estate? One particularly helpful pamphlet provides a succinct answer: "Depreciation and Capital Gain Are the Vital Keys to Tax Savings in Real Estate." Real estate veterans say, with considerable reason, that a third "vital key" should be added: inflation—rising real estate prices.

The case of Allen Ogilvie and the Providential Building illustrate how the depreciation-capital gain combination works. Mr. Ogilvie's attorney was able to convey the glad tidings that Ogilvie would come out nearly a million dollars ahead *on taxes alone*, with his sale of the building, because his depreciation

---

* All of these prospectuses involved real estate in New York City, where the fast-turnover tax angle has been worked far more vigorously than anywhere else in the country—so energetically, in fact, that some of these companies promised their investors too much in the way of tax-free payouts, and, as a result, have had to cut back or eliminate their cash dividends. Some are even in financial difficulties.

deductions* were taken at his regular top-bracket rate of 81
percent, while on his "book profit" on the sale, he paid only the
25 percent capital gains tax. The arithmetic works out this way:

A. Depreciation deductions taken by Ogilvie: $1,682,898
B. *Times* his 81% top-bracket tax rate†   x 81%
C. Equal his *tax saving* from the deductions $1,363,147
D. "Book profit" from sale of building $1,682,898
E. *Times* 25% capital gains rate   x 25%
F. *Equals tax he pays* on profit $ 420,724

   HIS NET TAX SAVING (C minus F) $ 942,423

In short, he saves 81 cents on the dollar, pays back only 25
cents on the dollar, and therefore "makes" 56 cents on the dollar.

Even without the capital gain advantage, depreciation deductions, being "paper deductions" (in that they involve no cash
outlay) offer a unique sort of tax pleasure. For a moment, indulge in the pleasant fantasy of holding $5,000 of cash income
in your hand. In order to claim a $5,000 deduction for, say,
medical expenses or taxes or interest, you have to actually spend
the cash for those purposes. True, your taxes have been somewhat reduced, and kindly Uncle Sam has paid a part of your
bill. *But the cash itself is gone.* It is unavailable to finance other
necessities or niceties of life. Not so with a *depreciation* deduction of, say, $5,000. You may claim the deduction on your tax
return, thus canceling out (and paying no taxes on) your $5,000
of income—*but still hold on to the $5,000.* It remains available
to buy food, or shoes for the baby, or, perhaps, that air-con-
ditioned hard-top convertible you've been coveting. In theory,

---

* These are simply the allowances the tax law makes for the wear and
tear of a building or machine. They permit the owner to recover his total
investment—including mortgages (see p. 150)—tax-free and, in theory,
help provide the funds to replace the property when it is worn out. Since
each owner is entitled to this, when a property changes hands, the depreciation deductions begin again, on the basis of whatever the new owner paid.

† In actual fact, depreciation deductions of this magnitude would cover
several tax brackets. The 81% figure is used here for simplicity.

the day of reckoning will come, when you'll have to provide the $5,000 to replace the building—but if you are as clever and as fortunate as Allen Ogilvie and are able to sell the building for a handsome price before you have to replace it, you avoid the day of reckoning.

You can compound your tax joy by buying a building with a small cash payment and a large mortgage, since the depreciation deductions are based not on the cash outlay, but on the entire purchase price of the building. For example, a 75-percent-bracket taxpayer exploiting this technique could realize nearly a 19 percent first-year *cash* return on his money.* Of course, large mortgages mean large interest payments, but to a taxpayer in the 75 percent bracket, this causes only minor distress, since the interest is tax-deductible and Uncle Sam therefore pays three-fourths of the bill.

An actual incident in New York City, told by Manhattan realtor Daniel Friedenberg in *Harper's* magazine, illustrates how handsomely a low-down-payment real estate investment can pay off. A real estate operator leased ground in Manhattan and borrowed what he alleged to be 65 percent of the cost of erecting a building. In reality, his borrowing amounted to 80 percent of the building's cost, thanks to padded cost estimates by the architect and engineer. When the building was completed, using double-rate depreciation,† *the tax savings alone in the first three years were sufficient to repay him his original cash investment!* His profits from rentals were over and above that. At the end of the three years, he liquidated the corporation that owned the apartment building and sold the building at a profit, thus returning his investment *a second time*, and paying only

---

* If he puts up $1 million cash for a $5 million new building, the first-year depreciation deductions would be $250,000. At his 75 percent tax bracket, this would mean added "keeping money" of $187,500. Treasury officials are at a loss to know how to curb the low-down-payment, high-depreciation practice, but they believe the problem would largely vanish if Congress were to eliminate "fast depreciation" and enact a "recapture plan," as described below.

†See p. 151.

the favored 25 percent capital gains tax on the profit. (Incidentally, it was the process of liquidating the corporation—which tax lawyers call "collapsing" it—that permitted him to pay the 25 percent capital gains rate instead of the regular 52 percent corporation tax on the profit. In certain respects, real estate corporations are easier to "collapse" than those in other industries.)

Are the depreciation deductions a true measure of the wear and tear on a building (and of its consequent loss of value)? Presumably, if they were, no one would want to pay more than its "book value." Yet buildings are constantly being bought and sold for considerably more than their depreciated worth. This leads Treasury Department officials to conclude that something is amiss—that the deductions do not, in fact, correspond to the building's *actual* loss in value. To the extent this is so, the Treasury contends, the deductions confer an unwarranted tax advantage on the building's owner.

The discrepancy is heightened, Treasury officials say, by the so-called "accelerated" or faster-than-average depreciation permitted during the early years of a building's life. The simplest method of depreciation is the so-called "straight-line" formula, whereby a uniform deduction is taken during each year of the building's "useful life" (e.g., for a $100,000 building with a twenty-five-year life, the deductions each year would come to $4,000). But on *new* buildings, twice this amount is permitted in the first year (so that the deduction would be $8,000 instead of $4,000), and on used buildings, one and one half times the average is permitted the first year. These deductions decline each year until, *theoretically*, in the latter years of a building's life, the lower-than-average deductions offset the larger-than-average deductions of the earlier years, and everybody comes out even.

That's the *theory*. But, here again, if the owner is as shrewd as Allen Ogilvie, and sells the building at the proper time, he avoids the unpleasantness of those lower-than-average deduction years. Not only does he end up ahead of the game, but the new owner starts at the beginning again, with renewed faster-than-average deductions. If he, in turn, sells soon enough, he too will escape the lower-than-average years, and the Treasury never catches up. And on each sale, the depreciation-capital gain advantage may come into play.

Treasury officials argue that this fast depreciation formula is the exact *opposite* of what is happening to the building. They contend that in reality, the value drops off more slowly in early years and faster later. This, they say, conforms precisely with the assumption underlying the repayment patterns mortgage bankers permit on real estate loans (slow repayment in early years, faster in later years).

To emphasize the discrepancy between these repayment practices and depreciation deductions, the Treasury has cited this example, taken from the magazine *Architectural Forum*:*

Five-Year Depreciation Deductions	*Five-Year Mortgage Repayment*
(Loss of Value in the eyes of the tax laws)	(Loss of Value in the eyes of the bank)
$203,600	$70,900

One leading real estate expert supported the Treasury contention when he told Congress that "it seems to be accepted in the real estate industry that depreciation is measured by mortgage amortization (loan repayment)—*the amount that you have to pay off on the mortgage, by and large, is considered about equivalent to current wastage* (wearing out) *of the asset.*" (Emphasis and parenthetical phrases added)

---

* Involving a $900,000 building on a $100,000 site, with a forty-year life, depreciated on a double-rate basis.

Real estate spokesmen say this evidence should not be given undue weight, for the repayment patterns in the lending industry are based on purely practical considerations, principally the popularity and success of the even-monthly-payment formula, which inherently involves low debt repayments in the early years. Nevertheless, says the Treasury, since sound lending institutions would not tolerate a discrepancy in values as large as that reflected in the *Architectural Forum* example, it supports the point that fast depreciation is not an accurate measure of wear and tear and value loss in buildings.

To remedy what it considers the unwarranted tax advantages enjoyed by the real estate industry, the Kennedy Administration proposed two measures:

(1) Discontinue "fast-depreciation" on buildings, and limit them to uniform yearly, or "straight-line" deductions.

(2) End the depreciation-capital gain tax advantage by taxing sale profits over "book value" at regular income tax rates instead of at the favored 25 percent capital gains rate.

The rationale of this second proposal is this: the fact that the building could be sold for more than its depreciated value *proves* that the depreciation deductions were "excessive" (i.e., were greater than the building's *real* loss of value). Hence, it is only fair that the tax advantage from these "excessive" deductions should be "recaptured."

In 1962, Congress accepted this reasoning for so-called "personal property" (e.g., machines and other movable assets). In fact, it conceded that the absence of a "recapture" makes possible a conversion of "ordinary income into a capital gain." Nonetheless, that conversion privilege, while denied to personal property, is still enjoyed by real estate, where it is most readily —and profitably—exploited.

The principal argument of the real estate industry against the recapture proposal runs something like this: When a man buys a building and lot for $10 million and sells it ten years later for $11 million, what accounts for the increase? It couldn't be the building, which is ten years older, its equipment, such as elevators and air conditioning and heating, less modern and more nearly in need of repair or replacement. So if it isn't the building that has gone up in value then it must be the land. It would be unfair, says the industry, to apply regular income tax rates to a gain in value of land, on two scores: first, no one else pays regular income tax rates on such a gain; and second, no depreciation has been taken on the land, and so there is no tax advantage to recapture.

The defenders of "recapture" offer several arguments in rebuttal:

First, argues the Treasury Department, the *purpose* of the depreciation allowance is to permit the owner to recover his original dollar investment in the machine or building. If he is able to recover this through the sale price, then the purpose of the depreciation allowance has been served and the deductions he has taken were needless. Besides, if a buyer is willing to pay more than the value-after-depreciation, this signifies that the building wasn't losing its usefulness as fast as the depreciation deductions assumed.

Second, the industry's argument would be more persuasive if a building could be picked up off its land and dangled on the end of a crane. Considered thus, separate from the land, the building is indeed more worn out and less useful. But obviously the building cannot be separated from the land. In fact, it derives its very value from the desirability of its location and shares in any increase in the location's value.

Third, the industry's own practices in assigning relative values to land and building are inconsistent with its argument against recapture. When a property changes hands, the bulk of the sale price is usually assigned to the *building* (in order to increase the buyer's depreciation deductions), directly contrary to the industry argument that it is the *land* that has gone up in value. In fact, one real estate spokesman acknowledged to Congress that a realistic allocation of values between building and land "would discourage somebody from buying real estate . . . *even though we know that it happens to be an accurate one and a true one economically.*" (Emphasis added)

Fourth, a recapture plan would turn what is now called "the one-way street" provision into a two-way street on which both the government and the taxpayer have equal rights. This one-way street operates not only through the full-deduction-capital-gain device so skillfully exploited by Allen Ogilvie with the Providential Building; it also operates through a special provision of the tax law which holds that where a building is sold for *less* than its depreciated "book value," the loss is deductible at regular income tax rates; but if it is sold for *more* than its book value, the profit is only taxed at the 25 percent capital gains rate. That is, if a 75-percent-bracket taxpayer sells a building for a $100,000 book *loss,* the government bears 75 percent of his misfortune. But if he sells it for a $100,000 book *profit,* the government gets only 25 percent of it. (Again—heads, the taxpayer wins; tails, the government loses).*

In 1962 and 1963, the Kennedy Administration modified its original proposal for a full recapture of all "book profits" and asked that for those holding a building beyond six years, the proportion of such profits subject to recapture would gradually decline, until after roughly fifteen years, they would all be taxed at capital gains rates, as at present. This sliding scale proposal, coupled with an elimination of fast depreciation on buildings would, it was reasoned, curb the tax-motivated fast turnover of buildings without penalizing the legitimate long-term real estate investor. But the House, in 1963, not only failed to eliminate the fast depreciation on buildings; it also foreshortened and reduced the Administration's sliding scale, starting it after only twenty months of ownership, so that after the ideal tax-

---

* Many realtors capitalized on the depressed real estate market at the outset of World War II by selling their properties at a fully-deductible loss, but leasing them right back, so that they would, in effect, still own the properties, meanwhile having effectively avoided the high war-time excess profits tax.

turnover time of seven to eight years, the "recapture" will be sharply diminished. Treasury officials, in short, see little in the new real estate provisions to discourage the Allen Ogilvies of this world.

A glance at the many books and pamphlets describing the tax glories of real estate investments confirms that thus far we have but scratched the surface of tax-saving devices.

Example 1: You are a successful real estate operator whose shrewd investments present you with the unpleasant prospect of large amounts of "unsheltered" income on which you might have to pay high income taxes. To forestall this unthinkable possibility you need some super-colossal depreciation deductions. Your trusted tax attorney, as usual, has just the answer: build a new office building with a forty-year life. "That won't do," you say impatiently. "On a forty-year life, the deductions will be too small."

"Ah," says your attorney, with a knowing smile, "but you haven't let me finish. What I have in mind amounts to your depreciating the building in twenty-five years, even though its useful life is forty years."

"Explain away," you respond admiringly.

"It's simple. Just put up your building on leased land. You'd want a long lease of course—say, a hundred and twenty-five years—to protect your interest in the building, but make sure the *initial term* of the lease is at least twenty-four years and a day, or play it safe and make it twenty-five years. Then take the rest in options to renew. That will get you your twenty-five year depreciation."

"But," you protest, "the useful life of the building is still forty years. How can I depreciate it in twenty-five?"

"Because, my friend, the tax laws say that if the *initial* term of a ground lease is sixty percent or more of the 'useful life' of the building, then you can 'amortize' the cost of the building— which amounts to the same thing as depreciating it—*over the term of that initial lease.* It simply amounts to increasing your depreciation deductions by forty percent. It fits your situation to a *T*."

Example 2: You own a piece of land ideally suited for a department store. You have two choices: either build the store yourself and charge $2,000 monthly rent, or lease the bare ground to a chain store for $800 a month and let *them* build the store. Your tax attorney strongly advises you to do the latter. After all, he argues, a wealthy man like yourself, in the 81 percent tax bracket, won't starve without that extra monthly rental and anyway, 81 percent of it would go to the government. Besides, you'll avoid the considerable headache of putting up the building. Most important, however—at the end of the ground lease you can get the building back tax-free. If and when you sell it, you pay a capital gains tax of 25 percent. As one real estate tax pamphlet puts it, by exchanging the higher rental income (taxed at your 81 percent regular income tax rate) for a later sale of the building (at the 25 percent capital gains rate), "in effect what you have done is to convert ordinary rental income into capital gain."

Example 3: You arrange to rent a building under a lease arrangement whereby you pay high rents during the early part of the lease, when the building is new, with lower rents during the later years, when the building is older. Thus, you get higher-than-average deductions (*at your ordinary income tax rates*) for the early-year rental payments you make. Then, just before the rents are scheduled under the lease to go *down,* you sell your right to the lease. Since the new rent levels are alluringly low, the lease will bring a handsome price (and you pay a *capital gains* tax on the profit). Result: you've done it again! You've achieved the effect of transforming ordinary income into capital gains. (But proceed with care. A recent Supreme Court decision frowns on arrangements where tax avoidance can be shown to be the only motive.)

Example 4: In Example 3, you were the tenant. In this example, you move to the other side of the table and become the landlord for a plot of land. You arrange a lease so that during the early years, the rental payments to you are low, with a provision for a reappraisal of the land value and a presumed rent increase later on. Just before the rent increase goes into effect, you sell the land, and, since the rental income from it is about to rise impressively, your land commands a generous price—and the profits from the sale are taxed at the 25 percent capital gains rate. What you have done, by accepting a lower initial rent, is avoid rental income (taxed at your regular income tax rates) in favor of a later sale of the land at a far lower-taxed capital-gain profit. You are clearly becoming a master alchemist at transforming ordinary income into capital gain.

Example 5: You put up a building. During the period of construction and the early years, your deductions for interest, taxes and depreciation are all taken at your own top-bracket rate which, let's say, is 75 percent. Later, when the bulk of these deductions have been enjoyed, and the building's income shows up as a profit on your tax return, you form a corporation, so that the profits are taxed at the 52 percent corporate rate rather than at your 75 percent personal rate. The effect: *full deduction* of the expenses, but only *partial taxation* of the income they produce.

Example 6: A 1963 tax pamphlet published by Prentice-Hall, entitled "Federal Tax Angles in Real Estate," cites the following:

Before 1962, if a Real Estate Investment Trust (REIT) earned $984,734* before providing for income taxes, here's how the melon was cut up:

To the Government, for income taxes . . . . $	478,500
To the shareholders, as dividends	506,234
	$ 984,734

* As the Real Estate Investment Trust of America actually did one year.

Assuming the earnings remain constant, here's how the melons will be cut up now:

To the Government, for income taxes . . . . . $ Zero
To the shareholders, as dividends   984,734
                                     $ 984,734

As the pamphlet aptly points out, "That's a whale of a different set-up—$478,500 more for the shareholders to divide among themselves."

What makes it different? A law was passed in 1960 which in effect excuses so-called real estate investment trusts from paying corporation income taxes (by permitting them to deduct their dividend payments to their shareholders in computing their taxable income).

In order to qualify for this, however, they must distribute at least 90 percent of their income to their shareholders, and the justification for excusing them from the corporation tax is that they act, in effect, merely as conduits for rental income, and not as ordinary corporations which actively reinvest their earnings in the business. On the other hand, as the law explicitly acknowledges, they are in every other respect exactly like other corporations. Thus, these groups are able to get all the *advantages* of doing business as a corporation, but unlike others who enjoy these advantages—even others who may *by choice* pay out 90 percent of their profits as dividends—they pay no corporate income tax.

No one should conclude from this chapter that real estate is just made up of splashy successes, ready buyers willing to pay rising prices, and sharp promotors interested in a fast buck and a clever tax angle. There are risks and failures and heartbreaks in real estate, just as in other industries which do not enjoy the tax advantages available in real estate.

Experienced real estate investors contend that these tax advantages hinge on rising prices for land and buildings; without the kind of real estate inflation we've had since World War II, they say, most of the tax angles described in this chapter would do little or no good.

This is generally true, but it is not a valid reason for not changing the tax laws pertaining to real estate. As the experience of the last fifteen years indicates, a rising market is not a freak exception; it can be the general rule—and is likely to be, in the long run, since the amount of land is as inevitably fixed as the population is inevitably expanding.

9 / *Missing: $5 Billion*

Every day, somewhere in the United States, events like these take place:

A housewife opens the mail on her way downtown, finds a dividend check for $10.20 and cashes it at the grocery store that same morning . . . A doctor, hurrying from one house call to another, gets a $5 bill from one patient and a $10 bill from another. He stuffs them in his pocket, and on the way home, uses them to buy groceries . . . A once-a-week maid collects her pay in cash at the end of the day, her employer fishing deep in a pocketbook to find the $5 bill and making no record of the transaction . . . A farmer sells his produce and spends the cash the same day on seed and feed . . . A worker cashes a savings bond, but in his mind the $6.25 profit he made isn't a separate item; it just becomes part of the $25 he needs to buy his wife a birthday present . . . A corner grocery owner puts the cash from the day's last few sales in his pocket instead of in the cash register (Who owns this business, anyway? he asks himself).

The law requires that every dollar referred to above be declared as part of the year's income when tax returns are made out. But under the particular circumstances described, chances are that, whether by forgetfulness, haste, ignorance, or deliberate cheating, not one of those dollars will be reported to the tax collector.

These are everyday occurrences—but in a year's time they add up to the staggering total of $25 *billion* of unreported taxable income, and cost the United States Treasury between $4 and $5 billion annually—in taxes called for under the law, but unreported and uncollected.

If the missing billions could be found and collected, it would be possible, without losing any revenue to the Treasury, to give everybody a 10 percent tax cut.

Thus, just as with the billions of dollars in revenue lost through the so-called "loopholes," the failure of some taxpayers to pay their full share—in this case because they fail to report all of their income—means higher taxes for the rest of the taxpayers.

Who doesn't pay, and why? How do they get away with it?

As to the "who," the $25 billion of unreported but taxable income for 1959 breaks down as follows:

Group	Income Unreported	Percent Unreported
Farmers	$ 5 billion ⎫	
Small Businessmen plus Professional Men (Doctors, Lawyers, etc.)	7 billion ⎬	28%
Wage and Salary Earners	6.5 billion	3%
Receivers of Interest	2.8 billion	34%
Receivers of Dividends	.9 billion	8%
Receivers of Pensions and Annuities	.6 billion	29%
Receivers of Rents, Royalties and Capital Gains	1.2 billion	11%

At first it may seem strange that such multi-billion dollar sums can slip through the hands of the 56,000 employees of the Internal Revenue Service. But the sleuthing job is formidable, because in reality the missing billions are made up of millions of tiny fragments scattered throughout some ninety-six million separate tax returns. Unless a return is individually reviewed and audited (and only one in twenty is), the government must rely on what the *taxpayer* states his income, expenses and taxes to be (Justice Jackson once said ours is "a system of taxation by confession"). The system of withholding some taxes from a person's paycheck greatly reduces this reliance, but where withholding is not in effect, the taxpayer's honesty, memory and records are crucial.

The main areas of under-reporting, therefore, are those where there is no withholding, where cash transactions are frequent, and where record-keeping is poor.

The example of the harried and overworked doctor was mentioned, at the outset of this chapter, although not all of the under-reporting by professional men is as unintentional. Tax prosecutors tell of one doctor who kept a large fishbowl in his office, advising his patients, "$3 in the fishbowl or I'll bill you $5." One dentist was discovered with $27,000 in cash filed away among his patients' x-rays.

Another doctor practiced for thirty-five years without ever filing a tax return. Revenue agents could not forgive him this oversight simply because during the depression he had charged only 75 cents for house calls and office visits, and was seldom paid in cash. Together with large quantities of currency found secreted among the doctor's pill bottles, tobacco pouches and other possessions were scraps of paper showing receipt of such things as "3 frogs @ 5¢—15¢ on account; 2 truck rides @ 5¢—10¢ on account."

Frequent cash transactions and a paucity of careful bookkeeping are prime factors behind the billions of unreported small business income. The corner grocer may be tempted, for example, to believe that the revenue agent will never know the difference if he occasionally by-passes the cash register in favor of his pocket. Many small businesses tend to pay off other creditors first, leaving their tax payment to the government to last. Some have even "borrowed" from the tax funds they have withheld from their employees, fully intending, perhaps, to pay over the sums to the government at the proper time. But if, in the meantime, they go bankrupt, Uncle Sam is left holding an empty bag.

The $6.5 billion of undeclared wages and salaries are believed to be mostly in the hands of casual or transient workers —the domestic servants who work one day a week for each of five or six employers; the itinerant farm workers whose peripatetic habits impede tax collection; the construction workers who float from job to job. "Moonlighters" are also a problem, since there is frequently no withholding of taxes from their second-job earnings.

Many hard-pressed wage earners overstate to their employers the *number* of their dependents so as to reduce the withholding from their wages and increase their take-home pay. Many, but not all, get caught, since in filling out their tax returns, they must list the *names* of the claimed dependents. Many resort to fictitious names, some even claim dead people. One tavern cook falsely claimed his mother-in-law as a dependent and when she protested, he told her to "forget it. I could claim a dog as a dependent," he went on, "and the government would never know the difference." He underestimated the tax collectors, however, for when another taxpayer, a Mr. Smith of New York, claimed, as a dependent, "Doris Smith—daughter," agents managed to discover that "Doris" was, in reality, Mr. Smith's dog "Duchess." Donkeys and pet birds have turned up as "dependents" and one revenue official recalls a truck driver listing his truck. A former movie and TV actor (who, ironically, always played the part of the law enforcement officer) was caught filing false returns on which he consistently listed, as dependents, six non-existent children bearing the first names of famous singers ("Grace" for Grace Moore, "Jenny" for Jenny Lind).

Taxi drivers, waiters and waitresses who fail to report all of their cash tips are another source of frustration for the tax collector. The courts do, however, permit revenue agents to compute "normal"' tipping income for, say, a New York taxi driver, and to tax him on such income even if he doesn't report it on his tax return.

Arriving at such a norm may be difficult for the headwaiters of popular restaurants or night clubs, whose palms are regularly and liberally crossed just at the crucial juncture when that ringside table suddenly becomes "available." Few such gentlemen, however, are as handsomely rewarded as Philippe of the Waldorf, who received some $300,000 in gratuities and kickbacks from caterers, but who was convicted for failing to share his largesse in proper measure with his government.

Among the devices for bilking the government, the filing of false refund claims is perhaps the most contagious. A taxpayer, after waiting a suitable interval after April 15, files a claim— sometimes several, using false names—for a refund to which he is not entitled. A false-refund prosecution has been known to produce a rash of similiar offenses in that same locality by people who acknowledge they got the idea from newspaper accounts of the trial. (Readers who may be similarly inspired by this account should be warned that electronic tax-checking will soon make false-refund claims highly hazardous.) One prisoner got the idea from a cell mate who had been jailed for such an offense, tried it himself when he was released, and ended up behind bars again.

Some taxpayers apparently cherish the thought that if they are very, very quiet and file no tax return whatever, revenue agents will never even know they exist. In 1961-62, revenue officials unearthed nearly a million instances in which required tax returns were not filed. How many other returns are among the missing and how much revenue they would yield is unknown, but few taxpayers could be as conspicuously forgetful as one local TV commentator who broadcast more than twenty special reminders on tax-filing requirements, but was later prosecuted for neglecting to file his own tax return in two consecutive years.

Farmers are by nature and training poor record keepers. For those who don't keep bank accounts, checks received are quickly cashed and spent, and thus may never be declared as income. Many farmers borrow against the future sale of their crop, so that when they part with the fruit of their labor and receive little or no cash in return, what income is there (they reason) to report to the government? Moreover, *deductible* farm expenses are easily comingled with *non-deductible* personal expenses (how much of that electric bill went to light the home, how much to run the milking machine?). Misunderstanding of the law is common: a farmer may regard the sale of some timber as simply reducing the value of his land; to be taxed for this is, to him, a violation of common sense.

Of course, such inadvertence or innocence does not wholly account for the $5 billion of unreported farm income. There are some willful violators, such as the farmer who neglected to report some $135,000 of oil-well income. When called before Revenue Agents to explain the omission, the farmer gave six conflicting stories. His attorney attributed this to his client's use of tranquilizers.

Tax officials believe that one factor behind the billions of undeclared farm income is that only recently has farm income become sufficient to be taxed in significant quantities. While other taxpayers have had several decades to become familiar with the tax laws, farm income until 1941 was so low that few farmers were required to pay any taxes. Hence, tax experts believe, there is a lag in farm tax knowledge that can only be overcome by an intensive education program.

Nearly $4 billion of the dividends and interest paid to Americans fails to appear on their tax returns. Some of this is mere oversight: the owner of a savings account may be unaware of the interest building up in his account; the redeemer of a savings bond may unwittingly forget the interest that has accrued. Revenue agents might, however, doubt the inadvertence of the real estate man who, in an actual Internal Revenue case, understated his dividend and interest income by $300,063 in a four-year period ($100,457 of it in a single year), or the lawyer who failed to report $32,570 in interest received during one year.

Some taxes are not fully collected simply because they are difficult to understand or enforce. The idiosyncracies of the retail excise tax, for example, would stump many a Phi Beta Kappa man, so the drug store clerk may be pardoned for not knowing that shampoos advertised for their *beautifying* qualities ("Adds Lustre To Your Hair") are taxable as cosmetics, while those touted for their *cleansing* properties are classed as soaps (provided, of course, they contain the requisite percentage of "saponaceous matter"). Cleanliness being next to godliness, soap is exempt from taxation.

Pity the poor revenue officer charged with the accurate collection of the cabaret tax since, by court interpretation, couples may dine early and remain through the 9:00 to 10:00 floor show but escape the cabaret tax by paying their bill at 8:55. How much of a night club's receipts are and aren't subject to the tax is likely, therefore, to be largely guesswork.

The gambling taxes are particularly difficult to enforce. Since gambling is illegal in most localities, the purchaser of the required $50 gambling tax stamp may subject himself to prima facie prosecution, and if the 10 percent excise tax on betting were paid, as required by law, this would more than wipe out the profit margin of most bookies. While Congress originally hoped to collect $400 million annually from the gambling tax, actual receipts have been less than $10 million a year.

Some revenue is lost through undetected mathematical errors, although electronic machines check the arithmetic on most returns. If pure chance were controlling—if there were no psychological factors at work—an arithmetical error might as easily favor the government as the taxpayer. Students of psychology might, however, find significance in the fact that the *number* of taxpayer mathematical errors is three to two against the government and to the taxpayer's advantage. The *dollar* errors involved in these slips-of-the-pencil favor the taxpayer two to one!

What can be done to close the $5 billion revenue gap? The biggest single step would be the enactment of a system of tax withholding for dividend and interest income, similar to that now in effect for wages and salaries. In a single stroke, this would collect between $650 and $880 million of revenue that now slips through the tax collector's fingers.

Under such a system, savings institutions and corporations would hold out a certain amount from dividend and interest payments to their shareholders and depositors (just as they now withhold a portion of their employees' paychecks) and would send the withheld amount to the government. At the end of the year, each stockholder or depositor, in making out his tax return, would report the amount withheld (just as a wage earner reports what has been held out of his paychecks), and this would be credited against his total tax bill.

Withholding has a venerable history. It dates back to the first U.S. tax, in Civil War days. It was also contained in the first income tax law sanctioned by the Sixteenth Amendment, enacted in 1913. The present day wage withholding has been in the U.S. tax system since 1943, and it has been called "the most important action ever taken by the Congress" in the field of tax collection. Mainly because of it, 97 percent of all wage and salary income is duly reported on tax returns; only three percent is unreported. By contrast, three times that proportion of all dividend income and eleven times that proportion of all interest income (where withholding is not in effect) fails to appear on tax returns.

This results in a profligate drain on the Treasury. In the decade from 1951 through 1961, the absence of withholding cost the Treasury a total of $4 billion in revenues!

If withholding has worked so successfully for wages and salaries, why hasn't it been applied to dividends and interest? Why has Congress sat by, year after year, and allowed the Treasury to be deprived of hundreds of millions—even billions —of tax revenue required by law to be paid? (Twice, once in 1951 and again in 1962, the House did pass a withholding provision, but both times the plan was killed by the Senate.)

The answer is that Congress—the Senate in particular—has permitted itself to be paralyzed into inaction by two objections to withholding that have little foundation in fact. The first is that low-income taxpayers or charitable institutions who owe the government little or no tax would supposedly suffer by having taxes unjustifiably withheld from their dividend and interest income and by having to wait for a tax refund to set matters right. The second objection is that withholding would impose an undue administrative burden on the savings institutions and corporations that would have to collect the withholding tax.

When the advocate of withholding tries to meet either of these two arguments, he quickly finds he can't win, whichever tack he takes. *Tack No. 1:* He proposes an across-the-board withholding system simple enough for banks and corporations to administer easily. *Result:* He is accused of working an unthinkable hardship on "churches, synagogues, orphanages, union trust funds, hospitals . . . and even little children" (all of whom are, by law, tax-exempt), not to mention "the aged, blind or indigent, earning less than necessary to pay income tax." *Tack No. 2:* His deepest sympathies aroused, our withholding advocate seeks to meet this objection by requiring banks and corporations to distinguish between their shareholders and depositors (sparing the non-taxable, while withholding from the taxable). The only reward for his solicitude is to be assailed for saddling the business community with an unconscionable administrative burden. (This, in capsule form, is precisely the sequence of events that led to the Senate's defeat of dividend and interest withholding in 1962.)

While the image of the over-taxed widow was evoked with

great effectiveness in the 1962 debate, there was a singular lack of senatorial sympathy toward the sixty million wage earners who for two decades have endured the rigors of wage withholding. Withholding opponents, for example, were concerned that there would be considerable *over*-withholding of taxes on dividends and interest, since no allowance would be made for differences in personal exemptions. The implication was that there were millions of widows, orphans or aged parents with their little caches of stocks and bonds who would anxiously await each morning's mail for the government check refunding their over-withheld tax. Scarcely any mention was made, however, of the fact that *nearly thirty-eight million wage earners have taxes over-withheld every year*—by an average of $142. In order to be over-withheld by $142 on dividend and interest income, a taxpayer would have to own roughly $17,500 in stocks or bonds—hardly the where-is-the-next-meal-coming-from type of citizen. Moreover, refunds to over-withheld wage earners are only paid once a year, in contrast to the four-times-yearly refunds proposed for dividend and interest recipients.

The following table highlights the senatorial inconsistency of August 29, 1962—when, after voting to reject dividend and interest withholding by a vote of 66 to 20, the Senate proceeded, by a 62 to 17 vote, to reaffirm its support of wage withholding:

	How many people have their taxes over-withheld?				
How many people subject to withholding?	Number	Percent of those subject to withholding	Total amount over-withheld	Average amount over-withheld	How often refunds made?
WAGES & SALARIES 60 million	37.8 million	63%	$4,766 million	$142	Once a Year
INTEREST & DIVIDENDS* 22 million	2.0 million	9%	$ 168 million	$ 84	Every 3 Months

* Figures based on withholding plan passed by the House in 1962.

The real-life statistics also drain the pathos from the vision of the impoverished widow or orphan dependent on every last penny of dividend and interest income. Among those earning less than $5,000 a year, only one in *twenty* receives any dividend income and one in *twelve* any interest income. Whatever they do receive from these sources constitutes, on the average, a scant 1 percent of their total income—hardly the difference between comfort and deprivation.

Upper income groups had cause to feel somewhat slighted by the senatorial preoccupation with the underprivileged widows and pensioners. By rights, the well-to-do, who receive a striking preponderance of the dividend and interest income, should have held stage center. Government statistics show, for example, that the *top 1 percent* of the taxpayers receive over *half* of all dividends and nearly a *fifth* of all interest income.

Although Congress failed to enact withholding for dividends and interest, it did require that savings institutions and corporations make more comprehensive reports on dividend interest payments both to the taxpayers receiving them and to the government. This has its ironic aspects, because instead of sparing corporations and banks, predictions are this added reporting burden will actually prove to be more onerous than withholding, because of the added paper work, and will collect far less revenue ($275 million annually compared with $880 million under withholding).

In 1962, several savings and loans institutions claimed, in "Dear-Saver" letters to customers, that dividend and interest withholding amounted to "trying to weed the garden with a bulldozer"—penalizing large numbers in order to catch "the few who do not report all of their interest and dividends." Clearly, though, the unreported dividends and interest—reaching the staggering total of $3,700,000,000—belong to more than "a few." If the garden metaphor is to be invoked, it would be more accurate to say that Congress' failure to enact dividend and interest withholding amounts to letting the garden become

overwhelmed by weeds for fear of damaging a few delicate
plants.

The second major hope for finding and collecting the missing
$5 billion lies in the initials ADP, which stand for Automatic
Data Processing, the electronic checking of tax returns.

By 1965, complete information about every taxpayer in the
United States will be recorded on reels of magnetic tape. A
single reel can store full information covering three years' returns of 116,000 taxpayers (punch cards containing the same
information would make a stack four hundred feet high). Electronic brains are able to "read" tax data from the magnetic tape
at a rate of 6½ million letters or numbers per minute.

Without ADP, the sleuthing job of the tax collector is almost
unmanageable. Not only are there nearly 96 million separate tax
returns to be reviewed, but the government receives close to a
third of a *billion* "information returns," such as the reports by
employers on the withholding from employees' wages and the
reports by corporations of their dividend payments of over $10.
These "information returns" contain valuable clues that can help
spot the tax evader, but because of their sheer mass and number, only scant use has been made of them. Most of them pile
up in government warehouses.

ADP will change all that. When it is in full operation, woe
to the "moonlighter" who neglects to report his second-job
earnings, or the taxpayer who forgets that dividend check of six
months ago, for ADP will make it possible, for the first time, to
take the data from the "information returns" on such things as
wage and dividend income and match it up against the tax return of the recipient.

The key to this matching operation is the tax-number that has
been assigned every taxpayer in the United States (identical to
his social security number, if he has one). In the future, a corporation, reporting to the government on its dividend payments to
shareholders, will state it has paid $183.25 this year to Taxpayer

Number 232-18-5432. This information will be recorded on magnetic tape, and the ADP machines, operating at 6½ million characters per minute, will seek out Mr. 232-18-5432's tax return and note the amount of dividend income he reported. If he has declared, say, only $10 of dividend income, the whirring tape machines will report the discrepancy, in readable form, at the remarkable speed of ten lines per second. It will not be long before Taxpayer 232-18-5432 will find a notice in his mailbox— or, if the discrepancy is large enough, an inquisitive revenue agent standing at his door.

These electronic wonders require no time out for lunch or coffee breaks and, if need be, they can easily work around the clock. Their stamina plus their almost limitless appetite for devouring, remembering, and analyzing information offers unexplored opportunities for the tax collector. It would be a simple matter, for example, to feed into the ADP system tape-recorded data on the billions of government subsidy payments to farmers and others, and check them against the recipients' tax returns. And while Internal Revenue is not now considering the step, it would be entirely possible to require taxpayers claiming a large deductible legal or medical expense to list the name *and tax number* of their lawyer or doctor, so that electronics could quickly detect any failure on his part to report the payment.

Information-matching is only one way ADP will provide clues to tax evasion. Over the years, the analysis of tens of millions of tax returns has produced certain norms for nearly every category of taxpayer. For example, in the aggregate, auto dealers of a certain size have certain normally expectable payrolls, maintenance costs, profit margins, and so on, in relation to their sales. By matching the *actual* tax return of, say, Auto Dealer John Smith of Tonawanda, Michigan, against a hypothetical "normal" return for dealers of his size in his area, ADP will be able to spot any unusual discrepancies. While these in themselves will prove nothing, they will suggest where revenue agents should do some more probing.

If, for instance, Mr. Smith's "maintenance and repair expenses" are three times the norm, revenue agents will want to know why. It could be that Mr. Smith has a perfectly logical explanation ("Sir, our Johnson Rod Gnarling machine broke down and had to be repaired on overtime because we had an unusual backlog of Johnson Rods waiting to be gnarled"). It could also be that Mr. Smith rebuilt his own garage at home and conceived the brilliant notion of listing it as a "garage repair" expense on his business return. It has been known to happen.

The computers would also send out an appropriate warning signal if they should run across the return of Factory Worker John Jones, which reports that the $4,000 he earned tending a blast furnace was supplemented with a tidy $2,000 of stock dividends. $2,000 of dividend income indicates that worker Jones owns some $50,000 of stocks—a fact which would prompt a curious revenue agent to wonder where the $50,000 came from and whether it had been duly reported on tax returns when it was received.

If the corner grocer's profit margins are abnormally small, compared with the norm of other comparable corner grocers, Internal Revenue may wonder if cash is by-passing the grocer's cash register—and his tax return.

Automation can also spot less-than-standard tip income reported by a waiter or taxi driver, and, by perceiving unusually high expense-account deductions, ADP could put government auditors on the trail of yachts or hunting lodges used primarily for pleasure but charged off as business expenses.

When automation is in full swing, there will be a far greater chance that your tax return will be checked for error or violation. Under present manual methods, less than a third of all income, estate and gift tax returns are even screened for possible full audit. The returns of all corporations, all top-income individuals, all those entitled to large tax refunds, and most unincorporated businesses are automatically reviewed. But among lower-income returns, only a sample number is screened, and the sample becomes sparser as the income level drops.

ADP, however, will be able to scan *all* returns for deviations from the norm, and will enable government auditors to concentrate their attention on the most potentially productive returns.

The electronic tax-checkers are not omniscient; nor are they lie-detectors. They may not be able to discern that Auto Dealer Smith charged personal home repairs to his business. Cash transactions under the table can easily escape detection. But the enthusiastic ADP experts contend that as they and the machines gain experience, there will be little the computers won't be able to catch. They may even be able to suggest whether that relative you claim as a dependent is alive or dead, existent or nonexistent.

The very awareness that the electronic wizards stand behind the tax collector appears to have a salutary psychological effect. Already, the publicity given ADP has caused guilt-ridden taxpayers to confess, in a single month, tax errors totaling $600,000, some of them dating back to 1918. Revenue officials cannot guarantee immunity from prosecution to the taxpayer who voluntarily discloses an offense, but they can weigh the confession "along with other facts and circumstances" in deciding whether to prosecute.

ADP has other advantages. The assignment to every taxpayer of his own tax number will eliminate the confusion among the 47,000 John Smiths or the 19,676 John Browns in the United States and facilitate the detection of multiple-refund claims by a single taxpayer. The computers will not approve any refund payment until they have checked other tax debts the claimant owes Uncle Sam. The half million refund checks undelivered every year due to changes of address will be electronically credited to the taxpayer's account and saved until claimed.

Using information from telephone directories, registry and license lists, the "memory units" of the computers can help track down those who fail to file any tax return.

Many economy-minded Congressmen envision the electronic marvels replacing revenue agents and reducing the payroll of the Internal Revenue Service. But for all their prowess, the machines can't pound the pavements or ring doorbells or interview corner-cutting taxpayers. In fact, by uncovering more and more investigative leads, ADP will create a need for *more* enforcement personnel. Unhappily, if past experience is any indication, Congress is unlikely to respond fully to this need. Despite documented claims by IRS that every added dollar for enforcement staff brings $6 in increased tax collections, Congress has consistently denied IRS the enforcement staff it has requested.

The present Commissioner of Internal Revenue, Mortimer Caplin, wants added personnel not just for tougher crackdowns but for better taxpayer education and assistance. In his view, long-run improvements can only come about through voluntary compliance—"preventing the tax errors *before* they occur." For instance, tax collectors are now visiting newly-opened businesses to explain to the new proprietor his tax responsibilities and prospective tax problems.

No one knows, of course, how much of the $25 billion "income gap" is willful, how much inadvertent. One official surmises that most of it is willful in the sense that at some point most taxpayers are conscious they are omitting something. Another puts it this way: "In our self-assessed tax system, we are expecting people to be more honest with Uncle Sam than they are with their wives or their business partners. The tax collector can't change human nature. He has to work with what he has."

Viewed in this light, the U. S. tax system is remarkable. It collects 96 percent of what is due under the law (at a cost of one-half cent for every dollar collected) and 97 percent of this comes in voluntarily—without enforcement action. "That a people so numerous, scattered and individualistic," said Justice Jackson, "annually assesses itself with a tax liability, often in highly burdensome amounts, is a reassuring sign of the stability and vitality of our system of self-government."

10 /

The Favored Few

QUESTION: What percent of the taxpayers of the United States make more than $25,000 a year?

What percent make more than $50,000? More than $10,000?

In the course of writing this book, I have asked these questions of a large number of people. I have encountered almost no one—even among people sophisticated in the facts of economic life—who could come anywhere near answering them correctly.* Many of the answers were off the mark ten-fold.

Can you do better?

Before turning the page, make your own guesses.

---

* This is not because the figures are particularly unavailable. They are published every year by the Internal Revenue Service, in a statistical portrait of American taxpayers entitled *Statistics of Income*.

The answers are:

—If you make more than $25,000 a year, you are in the top 1 percent of U. S. taxpayers.

—If your income is more than $50,000 a year, you are in the top *two-tenths of one percent.*

—If you make more than $10,000 a year, you are in the top 10 percent of all taxpayers.

Now, if you're not in that top 1 percent—if you don't make $25,000 a year—take fair warning. This chapter is not about you. As a matter of fact, chances are this chapter doesn't mention you unless you're in the top two-tenths of one percent. (But don't skip over the chapter—these tax features have a direct bearing on you: they cause you to pay higher taxes to make up for the billions of revenue they cost the Treasury every year.)

Do corporate dividends, for example, comprise more than 2 or 3 percent of your income?

Do you own any (or many) tax-exempt bonds? Do you happen to have a "stock option" arrangement with your employer? No? Then none of the tax preferences described in this chapter will do you any good.

If, however, you *are* a beneficiary of these particular tax preferences, you are indeed blessed, for great are the tax savings therefrom.

How great? Up to a billion dollars annually to the owners of state and local tax-free bonds. Nearly half a billion to corporation stockholders. $80 to $100 million to the fortunate holders of corporate stock options.

Since in each case, these bountiful tax favors are shared by only a comparative handful of taxpayers, the savings for each can be mighty.

Take, for example, the case of Mrs. Horace Dodge, Sr., who, according to *Fortune*, sank her entire $56,000,000 legacy into state and local bonds, the interest from which is nontaxable. At an average yield of 3 percent, Mrs. Dodge could enjoy the comfort of a $1,680,000 annual income, *without even having to bother filing a tax return.* Her probable tax saving: between $1,000,000 and $1,500,000 annually.

Or take Charles Stewart Mott, at one time General Motors' largest stockholder, with over 2,600,000 shares. To him the so-called "dividend tax" meant roughly $315,000 of extra spending money per year.

Or consider the case of E. R. Breech, former president of the Ford Motor Company, who realized some $3,200,000 of gain on his corporate stock options, and enjoyed a tax saving thereon of at least $1,600,000. Governor George Romney of Michigan, when president of American Motors, enjoyed stock option bene-fits of about $1,300,000, for a minimum tax saving of $650,000. And Roger Blough of U. S. Steel, famed for his eyeball-to-eyeball confrontation with President Kennedy in 1962, had op-tion benefits of around $2,000,000 and saved at least $1,000,000 in taxes.

Great, therefore, are the blessings, but few are the blessed, since the ownership of tax-free bonds and corporation stock, and the benefactions of stock option arrangements are heavily con-centrated in that top 1 percent of the population fortunate enough to make more than $25,000 a year.

Particularly is this true of executive stock options, which are available only to the top executives of roughly 1,500 corpora-tions in the entire country. The *average* 1960 salary of 215 optioned executives was $102,500. Rarely does an option plan include an official making less than $25,000.

An actual case will show how a stock option arrangement works. In 1956, the International Business Machines Corpora-tion (IBM) granted to its president, Thomas J. Watson, Jr., the right, for ten years, to buy a total of 11,464 shares of company stock at $91.80 per share. The price of IBM stock soared, and five years later when the stock was selling at $576 a share, Mr. Watson exercised his purchase rights on 3,887 shares. A sale by

Mr. Watson at the $576 price* would have netted him a $1,882,085.40 profit—*all taxable at the favorable 25 percent capital gain tax rate.* Assuming (conservatively) Mr. Watson is in at least the 75 percent tax bracket, his tax saving from the special 25 percent rate would have been at least half† of his $1,800,000 profit—that is, about $950,000. To the extent he elects to hold on to his stock until he dies, he will never pay any income or capital gains tax on this handsome profit (see p. 92).

A prime feature of a stock option arrangement is that if IBM stock had gone *down* in price, Mr. Watson would have risked and lost nothing, since there was no obligation on his part to buy the stock. That is, heads he wins, tails he *doesn't* lose.

Mr. Watson's good fortune is not unique. One manufacturing company president bought 30,000 shares of stock at $19.00 (market price that day: $52.00; profit: $990,000); an electric company president bought 25,000 shares at $30.00 (market price that day: $75.00; profit: $1,125,000); a drug company president bought 27,318 shares at $7.72 (market price that day: $50.00; profit: $1,100,000).

The crux of the tax advantage lies in the capital gains treatment accorded the stock option profits which, the Supreme Court has held, are essentially salary supplements. For most people, of course, salaries are taxed at the regular income tax rates of up to 91 percent. But Mr. Watson and other fortunate optioned executives are not "most people."

Actually, the term salary "supplements" may unfairly belittle option benefits, for in many cases, they loom far larger than the regular salary. During the 1950's, option benefits to Charles H. Percy, head of Bell & Howell, came to $1,400,000—twice his regular salary; for L. S. Rosenstiel of Schenley Industries they came to $1,267,000, more than 2¼ times his salary; and for

---

* He would have to hold the stock for six months to qualify for the 25 percent capital gains tax rate; but since IBM stock was rising at the time, he could easily have realized at least $576 per share.

† 75 percent minus 25 percent equals 50 percent.

W. R. Stevens of the Arkansas-Louisiana Gas Company, they amounted to ten times his regular salary. While these ratios are exceptional, the option benefits in one sample survey averaged two-thirds of executives' pre-tax salary—not bad for a supposed salary "supplement."'

All the option profits mentioned so far are those *realized* through the exercise of the purchase right. The *potential* gain from unexercised options is even more staggering: about $136,-000,000 for U. S. Steel executives, $109,000,000 for Ford officials, $164,000,000 for Alcoa executives, according to a 1959 AFL-CIO analysis.

Almost unknown prior to 1950, stock option plans have mush-roomed (increasing seven-fold from 1951 to 1961) since Congress accorded capital gains treatment to option benefits, with two apparent purposes in mind: (a) to enable companies to attract and hold executive talent; and (b) to give officials a "proprietary" (i.e., ownership) interest in their companies, as an incentive to better performance.

Critics acknowledge that stock options have succeeded brilliantly in bestowing lavish tax benefits on favored executives. But, they charge, options were either not needed and/or were poorly tailored to achieve either purpose (a) or purpose (b). As to attracting and holding executive talent, they say, a great majority of the option rights have been accorded senior executives already established in their companies and therefore the least likely to move. (One firm, for example, allotted over half its optioned stock to nine executives who *averaged* over 60 years of age and 35 years of service.) Moreover, option opponents ask, what is gained by bestowing a tax advantage to the Thomas J. Watsons of this world, who already have large holdings of their companies' stock (Watson owned outright or in trust $40 million of IBM stock prior to his option purchases) and who therefore feel the requisite proprietary love for their companies even without stock options?

Some contend that stock options have simply introduced an artificial element into inter-company competition for executive talent, and that repealing this tax feature would still leave all companies on an equal footing in trying to entice executives into their employ. In fact, it is argued, there would be even greater equality, since the law places small, new companies at a disadvantage in setting up option plans (see p. 187).

Critics also maintain that the suitability of stock options for achieving purpose (b) (providing executives with a performance incentive) rests on a demonstrably false assumption: namely, that a company's success or failure on the stock market is an accurate reflection and result of managerial performance. Often, a single company's stock may *rise* in price, even though its profits and earnings per share *decline** (connoting *poor* management). But, massive rises in over-all stock prices may be due not to any display of managerial genius but simply because investors as a whole are willing to pay higher prices for stocks. Between 1950 and 1962, for example, corporate profits as a whole rose only 15 percent, *but over-all stock prices trebled,* because investors were satisfied to pay nineteen times earnings-per-share, compared with only 7½ times earnings-per-share a decade earlier. Thus, optioned executives stood to gain handsomely, thanks largely to the expansiveness of the investing public.

One study sought to determine the effectiveness of stock options in a commendably scientific way: by comparing the stock market success of 38 matched pairs of option and non-option companies, with results not overly kind to option plans. While in 14 cases, the option company did appreciably better than its mate, in 19 cases it fared appreciably worse. (Five cases were a draw.)

Stock options rest on another sharply questioned premise:

---

* Examples: between 1950 and 1960, the earnings per share of Bethlehem Steel and of Westinghouse Electric *declined* 17 percent. Nevertheless, the price of their stock rose 225 percent and 188 percent, respectively.

namely, that the process of making a company official an actual
or would-be stockholder, via options, inherently imbues him
with a sense of oneness with other shareholders. Ah, say the
critics, but while optioned executives share the bliss of other
stockholders if the market price *rises,* they do not share their
misfortune if the stock happens to *decline.* They have no obligation to buy the proferred stock and unlike other shareholders,
they have risked nothing. In fact, under some option arrangements executives have actually benefited from such a decline,
for the old options have been cancelled and new ones issued
at a lower price. Example: When the stock of the Aluminum
Company of America (Alcoa) plummeted from $120 to $70 a
share, a committee of six top Alcoa officials, labeled by financial
columnist J. A. Livingston as a "fairy godmother committee,"
decided "to spare themselves and some 300 other officers and
employees a similar indignity" by cancelling options issued at
$177.25 and reissuing them at $68.50. The committee lacked the
ethereal objectivity usually associated with fairy godmothers:
four of its members themselves held Alcoa stock options, and
hence stood to benefit handsomely by the wisdom of the committee's decision. The tax bill passed by the House in 1963, in
effect, does away with these repricing practices.

Some detractors contend that options can actually create a
conflict (rather than a oneness) of interests between optioned
officials and other shareholders. Tennessee's Senator Albert Gore
says that corporate insiders have told him of instances where,
in order to "show a good profit and loss statement" and "run up
the price of [company] stock" just prior to selling some optioned
shares, executives have cut "to the bone" such things as advertising and research expenditures, without due regard for the
long-run well-being of their company. Doubtless this is the exception rather than the rule; nevertheless, say seasoned corporate observers, stock options, with their premium on short-run
flashy profit and market showings, create a temptation to sacri-
fice long-range corporate growth.

A true identity of interests between management and stockholders would be far better achieved, some contend, by encouraging and, perhaps, helping executives to acquire company stock on the open market (rather than through risk-free stock options) so that they would share adversity as well as prosperity on the same basis as other shareholders.

The catalogue of objections to stock options does not end there. Other criticisms:

—*The true cost of stock options is not made sufficiently apparent to the stockholders who bear that cost:* For one thing, options involve issuing more shares of stock, which means that each existing share gets a smaller share of the dividends. For another, when new stock which would ordinarily bring $1,000,000 in the open market is sold to an optioned executive for only $600,000, the cost to the company is $400,000. But shareholders will look in vain through the glossy four-color annual report of their company for a listing of any such costs. Some information on executives' options may be contained in the "proxy statements" mailed out in advance of annual meetings, but unless a shareholder (a) saves these from year to year and (b) is an astute mathematician, he is unlikely to glean any useful information as to the outcome and true cost of the options.

—*Stock options are far costlier to corporations than straight salary bonuses:* Option benefits, unlike salaries and bonuses, are *not* tax-deductible to corporations, hence involve more than twice the "out-of-pocket" costs. For example, if the $400,000 option benefit in the example above had been paid as a tax-deductible bonus, Uncle Sam would have borne 52 percent of the cost* and the corporation would have been out of pocket only $192,000 instead of the full $400,000. Of course a bonus would not bring the executive the tax pleasures of a capital gains stock option. Even so, for many optioned executives (those with taxable income below $64,000), a $208 bonus would work out better, after taxes, *both for the corporation and the executive,* than a $100 option profit.

---

* Since the pre-1964 corporation tax rate has been 52 percent.

Why, then, do companies persist in using stock options, rather than salaries and bonuses, even when they are more costly? Two stock option authorities, writing in the *Harvard Business Review,* have suggested some reasons. Some firms, "notably small and rapidly growing" ones, perenially starved for capital, prefer to avoid the cash drain of high salaries. Moreover, say these authors, salary increases are "immediately and painfully evident," and may prompt workers and stockholders to demand higher wages and dividends. Stock options, on the other hand, are far subtler. For example, Bethlehem Steel stockholders instituted a suit against company directors in 1957, charging that excessive salaries were being paid company executives. The firm adopted a stock option plan, and over the next several years *reduced* the regular salaries of their officers. There was no stockholder complaint about the options.

—*To the extent executives sell their optioned stock—and the law leaves them quite free to do so—the incentive effects of stock options are negated:* An executive who has sold *all* his optioned stock (and a 1958-60 survey indicates the proportion of such executives is sharply increasing) may experience a residual gratitude for the low-taxed profit he made on the deal, but now that he is no longer a shareholder, the much-touted feeling of *proprietary* devotion may wane. This problem would be eased somewhat by a requirement, added by the House in 1963, that executives hold their optioned stock for three years before selling.

—*Stock options may be unavailable to the very companies that need them the most:* under existing law and regulations, companies too small or too new to be listed on stock exchanges (those most likely in need of talent lures) are handicapped in qualifying for tax-favored option plans, which call for precise valuations of company stock on the date an option is granted. For listed companies, the quoted market price suffices nicely, but for unlisted firms, the valuation problem is serious and the penalties for a miscalculation may be severe.

—*Stock options, unlike other tax-favored pay schemes, are*

permitted to discriminate against company employees and are
profitably used by owners of closely-held businesses: In order
to qualify for favorable tax treatment, pension and profit-
sharing plans must cover a reasonable number of employees in
a non-discriminatory manner. Stock option plans, by contrast,
may be as discriminatory as the company desires, which has
had happy consequences for executives who own a controlling
interest in their companies. In July, 1957, for example, the
board of directors of a large drug company judiciously voted
stock option rights to a lone officer—the firm's president, who
also controlled 51 percent of the voting stock—who later trans-
lated these rights into a $2,450,000 profit. A large metals com-
pany granted options to two members of the family that
controlled 54 percent of the voting stock, the benefits of which
later totaled about $2,200,000.

These statistics illuminate the cardinal objection to stock options: the inequity of singling out a highly restricted group of
taxpayers for an especially gentle tax treatment of their
compensation-for-services-rendered, a favor unavailable to most
wage and salary earners. Not only are option benefits accorded
the 25 percent capital gains rate; but if a stock option beneficiary
holds his stock until his death, he entirely escapes any tax on
the gain.

Financial columnist J. A. Livingston summed up the "equity"
argument against stock options:

They [stock options] create a tax-sheltered elite. School
teachers, professors, government officials, factory workers,
union leaders, office employees and even most newspaper-
men, such as I, don't have a way of escaping high income
taxes through risk-free capital gains. Nor do doctors, lawyers or most other professional persons.

It seems to me that if income taxes are too high in the
upper brackets, rates ought to be lowered and special
escape hatches not made available to special classes of

people so that they can create their own manner of tax avoidance.

On the other side of the question, devotees of stock options are as convinced of their merits as critics are of their deficiencies. Henry Ford II, for example, while declining any stock options for himself, has been an enthusiastic supporter of options, both publicly and in his own company (three Ford executives have realized benefits totaling $6,300,000), and has enumerated their values. By leading an executive to think and act "less as a hired hand . . . and more as an owner-manager," he says, stock options "align the executive's personal interest closely with those of stockholders and thus, from their standpoint, affect favorably his day-to-day business actions and decisions, [strengthening] his interest in the long-term growth and health of the organization." This enhanced executive and corporate performance, says Mr. Ford, contributes to the well-being of the entire economy as well as of the individual enterprise.

Stock options are necessary, he contends, to prevent talented executives from leaving to form companies of their own so as to take advantage of the favorable capital gains rate (many Ford sales executives have done just that, he says); necessary, too, because "at present levels of progressive taxation it is almost impossible for a top-salary executive to create a substantial estate out of income." He also points out that options cause no net revenue loss to the Treasury (which the Treasury Department acknowledges).

Dr. Herbert W. Robinson, president of CEIR, a spectacularly expanding research and electronic data-processing company, extols the virtues of stock options from the point of view of a small, fast-growing concern. His company, he says, had to compete not only for business but also for talent with the large established computer firms, and could not "have obtained the highly trained professional and executive talent . . . on the basis of salary alone." The company has benefited too, he says, from "many hours of unpaid overtime and . . . extra devotion to duty." CEIR has "been able to make capitalists out of each of [the optioned] employees and given them a permanent stake in the future of the company they are building." Eliminating employee stock options would, says Dr. Robinson, "tend once again to promote the concentration of significant stock ownership in the hands of the wealthy."

If capital gains were taxed at the same rates as ordinary income, as suggested in this book,* then there would be no cause for complaint about stock option arrangements, since option beneficiaries would be taxed the same as everyone else. If the preferential capital gains rate is retained, however, why shouldn't option benefits be taxed at the same rates as other salary payments? After all, the Supreme Court itself has said that the two are essentially the same.

The advocates of stock options really shouldn't have any objection to this—*if*, that is, their true objective is to provide *ownership-incentives*† and not simply windfall tax advantages to favored executives. After all, even if the benefits were taxed at the regular income tax rates, corporations who believe in the ownership-incentive principle could go right on granting stock options just as they do now.

But Congress did not see it that way and in 1963, while tidying up a few fringe abuses, such as the re-pricing of options when company stock falls, the House rejected the Kennedy proposal to end the capital gains treatment of stock option benefits. Thus, the top executives of the top corporations will continue to enjoy tax-favored treatment of much of their compensation.

Tax-free bonds

How would you like to have $1,680,000 of income every year and not even have to file a tax return?

---

* With, of course, some averaging device for spreading out the gain and avoiding the "bunched"-income problem.

† And, for small companies, to avoid the cash drain of high salaries.

All you have to do is inherit $56 million and put it all into state and municipal bonds (as Mrs. Horace Dodge did) with an average 3 percent yield, and you're all set.

Why, even with a million-and-a-half of income, wouldn't you have to file a tax return? Because as far as Internal Revenue is concerned, the interest you receive on state and municipal bonds doesn't even exist: page 5 of the Form 1040 instructions specifically lists it an "income which should not be reported" on your tax return.

Now if you were to ask around among your friends as to whether they own any state or municipal bonds—assuming your friends have fairly average incomes, chances are about a hundred to one the answer would be no. If, however, you happen to travel in a circle of, say, Long Island estate owners, you'd get a far different answer, for among *individual* bond owners (as distinct from corporations, banks and other institutions), people of wealth own virtually all the tax-free bonds, as graphically shown by the following table:*

This share of the population	⟶ *Owned* ⟶	*This share of* tax-free state and local bonds
The top 1/10 of 1 percent .... owned		45%
The top 3/10 of 1 percent .... owned		66%
The top 1½ percent .... owned		87%

There is a simple explanation for this difference in investment tastes. For one thing, the average $5,000 to $8,000 family rarely has any spare dollars lying around to invest; even if they do, a 2½ or 3 percent state or local bond is distinctly unalluring, what with savings and loan companies clamoring to pay 4.85 percent interest on deposits.

By contrast, to the Long Island estate owner, with plenty of cash to spare for investments, a 3 percent tax-free bond is in-

---

* Figures are for 1940, the last year in which state and municipal bond interest was reported on tax returns.

tensely appetizing. Ordinarily, under pre-1964 rates, he would expect between 75 and 91 percent of any investment income to be intercepted by the tax collector before it reaches him. But with state and local bonds, the entire 3 percent return comes to him untouched by Internal Revenue. If he is in the 75 percent tax bracket, it would take a 12 percent return on a *taxable* investment to leave him 3 percent after-tax "keeping money." The following table shows how the allure of the tax-free bonds increases as the owner's income rises:

If your taxable income is:	*A 3% tax-free bond is equivalent to a taxable stock or bond yielding:*
Under $4,000	3.75%
$20–24,000	4.8%
$32–36,000	6.0%
$88–100,000	10.7%
$140–160,000	15.8%
$300–400,000	30.0%
Over $400,000	33.0%

Thus, the well-to-do have not only an opportunity, but an almost irresistible temptation to take refuge in tax-free bonds and thus avoid paying the taxes others pay. This has unpleasant economic as well as philosophic consequences: some investments of the wealthy are diverted away from venturesome, high-risk investments that make for a dynamic economy, and into virtually riskless state and local bonds.

Individuals own about two-fifths of all tax-free bonds; most of the remainder belongs to commercial banks, corporations and other institutions, who also derive handsome tax benefits therefrom. Evidence of the popularity of "tax-exempts" among commercial banks may be found in the *Wall Street Journal* every July, when the annual statements of the big banks are published: $632,000,000 owned by Morgan Guaranty Trust (netting tax-free income of roughly $19,000,000 and tax savings of nearly

$10,000,000); $386,000,000 owned by the First National Bank
of Chicago (for tax-free income of $11,600,000 and a tax saving
of nearly $6,000,000), and so on. As a result of their untaxed in-
come, most of these banks have been able to pay taxes of only
38 to 45 percent, instead of the 52 percent ordinarily paid by
corporations prior to 1964.

Banks and insurance companies enjoy a double-edged advantage from their tax-free bonds. They are allowed *full* tax deductions on their interest payments to depositors and policy-
holders; yet they may turn around and invest the deposits and
premiums in tax-exempt bonds and enjoy wholly untaxed income. An important court test of this practice is pending at this
writing.*

Tax-free bonds date back to the original income tax law of
1913 when Congress, notwithstanding its new power under the
Sixteenth Amendment to tax incomes "from whatever source
derived," voluntarily relinquished the taxes on state and local
bond interest. Why? Because of assurances given key governors
while the Sixteenth Amendment was before the states for ratifi-
cation and because there existed, then, a doubt as to the constitutionality of taxing the states.

But as the volume of state and local bonds has risen to $72
billion, their small cost in 1913 has grown into a billion dollar
annual revenue loss to the Treasury. Up until 1953, most Secretaries of the Treasury—including such conservatives as
Carter Glass and Andrew Mellon—recommended repeal of the
exemption, but the howls by the states and cities always killed
the proposal dead in its tracks.

To hard-pressed states, counties and towns, taxation of their
bond interest raises the specter of higher borrowing costs, since
it is the tax exemption that makes the bonds attractive even at

---

* Commercial banks also enjoy another special advantage: they are permitted to deduct *all* the expenses of administering their tax-exempt investments, whereas personal trusts that own tax-free bonds are disallowed
deductions on a proportionate share of their administrative expenses.

unusually low rates of interest. Yet the federal Treasury *loses* far more revenue (perhaps twice as much) than the states and localities *save* in lower borrowing costs. Hence, it is argued, the federal government could well afford to pay a direct subsidy to states and cities to prevent a rise in their borrowing costs and still come out comfortably ahead on revenue (not to mention improving the equity of the federal tax system.)*

Some contend that such an outright federal subsidy would reduce the independence of the states and localities. Yet the existing tax-exemption of their bond interest is nothing but a subsidy—and one that has little reason or equity. In a sense, it is an encouragement to fiscal irresponsibility on the part of the states, for the deeper a state goes into debt, the greater its subsidy. Sadly enough, the poorer states, whose need for public services is probably the greatest, tend to borrow (and hence benefit) the least. The average per capita debt in the Southern and border states in 1957, for example, was only $180, compared with nearly $569 in affluent New York. Moreover, the neediest communities—those with the poorest credit ratings and the highest interest rates—receive the least assistance under the existing system. Under a direct, federally appropriated subsidy, Congress would have an opportunity to correct some of these incongruities.

Some see an additional reason for eliminating the exemption: the fact that its benefactions are not confined to the states and cities but extend as well to private, profit-making companies, via the issuance of so-called "industrial development bonds."

To illustrate: A few years ago, the city of Florence, Alabama, sought new industry to perk up the town payrolls. At the same time, the Stylon Corporation of Milford, Massachusetts, makers of ceramic floor tile, was casting about for a new plant location

---

* The states would gain a side advantage from this: since the "truce" would be ended, they could begin taxing the interest on federal bonds and would pick up an added $180 million of revenue for themselves by so doing.

where production costs would be lower. This mutuality of interests was cemented when Florence issued $1,300,000 of tax-free "industrial development bonds," using the proceeds to build a city-owned plant made-to-order to Stylon's specifications. *Advantage No. 1:* Since the bonds were tax-free, they bore low interest rates; low borrowing costs meant offering Stylon an attractively low plant rent. *Advantage No. 2:* Since the plant legally belonged to the city, there were no state or local property taxes—another saving that could be passed on to the company. *Advantage No. 3:* As a sweetener to the deal (to encourage a permanent stay in Florence), Stylon was offered an option to renew the initial lease for an even lower rent. Thus Stylon, without laying out a cent, got a brand-new plant at a bargain rent (and in an area where operating costs are 10 to 12 percent lower than in Milford, Massachusetts); and the city of Florence was blessed with new steady payrolls. Only the town of Milford and the former employees of Stylon had reason to be unhappy with the arrangement.

Other small towns have strained their limited credit ratings with huge industrial development borrowings: Cherokee, Alabama (population 1,349)—$25,000,000 for an Armour fertilizer plant; Opelika, Alabama (population 15,678)—$21,000,000 for a U.S. Rubber Company plant.

Opponents of these arrangements, such as the Investment Bankers Association, feel that *private* companies are, in effect, exploiting the tax-free status supposedly reserved for *public* bonds to gain unfair competitive advantages. It was Armour's credit rating and not Cherokee's, says the IBA, that enabled such a tiny community to sell such a mammoth bond issue. Moreover, others ask, why should towns like Cherokee be straining their borrowing power, perhaps cutting back on other badly needed public improvements, to build a plant for a $430,000,000 giant like Armour?

Labor unions object to the use of these bonds to entice the transplantation of factories into non-unionized, low-wage communities. *Example:* The Borg Warner Company moved from Detroit to a tailor-made plant in Greenwood, Arkansas, leaving behind some 1800 production workers, nearly half of them over the dangerously unemployable age of forty.* *Example:* According to the United Auto Workers, when Lyon, Inc., for thirty years makers of wheel covers in Detroit, moved to Granada, Mississippi, it notified its four hundred most senior workers, that it had "agreed to give first opportunity for jobs in the new plant to people of that community in exchange for certain tax considerations." The problem has been aggravated, the unions maintain, by a Supreme Court decision holding that when a plant moves, the seniority and first-hire rights of its former employees do not move with it.

Still another tax wrinkle can be added if a company buys the very tax-free bonds floated to finance its own new plant, thus not only ending up with the plant but *deriving untaxed income for making this happy event possible.*

Some localities, not content with wooing industries with the offer of a new plant, have actually bought whole companies and moved them bodily. In 1959, for example, the town of Deming, New Mexico (population 6,764) issued $4,500,000 of tax-free bonds to acquire the Auburn Rubber Company of Auburn, Indiana and moved it to Deming. Purchaser of the bonds: The Teamsters' Central and Southwest Pension Fund. Subsequently, there was a labor election in the new plant between the Teamsters and the Rubber Workers. (P.S. The Teamsters won, hands down.)

Against the criticisms of tax-free industrial bonds, their defenders point out that they constitute only less than 1 percent of all tax-exempt securities, and that the overwhelming majority of plants built with such bonds are net *additions* to companies' facilities rather than "runaway" replacements for plants closed down elsewhere. Moreover, they maintain, the attracting and

---

* Borg Warner says it made extensive efforts either to transfer or find new jobs for its Michigan employees.

fostering of industry is a well-established public function regularly engaged in by states, localities and the federal government, and that the issuance of public bonds for this purpose is, therefore, hardly an abuse of a governmental privilege.

Advocates of retaining the existing *over-all* exemption for state and local bond interest cite their constitutional doubts about federal taxation of the states (which the Supreme Court has all but resolved); their distaste for direct federal subsidies, and their fear that without such a subsidy, the rise in the state and local borrowing costs would jeopardize badly needed public facilities.

Yet due regard for both the federal revenues and the equity of the federal tax system calls compellingly for an end to this exemption*—and if Congress wishes to continue subsidizing state and local borrowing, let this be by direct rather than indirect means. Most tax authorities do not share the cataclysmic view of one rhetorician, who predicted that an end to the exemption "would be destructive of our political institutions . . . an opportunity for centralization of all sovereign powers [and the possible demise of] state and local self-government in America." Ultimately, the arguments for repeal of the exemption return to the anomaly of Mrs. Dodge, her $56 million of tax-free bonds, and her $1,500,000-plus of wholly untaxed income.

The dividend tax credit

Few sounds or sights are as poignant as the congressional rhetorician in full flight, bemoaning the plight of the "little stockholder—the widow, the orphan, the retired and the aged," who, you are led to believe, make up the bulk of the investing and stockholding public in America.

---

* This would involve the thorny decision of whether to repeal the exemption for future bond issues only or for existing bonds as well. Either method presents problems, but of the two, a repeal for all bonds seems preferable.

Few affirmations are as thoroughly contradicted by the cold, hard facts, which are that:

—Only about one family in ten owns any public corporation stock. Nine-tenths own none.

—Less than 1 percent of all families hold 70 percent of the value of the personally-held shares.

—Ninety percent of all the stock is owned by the top half of American families.

—The lowest 50 percent of all shareholders own only 1 percent of all outstanding stock.

—The families of wage earners hold only 3/10 of 1 percent of all stock.

Hence it should come as no surprise that when Congress in 1954 eased the taxation of corporate dividends, over half of the tax cut went to the top 1 percent of the taxpayers, with whom this chapter is concerned.

The 1954 congressional action was designed as an attack on the alleged problem of "double taxation" of corporation dividends arising, it was said, because each dollar of dividends is taxed once when received by the corporation as part of profits, and a second time when it is received by the individual share-holder in the form of a dividend.

The 1954 law offered a two-fold remedy. First, taxpayers were permitted to omit the first $50 of their dividend income when they make out their tax returns (thanks to the so-called dividend "exclusion"). Second, after figuring out what they owe the government, they are permitted to reduce this figure by 4 percent of their dividend income. That is, the husband who, at 4 A.M. of April 13, reaches the unpleasant conclusion that his tax bill is $2,020 can find a small ray of sunshine in the so-called "dividend credit," for if he is blessed with, say, $500 of dividend income, he can subtract 4 percent of that ($20) and write out a check to Uncle Sam for an even $2,000 instead of $2,020. While perhaps this added $20 brings only a modicum of joy, to the top

306 taxpayers of the country, with an average dividend income of nearly a million dollars, the dividend credit offers substantial tax pleasure, in the form of about $40,000 of extra spending money.

All told, the "exclusion" plus the 4 percent "credit"—both of which President Kennedy asked be repealed*—cost the Treasury nearly half a billion dollars a year.

Is "double taxation" *per se* an intolerable inequity, as the defenders of this half-billion dollar tax preference contend? If so, Congress must lose no time in performing major surgery on the entire tax system to relieve the oppressed. General Eisenhower's celebrated 1952 campaign complaint about the hundred different ways eggs are taxed was a graphic (if slightly exaggerated) reminder that our tax system is shot through not just with double taxation, but with multiple taxation. As another illustration, do you remember the last time you bought a TV set? You paid an excise tax, using the already-taxed dollars of your take-home pay, and thus were the victim of "double taxation." But that is not the whole story, for the price of the TV set also included allowances for taxes paid by the retailer, and the wholesaler before him and the manufacturer before him and the parts supplier before him.

Hence, you may be prompted to wonder why a single class of taxpayers—the corporation shareholders—should be singled out for relief from mere *double* taxation, while you remain prey of *multiple* taxation on your TV set and, if General Eisenhower was correct, a full hundred taxes on your morning egg.†

Furthermore, it is far from clear just how much "double tax-

---

* The bill passed by the House in 1963 repealed the credit, but doubled the exclusion.

† Some tax economists say the "double taxation" argument is spurious in that our tax system has always levied different taxes for different purposes against different persons at different points in the economic process. For example, just as the income and the estate tax are two different *kinds* of taxes, so are the personal and the corporate income tax.

ation" of corporate dividends really exists. Many—including, significantly enough, some of the most ardent defenders of the dividend tax preferences—believe that corporations do not bear the burden of the corporate tax, but pass it along either to consumers (in higher prices) or to workers (in lower wages). The very sponsor of the dividend credit, the late Representative Daniel Reed, blamed "inordinately high" consumer prices in part on the fact that "all products are increased in price in the exact proportion of taxation." And the redoubtable former Speaker of the House, Representative Martin of Massachusetts, has affirmed that "any graduate economist can tell us that corporations compute profits after taxes, and not before, and their price scales are adjusted accordingly."

Most economists are not so dogmatic. The more modest will acknowledge that in any given instance, no one knows just how much a corporation bears, and how much it shifts, its tax burden, but most believe there is always some shifting, and to this extent, the "double taxation" problem is lessened.

It is also eased by the fact that stock market investors take account of the corporate tax in calculating the price they are willing to pay for their share of stock (i.e., they pay less for stocks than they would if there were no corporate tax and if 100 percent of company earnings were available for dividends). Therefore, it is argued, to the extent they have already allowed for the corporate tax in the lower purchase price of their stock, shareholders are unaffected by "double taxation."

Whatever the extent of "double taxation," even Dan Throop Smith, top Eisenhower tax advisor and a principal architect of the 1954 dividend relief provisions, acknowledges that "for both equity and budget reasons, *full elimination of double taxation does not seem appropriate or feasible.*" (Emphasis added)

If the architect himself acknowledges that perfect symmetry and grace are not attainable, how close to the ideal was his design? How much relief from "double taxation" was in fact accomplished—and for whom—by the 1954 dividend provisions? Look closely at architect Smith's creation and you will find:

—*That prior to 1954, the wealthy were far less burdened than the unprosperous by such "double taxation" as may have existed.* For each dollar of corporate earnings, "double taxation" (to the extent it existed) caused extra taxes of only 4.7 cents for a top bracket taxpayer, in contrast to 41.6 cents of extra taxes for a lowest-bracket taxpayer (see line G in the step-by-step chart below).

—*That the 1954 dividend "credit" relieved 40 percent of the top-bracket taxpayer's "extra burden," but less than 5 percent of the lowest bracket "extra burden."*

The following step-by-step chart shows why this is so. It compares what happens to $1 of corporation earnings paid, respectively, to a *top-bracket* stockholder and a *lowest-bracket* stockholder (1) under so-called *"double tax"* conditions (line E) where both the corporation and the shareholder are taxed; and (2) under hypothetical *"single tax"* circumstances (line F) —no corporation tax, *all* profits distributed to shareholders:

	Lowest-Bracket Stockholder	Top-Bracket Stockholder
	(TOP TAX RATE: 20%)	(TOP TAX RATE: 91%)
A. Corporation earns	100¢	100¢
B. Corporation pays 52% corporation tax	52¢	52¢
C. Corporation pays balance as dividend	48¢	48¢
D. Stockholder pays personal tax on dividend (48¢ times top tax rate, above)	9.6¢	43.7¢

E. Total tax under "double tax"
condition (B plus D)   61.6¢   95.7¢

F. Tax under "single tax" condition
(no corporation tax) (100¢
times stockholder's top tax
rate, above)   20.0¢   91.0¢

G. *"Extra burden" caused by
"double taxation"* (E minus
F)   41.6¢   4.7¢

H. Relief from double-tax "burden"
via 4% credit (4% of 48¢)   1.9¢   1.9¢

I. *Percent of "double-tax burden
relieved" by 4% credit*
(H divided by G)   4.6%   40.4%

The following table will enable you to determine just how "burdened" you supposedly were by "double taxation," prior to 1954, and the extent to which the dividend credit solved your problem:

Income Level*	"Extra burden" from "double taxation" of $1 of corporation earnings	Percent of this "extra burden" relieved by dividend credit
$4–8,000	40.6¢	4.7%
$20–24,000	32.2¢	5.9%
$32–36,000	26.0¢	7.3%
$52–64,000	19.8¢	9.6%
$100–120,000	13.0¢	14.6%
$180–200,000	6.8¢	27.9%
$400,000 and over	4.7¢	40.6%

* Taxable income (assuming you are married and file a joint return).

In summary, the critics of the 1954 dividend credit provision contend that there was no unique "double taxation" problem to begin with, and that the purported solution to this non-existent problem *created* more unfairnesses than it eliminated.

They also argue that the hoped-for side advantages of the 1954 provisions failed to materialize. For example, the dividend credit was supposed to bring on a new surge of public stock buying, and this, in turn, was to make it possible for corporations to meet more of their capital needs through stock issues rather than by going into debt. Alas, the dream did not come true. Since 1954, the volume of net stock purchases and the portion of public savings going into the stock market have both declined, even while the number of shareholders was increasing. And in the four years after 1954, new stock issues played a smaller, not a larger role in fulfilling corporations' capital requirements than they had in the four years prior to 1954.*

Because of the widespread ownership of corporation stock—seventeen million owners, according to the New York Stock Exchange—some may wonder why the dividend tax provisions were included in this book under the heading of "The Favored Few" instead of "The Favored Many" (see next chapter). The following facts will explain why:

WHO BENEFITED IN 1960 FROM THE DIVIDEND TAX CREDIT

This income group →	Comprises this percent of all taxpayers →	And received this percent of the benefits from the dividend tax credit
Over $50,000	2/10 of 1%	34.1%
Over $25,000	9/10 of 1%	54.1%

* Even such a staunch defender of the 1954 dividend provisions as Representative Thomas Curtis of Missouri acknowledges that the corporate penchant for borrowing rather than new stock issues is not due to any lack of investor demand but to sheer management preference, partly because of the tax-deductibility of interest payments on borrowings and partly because of stockholder distaste for any dilution of their existing shares by the issuance of new ones.

HOW MANY ACTUALLY RECEIVED
DIVIDENDS IN 1960

Income group	How many in this group reported any dividends	How much of this group's income came from dividends
Under $5,000	1 in 20	1.0%
$5,000–$10,000	1 in 10	0.9%
$20,000–$50,000	3 out of 4	10.4%
$100,000–$200,000	95 out of 100	31.1%
$1,000,000 and over	97 out of 100	47.1%

11 / The Favored Many

By now, you may be feeling somewhat left out. You have no stock option, no tax-free bonds. Perhaps you own a few shares of corporation stock; but not enough to make much difference. Nary an oil well, nor office building, nor brood cow do you possess.

"Where's *my* tax gimmick?" you may be asking.

You've got your tax gimmicks, I reply. Lots of them.

"Not me!" you say. "I just figure up my income, take my deductions—just like everybody else—go to the regular tax table and find out how much I owe. How can *I* have any gimmicks working for me?"

Well, here are a few questions.

Did you serve in the armed forces? You paid no tax on your mustering-out pay, did you? How about your veteran's pension? Or your disability benefits?

Do you own your own home? Have you ever compared notes with your neighbor, who rents his? Try it. You may be surprised about the "gimmicks" you have working for you. (See pp. 212-216.)

Are you over 65? If so, whether you're rich or poor, you're automatically entitled to two tax favors, and, if you're not working, to a third. Your neighbor, who won't turn 65 until next year, doesn't get any of them.

Are you getting social security benefits? Did you declare them on your tax return? Of course you didn't. Social security benefits bear a zero tax rate, just like the interest on state and local bonds, or capital gains on stocks and bonds you hold till your death.

Perhaps your son or daughter has a scholarship. Is anyone paying taxes on it? And what about the interest your life insurance premiums are drawing? There's no tax on that income, either. Not only that; all your interest payments are tax-deductible.

"But," you protest, "my interest deductions just amounted to a few dollars last year—hardly saved me anything on my tax bill. Why make such a fuss about it?"

Because your "few dollars" of interest deductions, along with those of nearly nineteen million other Americans, added up to nearly *ten-and-a-half billion dollars* in 1963—and cost the Treasury two-and-a-half billion dollars!

The provisions we're talking about here are far different from from stock options and capital gains and tax-free bonds, which bring massive doses of tax relief to a comparative handful of taxpayers. By contrast, the tax favors in this chapter are more like aspirins: they bring a little relief—but, to millions or tens of millions of taxpayers.

These favors bite deeply into the public coffers. Give a $100 tax saving (just $2 a week) to ten million taxpayers and you've lost $1,000,000,000 of revenue in a single stroke.

In all, the tax favors described in this chapter—for the elderly, for veterans, home owners, factory workers and the like—*cost the Treasury over $25 billion a year.* Repeal them all tomorrow, and there could be an immediate 33 percent cut in all tax rates

—that is, we could come fairly close to the 11 percent to 50 percent rate schedule suggested in Chapter 17—without creating any budget-unbalancing problems.

Therefore, while you may have an ideological attachment to one or another of the tax preferences for the Favored Many, don't forget that each has its price tag. And, just as with every government *spending* program, everyone has to pay that price through higher taxes—a full one-third higher, considering all the Favored Many tax preferences together.

Congress boasts of great frugality with public moneys, and often spends hours debating appropriations of a few million (or even a few hundred thousand) dollars. In striking contrast, however, most of the multi-billion dollar dispensations to the Favored Many have been enacted with little or no debate. Year after year, they dwell comfortably in the tax law, their security only rarely disturbed by some meddling questioner inquiring: *Why* a special tax exemption for the blind—and for no other handicapped persons? *Why* no tax on social security benefits or veterans' pensions or mustering-out pay? *Why* tax relief for the aged, whether rich or poor? Why permit deductions for interest costs, but not other personal expenses? Is the charitable deduction the best and fairest way of fostering philanthropy? Are these provisions helping the people we want them to help? Is the price tag right? Are the original purposes still valid?

Consider, for example, the array (some might call it the disarray) of tax favors for the elderly.

While in other respects you may be dreading your 65th birthday, from a tax point of view it will be a red-letter day. You will suddenly find yourself entitled to an extra $600 exemption, more liberal medical deductions, more lenient taxation of your dividend or interest income, and tax-free social security benefits.

Why these sudden blessings? Chances are you look and feel much the same as on the day before your birthday; you may have no thought of retiring; you may be millionaire or pauper.

No matter; the tax blessings are yours—because it's your 65th birthday.

As Congress sees it, the elderly, as a group, are deserving of these tax advantages because their incomes are, on the average, unusually low, "reflecting the fact that the group as a whole is handicapped in an economic, if not a physical sense," and because "unlike younger persons," they cannot supplement their meager incomes "by accepting full-time jobs." Hence, they suffer "with unusual severity" from rises in prices and taxes.

There is no denying that the aged, as a group, have shockingly low incomes. In 1960, half of those over 65 had incomes of under $1,000, three-fourths had incomes of less than $2,000. Where the head of the family was 65 or over, the median family income was just *half* that of families headed by a person under 65.

But poverty is by no means the exclusive province of the elderly; nor are they alone in their inability to take jobs and supplement slender incomes so as to combat rising prices. If low incomes and unemployability are proper reasons for granting tax concessions, then surely the humane tax legislator should not ignore those living in chronically unemployed or depressed areas such as those in West Virginia or Eastern Kentucky. Special dispensations should also go to the ill-educated and ill-trained, for whom jobs may be scarce—in short, to *all* the poor and under-privileged, *whether young or old*.

Look at the question from the point of view of "ability to pay": Is a *childless* couple aged 66 with $5,000 of income necessarily less able to pay taxes than a younger two-children family trying to live on the same $5,000? Government studies have, in fact, shown that over-all living expenses for the elderly are somewhat *lower*—some 10 to 15 percent lower—than a comparable budget (supposedly to provide a "modest but adequate level of living") for a younger family.* To this extent,

---

* The survey comparison allowed for such factors as family size, child expenses, and differing requirements for clothing, transportation and, above all, medical care.

older people may be *better* able to pay taxes than younger people *with the same income.*

Nonetheless, it is apparently a matter of national conscience to ease the lot of the elderly in every possible way—in part through direct-benefit programs such as social security; in part, too, through indirect means such as tax concessions. But the tax advantages *now* accorded those over 65 may be more effective in easing the national conscience than in actually *helping* the aged.

Consider for instance the liberalized medical deduction—the permission, at age 65, to deduct *all* medical expenses instead of just those that exceed 3 percent of income. It is, of course, common knowledge that older people are more prey to illness, and hence need more medical attention, than younger people, and so, on the face of it, the larger medical deduction seems eminently sensible—*until you realize that four-fifths of the elderly get no help whatever from it* because their incomes are so low they are nontaxable anyway.

Even for a couple with $10,000 of income, the provision means an added deduction of only $300 and a tax saving of about $66 (enough to cover about three days hospital expense), while, by contrast, for someone with a hundred times that income, the way is paved for added deductions of up to $30,000 and a possible tax saving of $27,300.

The point is that the least helpless get the most help, while those in greatest need of assistance get none at all. Besides, for all but the very wealthy, the tax savings from the added medical deduction won't pay the doctor or hospital bills. Only enhanced income or medical insurance, private or public, will provide the wherewithal.

Consider, too, the extra $600 exemption enjoyed by the elderly, another of the government's 65th birthday gifts, bestowed on rich and poor alike.

Compassionate? Certainly.

Expensive? It costs the Treasury some $380 million annually.

Effective? For roughly three-fifths of the elderly—those with incomes of less than $1,200—it provides no tax relief whatever.

Equitable? For those in the lowest tax bracket (20 percent), it means a tax saving of $120; for top-bracket taxpayers (91 percent), it means a saving of $546. Equally important, it ignores— in fact, it discriminates against—those who may be just as impoverished and needy, but who happen not to have reached the age of 65.

The elderly also receive all their social security benefits tax-free. For this favor, Congress may not claim credit (or blame): it resulted from a Treasury Department ruling in 1941 which doubtless had little impact on the federal revenues at the time, but today costs more than $1.5 billion annually, now that social security benefits are running at the rate of $14.3 billion a year.

Well, you may say, it wouldn't make much sense for the government to hand out social security benefits with one hand and turn around and tax them with the other. While this reasoning has the force of logic, it did not, over the years, salve the wounds of others—mainly teachers and state and local government employees—who, unlike social security recipients, had to pay taxes on their pension incomes. In 1954, Congress heeded their cries of anguish and enacted the so-called "retirement income credit" (see Glossary). As is so often the case with the spreading of tax preferences, this new provision went beyond correcting the discrimination against government employees' *pension* income; it also eased the taxation of the *dividend* and *interest* income of *all* the elderly, on the theory that those who had provided for their old age by virtue of their own frugality and savings should not be penalized as compared with pensioners and annuitants.

The thrifty were thus spared, but the industrious and energetic were penalized. Woe is the man or woman who goes on working beyond 65 and earns as much as $2,400, for he or she is wholly denied the benefactions of the retirement income credit. (Those over 72 may, however, work to their hearts' content without lessening the tax pleasure they derive from the retirement income credit.)

President Kennedy in 1963 proposed repealing the double exemption and the retirement income credit and substituting a flat $300 tax reduction for all those over 65. Assuming you have accepted the *principle* that old age is, in and of itself, a good and sufficient reason for a tax favor, the Kennedy plan has much to recommend it over the amalgam of tax preferences now accorded the aged. It would simplify the tax form and end the penalty against the industrious elderly who continue working (and three out of four do). All who benefit from it would receive equal dollar savings, and a greater portion of its benefits would go to those with lower incomes who most need help. It also would lessen considerably the remaining preference enjoyed by social security recipients.

Improvement though it would be, the Kennedy plan (which the House rejected) cannot escape the cardinal charge leveled at the existing concessions to the aged: it still fails to extend a helping hand to those who most need it—those whose incomes are so low as to be nontaxable. And at best, an extra $300 will be a help, but far from a solution when major illness strikes and medical bills pile up. To paraphrase one writer, "The income tax can avoid taking the shirt off a man, but it cannot provide a shirt for a naked man."

Social security benefits are by no means the only government payments that are free from taxation. Also exempt are the following:

Railroad retirement benefits	$1.1 billion*
Relief payments	$3.6 billion
Veterans' benefits	$4.7 billion

* Figures are estimated *total* payments for 1963, some portion of which goes to persons whose incomes are so low as to be nontaxable.

Unemployment compensation	$2.8 billion
Workmen's compensation (for injuries, etc.)	$1.5 billion
Servicemen's mustering-out pay, combat pay, subsistence and rental allowances	$1.0 billion

All told, the tax-free status of these government payments costs the Treasury roughly $3.5 billion in revenues every year. End the exemption and all tax rates could be cut 7 percent without contributing to the government deficits. Not, of course, that this could be done without evoking cries of anguish from aggrieved veterans, servicemen, and others, which leads some to argue that Congress would respond by increasing government benefit payments to make up for the taxes, and the Treasury would be no better off. Maybe so and maybe not, but the basic question remains: Isn't a dollar of, say, mustering-out pay exactly the same as a dollar of wages or salary in enabling a man to buy food and clothing or a present for his wife—or, for that matter, to pay taxes? If so, then why, on the face of it, should one be taxed and not the other?

Besides, under the general principle of "equity" in taxation (more fully described in Chapter 15) once one government benefit has been freed from taxation, "equity" requires that other benefits be given similar tax-free treatment, and the leak in the Treasury grows and grows. All in all, then, it would be better, from the point of view of tax fairness and of preventing growing punctures in the tax system, to *tax*, rather than *exempt*, the billions of government benefit payments, even if Congress *were* to increase them to offset the taxes.

ATTENTION HOMEOWNERS: Did you know that you and your fellow homeowners are enjoying nearly $7 *billion* of tax-free income every year?

Specifically, did you know that if you're living in a $20,000 house, you're enjoying somewhere around $350-400 of untaxed income a year? If your house is worth $35,000, your tax-free income is about $650. For a $150,000 house, the untaxed income amounts to roughly $2,600 annually.

What is all this supposedly "untaxed" income?

It is, in effect, the rent you don't have to pay because you own your home.

Now, you may feel you can't see or feel this "income," but it's there, all right. Just compare a few notes with your neighbor, who *rents* his house, and you'll see how and why.

It so happens that you and your neighbor are alike in most respects. You both hold $10,000-a-year jobs, you're both married and have two children. You both managed, as of a year or so ago, to accumulate $10,000 of savings—but here you and he followed different courses. Your neighbor put his $10,000 into bonds and you put yours into buying your $20,000 house, on which you have a $10,000 mortgage.

Your taxes and mortgage interest come to $800 a year and your maintenance and repairs and insurance cost you $600 a year. So you lay out $1,400 a year as the out-of-pocket cost of living in your home.

Your neighbor, on the other hand, has to pay $150 a month rent, or $1,800 a year, so you're $400 ahead of him on housing costs.

One way of looking at it is that you and your neighbor both made investments. He happened to invest in bonds, and the return on his money is the 4 percent interest he receives. You happened to invest in a piece of real estate. If you had rented it out to someone else, you would have paid a tax on the net rental income (i.e., after your expenses). But instead, you found another tenant—namely, yourself.

So what's the return on your investment in real estate? It's the $400 of housing costs your neighbor pays and you don't.

"But why should I pay taxes on that four hundred dollars?" you ask. "I can't see it or feel it—nobody *paid* me rent on my house. How can you call that 'income'?"

Your neighbor might answer your question with one of his own. He paid taxes on the return on his $10,000 investment. Why shouldn't you? Besides, your $400 return *is* real: you can see it, feel it, and spend it—for you, the $400 you *didn't* pay for housing made you end up with the same number of spendable dollars as your neighbor with his $400 of income from his bonds. The following chart makes this clear:

	You (Home *Owner*)	Your Neighbor (Home *Renter*)
Salary	$10,000	$10,000
Interest income from bonds	—	+400
Rent (or housing cost)	−1,400	−1,800
SPENDABLE DOLLARS REMAINING	$ 8,600	$ 8,600

It's your $400 return on your house investment, and like amounts enjoyed by the 35 million U.S. home owners that make up the nearly $7 billion of untaxed income. If we were to tax that $7 billion—as the English did until 1963,* and as other countries still do—*the Treasury would gain $2 billion in revenue,* which would make it possible to reduce everyone's taxes.

But we haven't really finished the comparison. Your neighbor (poor fellow) laid out $1,800 for his housing cost, *but none of it was tax-deductible.* By contrast, $800 of your out-of-pocket cost—the interest and taxes—*are* deductible. Result: Although you and your neighbor have the same amount of *spendable* income (and might expect, under a Utopian system of justice, to pay the same taxes), *you end up with $1,200 less taxable income than he*:

---

* The British government attributed the repeal of this tax to the increase that would result in an updating of real estate valuations and to its characterization of the rent-equivalent as "notional income"—which the *Economist* branded "double talk." In abolishing the tax, the government was acting counter to the recommendation of a 1955 Royal Commission on Taxation.

	You (Home *Owner*)	Your Neighbor (Home *Renter*)
Salary (assume all taxable)	$10,000	$10,000
Interest from bonds	—	+400
Deductions (for mortgage interest and taxes)	−800	—
TAXABLE INCOME	$ 9,200	$10,400
Taxes	$ 1,992	$ 2,304

In other words, you're allowed to take tax deductions on your interest and taxes as if you were a landlord, but at the same time you're excused from paying taxes on your landlordly income. In the example above, having your cake and eating it too gives you a $312 tax advantage.

"Now, just a minute," you say a bit heatedly. "First you want to tax me on income I can't even see and now you want to take away my tax deductions on my home. Don't you think it's worth encouraging a man to own his own house?"

Well, I counter, worth how much? Worth a billion dollars? Or would *two* billion dollars worth of encouragement be about right? After all, with two billion dollars a year, we could build a lot of houses for people who don't have any, or for people who live in slums—so this "encouragement price tag" is important.

The fact is that today, we're paying not two billion, but *well over three billion dollars a year* to encourage home ownership— about six times what the Federal government was spending in the mid-fifties for *all* housing and community development programs.

Now some argue that these billions are far better spent encouraging *private* home-building and home-owning than through a muscle-bound, bureaucratically-run *government* housing program. The proof of this particular pudding, they may well say, is in the spectacular rise in home ownership in America—up 50 percent since 1940.

Well, it would be hard to prove how much of this remarkable increase in home ownership was due to the tax spur and how much due to other factors, such as sharply rising personal income and the greater availability of mortgage credit. In fact, the tax incentives in existing law are a wasteful way to try to induce home ownership, since the greatest benefits go to those most likely to own their homes anyway—those least in need of encouragement. The higher your tax bracket and the more expensive your home, the greater your tax savings.

Taxing the equivalent net-rent value of owned homes presents two difficulties. One is the practical problem (that has apparently plagued the British) of keeping up-to-date appraisals of rental values. The other is the difficulty of drawing a logical and plausible line between home rentals and similar "imputed" income from other possessions, such as a car (which spares you public bus expense), or washing machine (which saves commercial laundry bills), not to mention the $5 billion of "imputed interest income" in the form of services provided free by commercial banks and other financial institutions in lieu of interest payments on deposits.

These problems could be avoided by simply disallowing the landlord-type deductions for interest and taxes now enjoyed by homeowners, and continuing to excuse them from paying taxes on their landlord-type income. The Treasury might, in fact, be better off, both from a practical and a revenue standpoint, by choosing this alternative. But a choice should be made; for why should homeowners continue to have their tax-free income and their deductions too?

Let's say you're a factory worker. Your taxes are taken out of your weekly paycheck before you even see them. You rent your home; you take no special deductions; you file the short-form 1040 and that's the end of it. Chances are you're convinced you're the proverbial "forgotten man." No special tax favors for you.

But think carefully.

Is there, by any chance, a company health or medical plan? Or a company-paid group-term life insurance arrangement? Or a pension or profit-sharing plan?

If so, then you, sir (or madam), are the proud possessor of a tax preference. So don't look so glum. Smile.

A smile will suffice—a full-fledged grin would probably be overdoing it, since the dollars-and-cents savings to you are probably pretty small. But to the United States Treasury, looking at these fringe benefits through the other end of the telescope, the theoretical revenue loss looks huge since, in all, there is no current tax on more than *eleven billion dollars*—ten billion of employer contributions* to various fringe benefits plus about $1.4 billion earned by pension trust funds.

That's the amount that is *theoretically* untaxed on a current basis. From a *practical* point of view, it would be difficult, if not impossible, to tax a great deal of it currently anyway. Still, it's worth listing some of the tax preferences enjoyed by those who receive fringe benefits:

—*Health and medical benefits*: Tax-deductible employer contributions to health plans total some $5.6 billion annually; yet the benefits of those plans are, by and large, untaxed when received by the employee. Trying to tax those benefits wouldn't produce as much revenue as you might theoretically expect (since employees in many cases could claim offsetting medical-expense tax deductions) and would create serious administrative problems, both for employers and for the government. Nevertheless, anyone covered by a company health plan, is getting, tax-free, benefits which others have to buy with after-tax dollars.

—*Company-paid group-term life insurance premiums*: This is another fringe benefit which most people have to pay for with

---

* There is no problem about the *employees'* contributions escaping tax-free since they were made with workers' *after*-tax dollars—i.e., were already taxed in the employees' hands.

after-tax dollars. Under pre-1963 regulations, there was no limit on the amount of company-paid insurance an employee could receive tax-free. The Kennedy Administration proposed limiting it to $5,000 of insurance, but in 1963, the House raised this limit to $30,000.

—*Miscellaneous employee benefits*: These take a variety of forms—discount sales, cafeteria services, low-interest loans, company-paid transportation and vacation facilities, and so on. While the total volume of these probably reaches into the billions, it would be impractical to try to tax most of them. Still, to the extent others are using already-taxed dollars to buy these same pleasures, a tax-preference exists.

—*Pension and profit-sharing benefits, plus earnings of pension trust funds*: These, in theory, are enjoyed only on a tax-*postponed*, rather than a tax-*free* basis, since they are, supposedly, taxed when received upon retirement. But in practice, the tax concessions granted those over 65 (the double exemption plus the retirement income credit) make it probable that a substantial part of these benefits are not in fact, taxed on receipt but escape taxation entirely.

Even if there were no side tax concessions to the aged and pension income were fully taxed when received, there would remain the advantage of tax postponement. After all, company pension contributions, like wages, are payment for services currently rendered (they're negotiated in the same bargaining "package")—but, unlike wages, they are not currently taxed. But this postponement advantage is hard to avoid, since in most pension plans, it is some years before an employee gets legal ownership (called technically, a "vested" right) in his pension. Clearly, it would be unfair to tax him on something he doesn't legally own, and it is often extremely difficult to unravel the "vested" from the "unvested" pension contributions.

There are two other wrinkles to "fringe benefit" tax preferences. One is the magical transformation of a delayed salary payment into a "capital asset"; that is, Congress has decreed that

if all your pension or profit-sharing rights are distributed to you
during the first year you're entitled to them, the dollars you get
are taxed at the preferential 25 percent capital gains tax rate
instead of the regular rates applicable to other salary income.*
The lump-sum payment beneficiary, with his 25 percent tax,
is not, however, as fortunate as the employee who gets sick (or
disabled) and is paid $100 a week "sick pay" in lieu of salary—
for on this $100, the tax rate is not 25 percent: it is zero.† This
resulted in the anomaly of a man staying home with, say, a
sprained ankle, savoring the thought of his $100-a-week tax-free
salary substitute, while his co-worker who braved it to work
despite a dizzying head cold was penalized for his conscien-
tiousness by paying taxes on all his earnings. Before the $100-a-
week limit was enacted, in 1954 however, the abuses were far
more imaginative. According to Dan Throop Smith, top Eisenhower tax advisor, insurance companies, in a cosy arrangement
with a closely-held business, would write a cost-plus policy
providing generous sick-leave privileges for the company's
owner-president—the cost of the policy being, of course, tax-
deductible to the company. Result: the company president
would take "a year or two of sick leave before retirement"
which, with its wholly tax-free benefits, "could be more useful
than an elaborate pension plan."

Even with the $100 limitation, the sick pay exclusion has ap-
parently been a highly popular and well-used tax favor, for when
President Kennedy proposed its repeal in 1963, he estimated
this would save the Treasury as much as $160 million in revenue.
The House rejected the outright repeal, but did curb the abuses

---

* The House would have none of President Kennedy's 1963 plea to remove this alchemistic tax feature.

† This $100-per-week tax-free "sick pay" was enacted under the princi-
ple of "tax equity" described more fully in Chapter 15. Prior to 1954, sick
employees covered by insurance contracts received tax-free sick benefits,
but those covered by company-paid rather than insurance plans were taxable on their sick benefits. "Equity" was achieved by extending the zero
tax rate to company as well as insurance sick benefits.

by requiring thirty-one days of absence (instead of seven) before the tax-free income privilege could begin.

A third fringe-benefit wrinkle, also a favorite among owner-managers of small companies, is to design a tax-deductible pension or profit-sharing plan that will satisfy the Treasury requirement of being reasonably non-discriminatory, but still funnel the lion's share of the benefits to the top one, two or three officers. (Recent Treasury regulations are making life difficult for such plans, however).

In all these cases, tax-deductible dollars are used to buy retirement and other benefits for certain employees which others must use after-tax dollars to buy. This point was a particular source of irritation among self-employed business owners and professionals (doctors, lawyers, and so on) who pleaded for—and in 1962 won—tax deductions on their own outlays for pensions, annuities and other retirement aids. The 1962 measure is expected to cost the Treasury about a hundred million dollars annually—but this is only a start. "It is only a matter of time," said Florida's Senator George Smathers, chief senatorial sponsor of the measure, before it is extended to include all those omitted from its gentle tax treatment, which could mean, some say, an estimated revenue cost of about three *billion* dollars a year.

Even if, by some miracle, you are neither ex-serviceman nor home owner nor over 65 and even if you have no fringe benefits and have never drawn any unemployment insurance, social security or other government benefit—you may well be enjoying a tax preference.

How? By virtue of your various tax deductions—for interest, taxes, medical expenses, charity gifts, and so on.

"Not me," you say, "I'm a standard deduction man myself. I just take the straight ten percent."

Well, if that's the case, you're simply getting the benefit of what really amounts to Congress' decision that it had set the

rates 10 percent* too high and thought they ought to be eased—
for that's really all the standard deduction comes down to.

But you're barely in the majority these days. Nearly half the
taxpayers now itemize their deductions—*and they cost the
Treasury $11½ billion dollars every year. If we eliminated all
the itemized deductions, all tax rates could be cut 20 percent
without costing the Treasury a cent.*

Considering the fact they open up an $11½ billion-dollar leak
in the United States Treasury, these personal deductions have
enjoyed an almost total immunity from public criticism or debate. How often do you hear questions asked such as: Why
give more favorable tax treatment to the repairing of a car
fender than to the setting of a broken arm?† Is it right when a
millionaire and a drug store clerk sit side by side in church and
put money in the plate, the millionaire should be out-of-pocket
only 10 cents on the dollar but the clerk 80 cents? Or, if the
millionaire's Cadillac and the clerk's Corvair collide on the street,
that the government should pay 90 percent of the cost of fixing
the Cadillac but only 20 percent of the Corvair repairs? Are
these really the ways we want to spend $11½ billion dollars of
federal revenue?

Not until the Kennedy Administration proposed a 5 percent
cutback on these deductions was public attention focused on
them.

Now, *business* deductions are fairly easy to understand: if
you incur some costs in getting your income (travel, office rent
and the like), it is generally accepted that those should be deductible and not taxed. But the same reasoning doesn't apply to
strictly *personal* deductions, where money-making is not involved.

Why, then, allow them? Their purposes fall into three main
categories:

---

* If the minimum standard deduction passed by the House in 1963 becomes law, the figure may be greater than 10 percent for some low-income
taxpayers.

† See p. 232.

—To stimulate (some might say "subsidize") a "socially worthy" activity—e.g., charitable giving or home ownership.

—To ease the blow of extraordinary, uncontrollable and unexpected expenses—e.g., medical expenses or losses from fire, collision, and so on.

—To avoid the possibly confiscatory—and emotionally grating—effect of imposing a "tax on a tax," which explains the deductibility of most state and local and some federal taxes.

Commendable ends, perhaps, but do the means suit the ends? Put a bright spotlight on the personal deductions and defects begin to appear—serious ones.

Some of the flaws have already been suggested. If we wish, in all compassion, to cushion the financial shock of an illness, why use a device that wholly by-passes those who most need succor—those whose incomes are so low as to be non-taxable? And if incentives to worthy activity are the order of the day, why give a 90 percent encouragement to a rich man (who probably needs it least) and only a 20 percent encouragement to one less prosperous?

The spotlight also reveals a practical shortcoming. Because ours is a self-assessment tax system, it is the taxpayer who initially *claims* the deductions, and if he abuses or misunderstands them, the burden is on the government to catch the error and to challenge it. With some sixty-one million tax returns, that presents Uncle Sam with a major enforcement headache, compounded by the fact that taxpayers seem especially prone to mistakes on their deductions, whether accidental or deliberate. A 1948 survey disclosed that one out of three itemized-deduction returns contained major errors in the claimed deductions. A reading of Chapter 13, about the charitable deductions, will illuminate some of the most vexing enforcement problems—such as, for example, a donated painting whose "value" (for tax purposes, of course) rose from $3,000 to $90,000 in the space of one month; or the ex-governor who found tax profit in placing a multi-thousand-dollar value on his gift to a university of his public letters and papers (cost to him: zero).

Ordinarily, Congress is very chary about, if not down-right hostile to, granting open-ended spending authority to the President or cabinet officer. Yet the lawmakers have, in effect, extended just such carte blanche authority to each taxpayer, who is permitted to decide (sometimes within limits, sometimes not) just how much revenue he wishes to drain from the Treasury for his own private purposes. Over the years, the practice has become an increasingly expensive fad among taxpayers, as the following table eloquently demonstrates:

Type of deduction	Amount deducted 1944 1950 1963* (billion dollars)			Percent of increase 1944-1963	1963 Revenue cost* (billion dollars)
Taxes	1.2	2.0	13.2	1100%	2.7
Interest	0.7	1.5	10.5	1650%	3.7
Charitable gifts	1.3	2.3	8.4	600%	2.5
Medical expenses	0.8	1.4	5.6	700%	1.4
Miscellaneous	0.9	2.0	5.3	563%	1.5
TOTAL	4.5	9.0	43.0	877%	11.9

* Estimated.

It was this prodigious growth in the use of these deductions, and the drain on the Treasury, that prompted the Kennedy Administration to propose a 5 percent cutback (by means of restricting a taxpayer to deductions in excess of 5 percent of his gross income). This 5-percent "floor" (which by itself would have added $2.3 billion to Treasury revenues) loosed a tidal wave of protest upon Congress and got nowhere. But perhaps it achieved its aim: it focused congressional attention on the problem and resulted in the first cutback in the personal deductions in many years ($520 millions of deductions for state and local taxes were disallowed in the 1963 tax bill passed by the House).

Heading the list in the amount drained from the Treasury are the deductions for taxes paid—not *all* taxes, just some. State income and sales taxes and property taxes *are* deductible. Federal income and excise taxes, death taxes and local improvement taxes are not.

These deductions are allowed in part because of the supposed objections to imposing "a tax on a tax." Evidently, however, this is not a matter of inflexible moral principle; if it were, then Congress should logically allow deductions for *all* taxes paid. Surely, too, these deductions cannot be defended on the ground that the payment of taxes reduces a person's "ability to pay" (the time-honored philosophic base of the U.S. tax system) —for why do we not permit a deduction for by far the heaviest tax of all: the federal income tax?*

If most state and local taxes stand justly accused of pressing more heavily on the poor than the rich (thus flouting "ability to pay"), their deductibility for federal tax purposes compounds the felony. To "ability-to-pay" devotees, a flat sales tax is heresy enough; but with federal taxes included in the calculation, the poor man actually ends up paying a higher rate of sales tax on what he buys than does the rich man.

Picture, for example, two cars drawn up on either side of a gasoline pump in New York City. On one side a millionaire's Rolls Royce, on the other a day-laborer's fourth-hand Chevy. On each gallon of gasoline, there is a 6-cent state tax, devoted to the care and building of public roads. Yet, after deducting this at their respective federal top-bracket rates of 90 and 20 percent, the millionaire ends up paying, out of pocket, only $\frac{6}{10}$ of a cent per gallon as his contribution to the public highways, while the day-laborer pays 4.8 cents a gallon out-of pocket.

---

* That tax was, in fact, deductible during the first four years of the American income tax, from 1913 to 1917.

Now suppose that when the millionaire and the day-laborer pull away from the filling station, both proceed, by sheer coincidence, to a local appliance store where each buys a $150 television set. City sales tax: ostensibly $6 for the millionaire, $6 for the laborer. Yet, after federal tax deductions, the worker finds himself out-of-pocket $4.80 for the sales tax, the millionaire only 60 cents—clearly a cause for hand-wringing and teeth-gnashing among "ability to pay" adherents.

Some argue that state *income* taxes, but no others, should be deductible for federal tax purposes, on two grounds. First, it is possible, in the case of the 91 percent federal taxpayer, to have more than 100 percent of his "top dollars" taken from him by piling a state tax on top of his federal tax. Second, so-called "consumption taxes" are, in effect, part of the price the buyer is willing, voluntarily, to pay for a given item, but a state *income* tax lacks such voluntary niceties, and therefore should be deductible.

Interest deductions are next on the list of Treasury-drainers, amounting to $10.5 billion in 1963, and costing roughly $2.7 billion in revenue.

Interest outlays for personal (as distinct from business) purposes have been deductible ever since the first federal income tax law of 1913. But why, critics ask, should they be? After all, they say, interest is only a part of the cost of buying things —for example, on many installment purchase loans, the interest payments are not even considered separately, but simply melt into the weekly or monthly installments. Why, therefore, should the interest cost be treated differently, for tax purposes, than the price of the refrigerator, TV set, or car itself?

In reply, two main reasons are usually advanced. The first is purely practical: namely, that it is simply not feasible to separate, for tax purposes, the interest on *business* loans (i.e., loans made to generate profits or income) from the interest on personal loans. It is a generally acknowledged principle, under our system of taxing business income, that all expenses incurred in generating income should be deductible. Under this principle, if a man borrows $5,000 to buy some shares of stock, rather than delving into his savings account, the interest on that loan is deductible. But really all he did was to make $5,000 of his savings available to buy that new car he'd been eyeing. So what was the *real* purpose or effect of the loan: to help him buy the stocks (tax-deductible) or the car (nondeductible)? Since no one can ever be sure (the argument runs), equity and simplicity demand allowing deductions for *all* interest costs.

The second argument is that whether you borrow or draw on your savings account to buy that new car, there is a cost involved that makes you that much poorer and hence less "able to pay" taxes. If you borrow, you pay out 4 percent interest on your loan (if you're lucky); if you draw down your savings account, you forego the 4 percent interest your money would otherwise earn.

Yet, counter the critics, *any* personal expense makes a man poorer and less "able to pay" his taxes—a logic that leads to the conclusion that all spending should be deductible and only savings should be taxed (a tenet hardly to be found in *Poor Richard's Almanack*).

Next in order of magnitude is the deduction for gifts to charity, limited, generally, to 20 or 30 percent of a person's income, and generally regarded as among the most unarguably worthy provisions of the tax law, clearly worth every penny of the $2.5 billion it costs the Treasury annually.

Yet there are some who view the present charitable deduction with less than total enthusiasm. Even leaving aside the problems and abuses described in Chapter 13, these critics find basic grounds for criticism. Why, they ask, should 90 percent of a wealthy man's generosity, but only 20 percent of an un-

moneyed taxpayer's, be financed by Uncle Sam? Is it sensible
to permit some $2.5 billion of public revenues to be strewn
broadcast, with little sense of order or priority, for such varied
causes as the Vegetarian Brotherhood of America, the Degree
of Honor Protective Association, and the Recreation Home of
the Salesmanship Club of Houston? Is it right, they ask, that
your neighbor should be allowed to divert some of *your* tax
money* to support a cause—be it vegetarianism or degree of
honor protection—that might not rank very high in your scale
of preferences, and to which, in fact, you may be violently
opposed? (In answer to the preceding two questions, some
argue vigorously that variety is the spice of democracy as well
as of life, and that privately financed good works can often
achieve what government spending via centralized decisions
either could not or would not.)

It has come to be unquestioned dogma that without the
incentive of the charitable deduction, philanthropy would
wither, and museums, colleges, churches and other worthy
institutions would fade or die on the vine. The facts, however,
do not support such an assumption. It was predicted, for example, that when the standard deduction was introduced in
1942 and millions stopped taking advantage of the particular
itemized deductions, charities would suffer. The pessimism
proved unwarranted. Moreover, even though the lure of a 20
to 30 percent allowable deduction has been dangled before the
taxpayers, the attraction has only been powerful enough to
induce those who itemize to give about 4 percent of their
income to charity.† Even more striking, perhaps, is the fact
that among 298 taxpayers with incomes of a million dollars or
more in 1960, 23 made charitable gifts of a thousand dollars
or less, 49 gave $5,000 or less and 67—nearly a fourth of the

---

* You have to pay higher taxes because of your neighbor's and everyone
else's charitable deduction privilege.

† This 4 percent has remained constant over the years, even while tax
rates (and hence, theoretically, the tax incentive to philanthropy) have
risen and fallen.

total—gave $10,000 or less of their million-dollar incomes to charity.

Some have suggested that charitable gifts should be tax-favored only to the extent they exceed, say, 2 or 3 percent of income (similar to the existing medical deduction). This is based on the philosophy that citizens might reasonably be expected to give a small share of their income to public causes without tax inducements, and that a tax concession should be reserved for *unusual* generosity—over and above the norm. This, it is argued, would substantially reduce the revenue loss from the charitable deduction, yet would have comparatively little effect on total volume of philanthropy, much of which even now comes from small contributions (especially to churches) from those who use the standard deduction.

Many strongly urge, moreover, that the tax incentive should be in the form of a uniform tax *credit* (e.g., for every dollar donated, a dollar could be substracted from your taxes, up to a reasonable limit) rather than a deduction, so that for a given gift, those with modest means would get the same tax benefits as the well-to-do.

The final major category of personal deductions is that for medical expenses, introduced into the tax laws in 1942 as a means of relieving the burden of extraordinary and unexpected medical expenses. Originally, only those medical expenditures in excess of 5 percent of income could be deducted. Later this "floor" was eliminated for those over 65, and reduced to 3 percent of income for others. Expenses for drugs exceeding 1 percent of income are deductible, although the 1963 House tax bill eliminated this "floor" for the elderly.

The weaknesses in the medical deduction have already been suggested (p. 209): the greatest help is accorded those who need it least, and none goes to those who need it the most.

Basically, the income tax system is a poor instrument for accommodating extraordinary and uncontrollable expenses of this sort. At best, its help is minimal, and it cannot place in a family's hands the dollars it needs to pay the often ruinous hospital and doctors' bills that come with major illness. Only health insurance, private or public, can do that.

Where will it all end? That is the question that troubles Treasury officials when they consider the range, magnitude and cost of personal deductions now permitted by the tax laws. Moreover, the pressures are strong for *expanding* the list of tax-deductible outlays. Bills have been introduced, for example, to make the cost of fallout shelters tax-deductible. And as of spring, 1962, more than a hundred senators and representatives had introduced bills to permit tax deductions for the expenses of sending children to college. Annual cost to the Treasury: $500,000,000 to $800,000,000. And if college expenses become deductible, why not private school expenses? Or outlays for vocational training? Or for correspondence courses or night school college courses for inquisitive adults?

As Chapter 15 demonstrates, once the procession of tax favors begins, it picks up momentum and becomes increasingly difficult to stop. Not only do inequities grow; but, as a smaller and smaller part of Americans' income is subject to tax, higher and higher rates are required to raise the necessary revenues. Reverse the trend, however, and start with a clean slate, as suggested in Chapter 17, and you pave the way for 10 percent to 50 percent tax rates, in place of the 20 percent to 91 percent rates in effect until 1963. Let the present trend continue, however . . . and who knows?

Every taxpayer, therefore; would do well to join in pondering the question, Where will it all end?

12 /

Some Moral
Preachments of
Our Tax Laws

The following is an attitude test. Do you agree or disagree
with these statements?

Agree | *Disagree*

1. Repairing a dented fender is
   more important than fixing
   a broken arm.
2. People should not try to edu-
   cate themselves for a better
   job, but should be content
   with their present job.
3. The boy working his way
   through college is less deserving than the football
   star on an athletic scholarship.
4. People should be penalized
   for continuing to work beyond age 65.

Agree | Disagree

5. People should be encouraged to go into debt rather than to live within their means.

6. Places of learning are less important than places of worship.

7. Machines are more important than people.

8. The inventor of, say, a new pretzel bender is more important than the writer of a new book, play, poem, song or symphony.

9. A blind person deserves financial help, but a paralytic does not.

10. People who work for a living are less deserving than those who don't.

11. The work of money is entitled to a greater reward than the work of people.

If you disagree with eight or more of the above statements, it is not time to see your doctor—but it may well be time to see your congressman or senator and ask him a few questions about our tax laws.

Why? Because every one of the above statements is contained in those laws. Of course, you won't find them stated in just the way they were in the attitude test; nor, in most cases, did the writers of the tax laws *intend* to make such value judgments when they framed the tax code—but no tax law can be free of such judgments. So there they sit, even though many of them don't coincide with what a preponderance of Americans believe.

Most people probably aren't even aware these judgments

exist. Even now, for example, you may be highly dubious that the tax laws really do draw the conclusions on which the attitude test was based. Where, for example (you may ask), does it say that repairing a fender is more important than fixing a broken arm? Well, Section 165(c)(3) of the Internal Revenue Code provides that all so-called "casualty losses"—even the most minor ones, such as dented fenders*—are tax deductible, whereas Section 213(a)(1)(B) states that for those under 65 *medical* expenses that come to less than 3 percent of your income are *not* deductible.

Americans schooled to revere the shimmering virtues extolled by Horatio Alger will surely be shocked to learn that the tax laws discourage initiative, self-advancement and the quest for knowledge. Yet consider the case of Nora Payne Hill, a Danville, Virginia, schoolteacher very much in the Horatio Alger tradition. Although Miss Hill could have fulfilled her state teaching requirements right in Danville, she chose to journey to New York to attend Columbia University summer school, in the belief that "she could do a better job in Danville by so doing." But the Tax Court sternly disallowed the deduction of her $239.50 of summer school expenses, applying the accepted rule of law that educational expenses incurred in the pursuit of a higher position are *not* deductible. The expenses of standing still—yes, those are deductible, but not those devoted to moving ahead in life. "However commendable [Miss Hill's] conduct may have been," the Tax Court found, her journey to the fount of knowledge was not necessary to maintain her present position. Besides, the court observed, "she said she loved to go to summer school."

Happily, a higher court reversed the Tax Court as "unreal and hypercritical" and allowed Miss Hill her $239.50 deduction —but only because it exonerated her of the sin of trying to

---

* The 1963 tax bill passed by the House allowed casualty deductions only for items in excess of the first $100; but these days, even a fender may well cost more than $100 to fix.

elevate herself to a higher station. Had the appeals court suspected her of such a sinister motive, it would have upheld the Tax Court, for the rule against self-advancement must be maintained.* A group of research chemists, for example, was not allowed to deduct the costs of attending law school in order to become patent chemists; and a psychiatrist was denied a deduction for the expenses of his own psychoanalysis, a prerequisite to his advancement to the status of a qualified analyst.

Now that being born in a log cabin has gone out of style, a modern equivalent for the aspiring politician is the claim of having worked his way through college—preferably by waiting on table. While such industriousness thus appears to enjoy great public approbation, the law takes a more critical view: it taxes the hard-earned income of the college waiter, but leaves untouched the athletic "scholarship" which enthusiastic alumni bestow upon the football hero (and which the law treats as a gift).

In order to ease what are commonly called the "twilight years," Congress has compassionately conferred on those over 65 a tax credit on the first $1,200 of their income from pensions, dividends or other investment income. But the elderly are encouraged to suppress any desire to supplement that income (and to keep busy) by working, for the moment they earn more than $1,200 a year, the tax credit begins to fade away. When their earnings reach $2,400, it vanishes entirely. Their *unearned* income, however, can rise to any height without penalty; so long as all remunerative work is meticulously avoided, the tax credit retains its full glory. Once they have safely reached age 72, though, they may once again join the ranks of the gainfully employed without adverse tax consequences.

---

* The rule is defended on practical grounds: unless some line is drawn to define what educational costs are "ordinary and necessary" business expenses, it is argued, *all* educational outlays would have to become tax-deductible, and the drain on the Treasury would be formidable.

Poor Richard's Almanack and similar fountainheads of wisdom are replete with admonitions about the evils of borrowing and the virtues of living within one's means ("He that goes a-Borrowing goes a-Sorrowing . . . The Borrower is a Slave to the Lender"). Benjamin Franklin would doubtless, therefore, be horrified by the manner in which the tax laws make the government of the United States an active partner in encouraging people to stray from the balanced family budget. For, after all, since interest payments are tax-deductible, Uncle Sam bears a part of the cost and makes borrowing less expensive. Modern-day economists, to be sure, might well applaud the ample use of credit; but Poor Richard could never condone the concomitant erosion of fiscal virtue.

Wherein do the tax laws either state or imply that institutions of learning are inferior in importance to institutions of worship? Section 511(a)(2)(A), states that if a college (or any other charitable organization) owns an "unrelated business," such as a macaroni factory, the profits of such a business are subject to regular taxes. However, if the same macaroni factory is owned by "a church, a convention or association of churches," the macaroni profits are immune from taxation. "The exemption conferred for our spiritual needs," observes Louis Eisenstein, "also embraces the worldly pursuit of profit."

Judging from the tax law, the inventors in our midst are clearly to be revered over our authors and composers, for while Section 1235 specifically confers a tax blessing upon the fruits of the inventor's imagination, Section 1231(b)(1)(C) just as specifically denies that tax favor (the special 25 percent capital gain rate) to authors, composers and artists. In the eyes of the tax law, it appears, *any* invention—whether it be a new kind of radar or a new pretzel bender—contributes more to the well-being of society than, say, a Faulkner or Hemingway novel, a Robert Frost poem, an Aaron Copland symphony, or, perhaps, a Rodgers and Hammerstein Broadway musical.

As to the preference shown the blind, the story is simple:

Congress has sympathetically conferred an extra $600 exemption upon those to whom sight is denied, but this expression of compassion for the handicapped mysteriously began and ended there.

And who, reading the tax laws, can doubt that machines are more important than people? After all, when a businessman invests in a machine he is entitled to take tax deductions on the cost of that machine over its useful life. But the tax laws give him no comparable merit points for investing in his son (by sending him to college).

Moreover, the tax laws are most understanding about the aging of machines: as indicated above, a year-by-year allowance is made as machines lose their zip and zest and approach the age of retirement. But leaving aside the minor concessions made at age 65 (pp. 207-211), the tax laws sternly forbid any recognition of the gradual aging of human beings—except, perhaps in one instance: the professional baseball and football players who are bought and sold precisely like indentured slaves, and whose initial purchase price may be "depreciable." But do not rejoice for the players, for they derive no benefit. Only the purchaser of the ball club is thus blessed.

Any youngster reading the biographies of the titans of America's past (the Franklins, Jeffersons and Lincolns, the Lewis-and-Clarks, the Andrew Carnegies and the Henry Fords) cannot escape the deeply-held American precept that it was heroic personal effort—hard work—that made these men and their country great. *Poor Richard's Almanack* confirms this wisdom ("Diligence is the Mother of good luck . . . Idleness is the greatest prodigality"). Yet in many respects, the tax law seems to frown upon those who work for their living—or, at least, to smile warmly upon those who don't. Some of these respects have already been mentioned: the comparative penalty, for example, suffered by those who work beyond age 65 or who wait on table to get a college education. Wives, moreover, may be said to be discouraged from remunerative activity, since this reduces the tax advantage their husband derives from matrimony (see p. 65). But these are peripheral compared with the dramatic preference accorded *unearned* income over earned income. Those blessed with large holdings of corporate stock, for example, derive their dividend income through the managerial efforts and talents of others but are nevertheless favored with the "dividend credit" (pp. 197-204), a tax concession denied those whose income is wholly earned. Others may, without lifting a finger, inherit great wealth generated by the efforts of their forebears, and pay not a penny of tax when they receive it.

But by far the greatest advantage enjoyed by unearned income is the special capital gains tax rate, which openly proclaims that the work of money is entitled to a greater reward than the work of people. Lawyers (and other high-paid professionals, such as doctors or engineers), it is said, live well, but die poor. Why? Because they perform the work of *people*, and for their prodigious efforts, they are taxed at the regular income tax rates, ranging up to 91 percent. Others, on the other hand, who have the means to put their *money* to work, are favored with a tax rate that rises no higher than 25 percent.

This is not to deprecate the value of capital, an essential ingredient in society. But capital without human effort counts for little; in fact, it is the addition of human effort and ingenuity that brings capital to life.

In times past, the American tax laws sought to favor this human factor through a preferential "earned income credit." But human effort requires no such preferential recognition. What is wrong with simple equality, which can be effortlessly achieved by taxing the work of money and the work of people according to the same rates?*

These and many other value judgments are scattered through-

---

* Including, of course, an averaging device for smoothing out "bunched" income of various sorts.

out the tax law. Few are as overtly stated as Section 152(b)(5), which expresses a deeply engrained American attitude toward mistresses (it denies their benefactors the right to claim them as dependents). Most are subtly buried in the inscrutable legal verbiage of the Internal Revenue Code. But, as the Duchess said, "Everything's got a moral—if only you can find it."

13 /

'Tis More Blessed
To Give— If You
Work It Right

Section 170 of the Internal Revenue Code states: "There shall be allowed as a [tax] deduction any charitable contribution . . . payment of which is made within the taxable year."

It is generally supposed that the cardinal purpose of Section 170, which now costs the Treasury $2½ billion every year, is to help the recipient charity, with benefits to the donor-taxpayer a strictly secondary means to that end. But in actual practice, it frequently works just the other way: the giver is far more blessed than the receiver. Section 170, for example, actually makes it possible to *make* money by giving money away (pp. 247-248). It also enabled one taxpayer to enjoy nearly $20 *million* of tax-free income one year (pp. 248-249).

One illustration of a donor benefiting more than the charity is that of a wealthy lady whose gift of nearly $40,000 worth of jewelry to her own private foundation was simply placed in a safe deposit box where, she said, it lay dormant. Benefit to the lady: a $39,400 tax deduction—which offset and made tax-free $39,400 of her income in the year she made the gift. Benefit to "charity": zero.

Or consider the instance of the gentleman who gave a large number of paintings to his private foundation (which had no place to hang them)—so many, in fact, that he had to store some of them in his office storeroom. While the donor was financially enhanced by his tax deductions, charity was left out in the cold.

Taxpayers have been known to claim thousand-dollar (occasionally, even multi-thousand dollar) tax deductions based on generous art-dealer valuations of paintings they contributed to a hospital "thrift shop"* which had never succeeded in selling a painting for more than $75. Often, the very dealers who had supplied the inflated appraisals would hurry down to the thrift shop and snap up the paintings at bargain prices. (If revenue agents can establish and assemble the entire chain of facts in cases such as this, they can take action; but the enforcement problem, especially where difficult-to-value paintings are involved, has proved troublesome in the past.)

Another taxpayer donated to his private foundation the commercially valuable waterfront rights to his lake-shore home. Charity could only benefit from this gift if the shore rights were actually sold, which could hardly have been the intent of the owner-donor. Yet, under the law, he was entitled to a tax-saving deduction on the market value of those rights.

Giving works of art to "charity" has been such a fertile field for tax savings that French & Company, one of New York's most distinguished art dealers, published a special pamphlet called *Taxes and Art*. "THE ASTUTE ART COLLECTOR," the pamphlet said, "HAS IT IN HIS POWER TO DRASTICALLY SLICE HIS OVER-ALL TAX BILL. As a matter of fact, through the sophisticated use of CHARITABLE DEDUCTIONS, he can cut his taxes by more than ONE-THIRD . . . It adds up to an attractive picture."

---

* These "thrift shops" sell donated objects and give the proceeds to a hospital.

Under the heading, "GIVE YOUR ART OBJECT AND STILL KEEP IT," the pamphlet described one popular tax-saving practice pursued by art collectors. This involves giving works of art to a museum, but retaining possession until the donor's death. Dual advantage to the giver: a lifetime of enjoyment of his art works, plus a handsome *immediate* tax deduction.

Placing proper values on works of art is a thorny problem. At best, art values are slippery, since even conscientious appraisals can vary widely, and honest opinions, the government has discovered, are sometimes hard to come by. Recipient museums may be tempted to err on the high side in their valuations of donated works, in the hope this will stimulate further gifts from the tax-satisfied donor. Dealers and professional appraisers have likewise shown themselves anxious to please, although few have gone to the lengths of one dealer, who offered to sell a painting for $7,000 and at the same time agreed to appraise it, for potential tax-deduction purposes, at $24,000. Another appraiser indignantly sued his client for failing to pay a kickback on the tax savings resulting from a phony art appraisal. New York art dealers have now formed an association in the hope of curbing such practices.

One artist thought highly enough of eight of her abstract works to give them to schools—and to value them at $169,000 for tax-deduction purposes. Internal Revenue thought this appraisal over-generous since she had never before succeeded in selling a single of her paintings. Later she did make one sale for $15,000 —but this was to an associate of her lawyer's who was not an art collector and had not previously purchased any painting for more than $50. Under the circumstances, the Tax Court held, it "would hardly be justified" in "according much weight" to this sale, and it knocked the deductions down from $169,000 to $9,300.

Other contributed paintings have exhibited remarkable increases in value. One taxpayer claimed deductions of $15,000 and $12,500 for donating paintings for which he had recently paid only $150 and $90, respectively. Another collector paid

$44,000 for a Velasquez painting that a few weeks earlier had sold for only $3,000. Several days later, he donated the work to charity and claimed a $90,000 deduction. Thus, in a single month, the painting's "value" had gone up 3000 percent.

Recently, a taxpayer claimed a $42,500 deduction on his gift to charity of five pieces of ancient jewelry for which he had only paid $15,000. His reason: the Lebanese merchant who had sold him the jewelry had told him it was worth $100,000. The Tax Court, however, felt that $15,000 was a more appropriate value, the Lebanese merchant to the contrary notwithstanding.

Internal Revenue will be greatly aided in spotting and disallowing such inflated claims by new regulations requiring a donor to show, on his tax return, all items of property contributed to charities, plus the date and cost of their acquisition. This will also be helpful in detecting padded values given old clothes and other miscellany that used to be concealed behind an apparently innocuous tax-return item such as "Contributions to City Hospital: $484."

Treasury rules do not permit claiming deductions for donating personal services, but this can be circumvented by contributing items made or created by the donor—paintings, manuscripts, papers and documents. One prominent ex-governor claimed a substantial tax deduction for his gift of gubernatorial papers and letters to a university, although their cost to him was zero.

Manufacturers may derive a tax advantage from donating their products to charity, since their tax deduction includes an allowance for their usual mark-up, even though the company is only out of pocket its direct production costs. One highly-publicized example of this was the donation of food and drugs by American firms to help ransom invasion prisoners from Cuba. The tax deduction to the contributing companies came to $46 million, although the actual cost to the manufacturers was considerably less than this.

In the so-called Pomona Plan (now curbed by Internal Revenue regulations), colleges found a profitable, if unidealistic, theme for fund-raising: not sentiment toward the old alma mater, not belief in higher education—but straight tax avoidance. Commercial advertising techniques were used to spread the message: "ELIMINATE CAPITAL GAINS TAX" was the headline in a newspaper advertisement by one California college. For a person with some stock worth $100,000 (original cost: $40,000), the Pomona Plan was most attractive. If he were to sell the stock himself and reinvest it, he would pay a capital gains tax of $15,000 and have only $85,000 left to reinvest. But under the Pomona Plan, he would give the stock to a college, retaining a right to the *income* from the stock during his lifetime. The college would then sell the stock and reinvest the proceeds, usually in tax-free bonds. But, being tax exempt, the college would pay no gains tax, and thus be able to put the entire $100,-000 to work on the donor's behalf. Result to the donor: (1) a sizable tax deduction at the time of the gift; (2) no capital gains tax; (3) a steady stream of tax-free income for life. Prior to the Internal Revenue clamp-down, this proved a successful college money-raiser. Said one official of Pomona College, where the plan originated: "A lot of our donors say they never heard of Pomona until they read our ads. They give us money just to save taxes."

"Private" foundations—charitable foundations which receive their funds from one or a few principal grantors, rather than from the general public—have become increasingly popular in recent years. The Foundation Library Center in New York says that of the 15,000 such foundations in existence in late 1963, 88 percent have been created since 1940, and roughly 1,200 new ones are created every year.

In addition to their charitable functions, these foundations can serve a variety of business purposes for their principal grantor. Some of these were listed in a 1960 law review article: "Tax avoidance . . . Perpetuation of [company] control . . . Public relations ("And now abideth faith, hope, charity, these three; but the greatest of these is charity." [I Cor. 13:13]) . . . Research and product development (for public and industry

benefit—and first use by the founder's organization is only fair)
... Prestige (puts the founder's name in the same category with
Ford and Carnegie's) . . . Competitive advantage (obviously,
over competitors who pay normal taxes) . . . Little regulation
(the lack of government supervision is a fact, despite 'public'
nature of foundations)."

Concludes the author: "Business purposes now so often are
dominant in the formation of 'charitable foundations' that the
importance of that motive hardly needs to be emphasized." And
Business Week observed, in 1960, that "the real motive behind
most private foundations is keeping control of wealth (even
while the wealth itself is given away)."

True, a foundation's income must eventually go to charity,
but, as the Kiplinger Tax Letter has pointed out, "There can be
a long time lag between income and disbursement. Many foundations accumulate for years in order to build enough capital. In
the meantime, they perform valuable functions for founders and
families."

These "valuable functions" take a variety of forms. One private
foundation, for example, played a key role in the proxy fight
for control of the Fruehauf Trailer Company. Dave Beck of the
Teamsters Union agreed to have the union buy a number of
Fruehauf shares, whose votes would be controlled by company
president Roy Fruehauf. The union was guaranteed its money
back, with a 4 percent return—a guarantee backed up by the
entire assets of the Roy Fruehauf Foundation, Inc. If Internal
Revenue is empowered to take action against the foundation for
this use of assets to benefit Mr. Fruehauf rather than charity, it
had not done so as of September, 1963, nine years after the
incident took place.

Similarly, in the titanic proxy struggle between two Texas
millionaire families, the Murchisons and Allan Kirby, for control
of the Alleghany Corporation and the New York Central Railroad, the Fred M. Kirby Foundation (of which Allan Kirby was
president) bought at least 91,110 shares of Alleghany stock.

Kirby later bought the stock from the foundation, apparently, his associates said, to forestall any questioning of the foundation's tax-exempt status.

Private charitable foundations offer an effective means of maintaining operating control of a family-owned or dominated business. The benefits of such control are vividly illustrated by a controversy between Lewis S. Rosenstiel, president of Schenley Industries, and his daughter, Mrs. Louise S. Frank. In a court affidavit, Mrs. Frank alleged that the Rosenstiel Foundation, which owned about $12,000,000 of Schenley stock, was being used by her father to "dominate" the firm and assure himself the "emoluments" thereof, including $300,000 in annual salary and lucrative stock options. Earlier, Mrs. Frank said, her father's "emoluments" had been even greater: in an out-of-court settlement of a previous stockholders' suit, Rosenstiel had agreed to relinquish benefits totaling more than $900,000—including reducing his annual vacation from three months to two. In reply, Mr. Rosenstiel said the entire matter had arisen because of his daughter's opposition to the appointment of three new directors for the foundation, whose grants since 1944, he said, had exceeded $6 million. At this writing, the matter is being settled, the partners say.

Continued family control, plus considerable estate tax savings, can be achieved by willing a majority of the stock of a family-held company to a family-controlled charitable foundation, when the principal owner dies. Later, the company (or the family) can buy back the stock out of profits.

Substantial loans by a private foundation to a principal donor or to one of his companies can be another "fringe benefit" of charitable giving. One foundation, for example, made a $200,000 loan (borrowing $100,000 in order to do so) to a distillery one-third owned by one of the foundation's principal grantors. In contrast to this $200,000 loan to the distillery, the dispensations to charity over a three-year period averaged less than $10,000.

Although the law requires reasonable security and rates of

interest on such loans, the borrower has the comfort of knowing
that renewals of the loan and extensions of repayment schedules
can be easily arranged. Some taxpayers have borrowed the entire
assets of their private foundation and then defaulted on the loan,
liquidating the penniless foundation and leaving Internal
Revenue powerless to take away its tax exemption.

"Bootstrapping" is the name given to another helpful use to
which private foundations have been put. A man sells his company (or part of it) to his private foundation—probably for a
generous price, agreeing to accept installment payments and
also "agreeing" to stay on as a high-paid executive. Over the
next few years, the company profits flow in to the foundation,
tax-free, and are passed on to the former owner to pay him for
the sale. Thus, the taxes that would ordinarily be paid by the
company are avoided.

Of the above practices, some may be preventable under existing law—*if* revenue agents can unravel all the facts with sufficient clarity, which is frequently difficult. Some are in a
shadowy "maybe" area; others are clearly permissible. Internal
Revenue is now "on" to the art abuses, and the new regulations
requiring full disclosure of property gifts will help in enforcement, although the vexing "valuation" problem will remain.

In the realm of the private foundations, some who have studied
their practices believe the law should more unequivocally confine the uses of charitable gifts to truly charitable purposes,
through such provisions as:

—*A flat prohibition against the use of a foundation's assets
for the benefit of a major contributor, his family or any of his
controlled businesses, whether through loans, purchases and sales
or exchanges.* The law now requires "reasonable" or "adequate"
security, rates of interest and prices on loans and sales of this
sort, but since these are not arm's-length business transactions,
these vague standards are easily stretched, and transgressions
are difficult to combat in court. Besides, if the true purpose of

the foundation is "charitable," why, it is asked, should there be any objection to divorcing its affairs from those of its major grantors?

—*Denial of a tax deduction when a taxpayer gives stock in a company he controls to a foundation he also controls.* The reasoning behind this is that a controlled foundation does not have freedom to dispose of the stock as it might see fit, as is the case in an arm's-length gift to an uncontrolled foundation or charity; hence, a true gift has not been made.

Both of these provisions were approved by the House of Representatives in 1950, but were either killed or considerably softened by the Senate.

Under the tax laws as now written, generosity and philanthropy may be rewarded in sharply varying degrees, depending on the wealth and possessions of the giver.

First, the affluent are more amply rewarded than the poor. Under pre-1964 rates, a top-bracket taxpayer only furnished 9 cents out of every dollar given to charity, the government, in effect, paying the other 91 cents. But for a lowest-bracket taxpayer, 80 percent of every contribution came out of his own pocket; the government was only a 20 percent partner. Some may say that this is simply a result of stiff progressive tax rates, and that it is only fair that what goes steeply up should come just as steeply down. But that is not the whole answer. Even with graduated rates, if the tax incentive to philanthropy were in the form of a tax *credit** instead of a tax *deduction,* then each person's philanthropy would be uniformly rewarded, regardless of his wealth.

But that is not the only distinction the law makes in rewarding contributors to charity. Equally important (although less well known), is the advantage enjoyed by those who give "appreciated property" (i.e., property that has gone up in value) over those who give cash.

---

* E.g., each person being permitted to subtract 50 percent of his charitable contributions from the taxes he owes the government.

Consider two men, each with $40,000 of taxable salary. A gives $5,000 of that salary to charity, takes a tax deduction, and thus successfully reduces his taxable income to $35,000. *But in order to do so, he had to part with $5,000 of cash.* His remaining spendable income: $35,000.

B is more fortunate. He owns some stock that originally cost him $1,000 but is now worth $5,000. He gives this stock to charity and takes the tax deduction, so that he, too, reduces his taxable income to $35,000. *But B was able to do so without parting with a penny of his salary.* His $40,000 is still intact. B's *taxable* income is the same as A's but he ends up $5,000 ahead on *spendable* income. In effect, he is able to enjoy $5,000 of tax-free cash income.

The crux of B's advantage is this: if he had sold the stock and then given the cash proceeds to charity, he would have had to pay a $1,000 capital gains tax. But because he gave the stock to charity instead, the law permits him to get the advantage of the gain (by allowing a tax deduction on the full $5,000) without paying any tax on it.

Whenever top-bracket tax rates are higher than 75 percent, as they were through 1963, *a high-income taxpayer can literally make money by giving money away.* Say he is in the 90 percent bracket and has some stock that has gone up in value by $10,000. If the sells the stock, he pays $2,500 capital gains tax and his spendable income is increased by the remaining $7,500. If, instead, he gives the stock to charity, his charitable deduction saves him $9,000. Thus, he is $1,500 better off giving the stock to charity than by selling it on his own behalf.

In the above example, the taxpayer came out ahead by giving his property away rather than selling it. But he might also gain by giving it away rather than *keeping* it—even under the lower tax rates of the 1963 House tax bill. Suppose a 70-percent-bracket taxpayer has a building that throws off a cash profit of $10,000 a year. If he keeps the building for the next ten years, he will get $100,000 cash, but will keep only $30,000. But if he gives the building to a charity for ten years (the building to return to his

wife thereafter) his immediate deduction would net him $58,-
000* of added spending money—nearly twice the $30,000 he'd
keep after taxes by holding on to the building himself. This remarkable result is achieved because the tax law permits him a
deduction on money the law assumes he never really owned.

In 1938, the House of Representatives approved a change
in the charitable giving law which would have ended the discrimination against cash charity-donors and solved the perplex-
ing problem of valuing gifts such as paintings: allow a deduction
on the basis of original cost to the donor, instead of its fair
market value at the time of the gift. But the Senate Finance
Committee would have none of it.

An alternative and less severe way of placing the property
donor more nearly on a par with the cash donor would be to
require him to pay a capital gains tax on the gain in his property's
value, just as he would have to if he were to sell the property
and give the proceeds to charity. After all, if a charitable donor
is going to claim a deduction on his capital gain, why should he
not pay the tax on it?

Have you ever, in a moment of special wrath against what
seems to you an unusually senseless governmental folly, wished
that you and you alone might be the judge of how your tax
dollars should be spent? Well, there are some taxpayers who
have realized that wish. They have won permission to divert
their entire tax into charitable uses of their own choosing. They
pay no taxes whatever to the government.

Who are they? They are the taxpayers who have earned the
right to an unlimited charitable deduction, and are not bound by
the 20 or 30 percent ceiling applicable to other taxpayers.

Their tax savings are sometimes prodigious. One taxpayer,
for example, was enabled to enjoy nearly $20,000,000 of income

---

* His tax saving comes to only $58,000 instead of $70,000 because the
$100,000 of income he is giving to charity is stretched out over ten
years. Thus it is not considered as valuable as a $100,000-here-and-now
gift, and a smaller deduction is allowed.

one year—without paying a penny of taxes. His tax saving: over $6,000,000 that year alone. He managed this by giving to his privately-controlled foundation some $21,600,000 of securities. Their original cost to him: $460,000—*about one-fortieth of their current value.* By giving this stock to his foundation, he was in a position to get all the advantages of a $21,000,000 capital gain without paying a cent of the gains tax, which would ordinarily have come to $5,250,000.

Qualifying for this unlimited deduction privilege sounds more arduous than it is in actual practice. In fact, if one manages his investments and tax affairs wisely, it can be simplicity itself. Before unlimited deductions may be taken, the law requires that in eight years out of a ten-year period, a person's federal taxes *plus* his charitable contributions must come to at least 90 percent of his taxable income. All taxpayers, of course, are permitted to give and deduct 30 percent of their income, and for one in the top bracket, the 90 percent requirement can be met without going far beyond that ceiling. Besides, for those owning stocks that have multiplied in value forty-fold, like the multimillionaire mentioned above, any charitable gift is vastly less painful than for the cash contributor.

But for the well-advised oil investor, the 90 percent hurdle can be cleared with almost no charitable gifts. Note that the 90 percent relates to a person's *taxable* income. Recall, too, from Chapter 2, that many oil investors are able, through special deductions, to reduce their taxable incomes to zero—or close to it. For such a person as the oil operator who has paid no income tax since 1949 (p. 19), a charitable gift of as little as a dollar a year will qualify him for the unlimited charitable deduction. Thus, should he ever wish to retire from the oil business and forego the depletion avenue of tax escape, another avenue will be ready and waiting.

Statistically speaking, Section 170 has been brilliantly successful in fostering philanthropy. Not only have the number of foundations multiplied; but the volume of charitable deductions claimed has nearly trebled in the last decade. There is a temptation to be dazzled by these statistics and by the thought of the manifold worthy causes that have been supported, thanks to Section 170, and to shrug off the abuses. Yet the cardinal purpose of this tax provision—and of the $2½ billion it costs the Treasury —is to help charity first and the giver only incidentally. But in all too many instances, the donor's cart is being put before the charity's horse.

14 /

Tax Precautions To Take Before You Die

Tax lawyer Joseph Prentice shook his head as he pushed away from the breakfast table to make the morning paper more maneuverable. "Incredible!" he said.

"What's incredible, dear?" asked Mrs. Prentice as she plugged in the coffee pot.

"Well, there's a story here about a college chemistry professor who thought up some fantastic invention, and made himself a ten million dollar fortune. He died recently, and it seems he's going to pay about six million in estate taxes."

"What's so incredible about that?" asked his wife, placing bacon strips in the frying pan.

"Why, nobody in his right mind pays estate taxes like that," replied Mr. Prentice. "But this poor fellow had some fetish about doing all his own research and he tried to look up the law by himself, without a lawyer. When he saw the rates called for a six million dollar tax on a ten million dollar estate, he figured

there wasn't anything he could do about it—left the whole ten
million to his daughters and told them to take care of their
step-mother. Can you imagine anyone taking those rates seriously?"

"Why shouldn't they?" asked Mrs. Prentice as the toast disappeared into the toaster.

"Why, with all the ways of getting around them, anyone's a
fool to pay those rates."

"Well, I must say," said Mrs. Prentice, "*that's* a fine attitude
for a lawyer to take. Don't you have any respect for the law?"

"Of course I do. It's all perfectly legal. Why, just by adding
one simple sentence to his will—'I hereby bequeath half my
worldly goods to my wife'—his tax could have been about three
and a half million dollars less."

Mrs. Prentice turned away from the sputtering bacon with a
new interest. "Three and a half *million*! You mean a man can
save that much by leaving money to his wife? I must say, I think
that's a pretty cute law."

"Cute, nothing," said Sam Prentice, their vacationing college
freshman son, who had just walked into the room. "It's nothing
but an outrageous sop to the rich—a steal. A giveaway." (Sam
was a zealous member of the campus Liberal Society.)

"Why, Sam Prentice. What a thing to say," said his mother, as
the first curls of smoke rose from the forgotten bacon.

"It's true. How are we ever going to break up the big concentrations of wealth when a man with a hundred million
dollars can leave fifty million of it to his wife, tax-free?"

"Of course, son," said Mr. Prentice, "he would have to be
a pretty trusting husband to do a thing like that. After all, his
widow might run off with some handsome gigolo and cut off the
children without a penny. But, of course, you wouldn't do a
thing like that to our Sam, would you, dear?"

"Oh, I don't know," said Mrs. Prentice, lifting the charred
remains of the bacon from the pan. "With fifty million dollars
and an attractive man, I might get pretty reckless."

"Now if the professor had come to *me* for advice," said Mr.

Prentice, "I probably would have advised him to leave some of his money to his grandchildren instead of his children—that could easily have saved him around six hundred thousand dollars in taxes."

The Liberal Society was momentarily forgotten as Sam perceived a threat to his own position in the Prentice will. "What? And by-pass his own children?"

"Well, he wouldn't need to by-pass them completely. They could have all the *income* from the property as long as they lived, and when they died the property would pass to their children tax-free."

"You mean you can skip a whole generation of taxes?"

"Why limit it to one generation?" said Mr. Prentice. "A good many really wealthy people leave their money to their great-grandchildren and skip *two* generations."

"What a steal," said Sam.

"Then again," said Mr. Prentice, "I could have saved the professor another million by advising him to start giving his money away to his children during his lifetime."

"Speaking as your son," said Sam, "*that* plan interests me. As a member of the Liberal Society, however, I am appalled. How can he save a million dollars that way? Wouldn't he have to pay a gift tax?"

"Not necessarily," said Mr. Prentice. "But even if he did, the gift tax rates are a lot lower than the estate tax rates. Of course, I wouldn't advise the professor to start making big gifts unless he looked pretty healthy."

"Why not?" asked Mrs. Prentice, who was now starting the second batch of bacon. "What could his health possibly have to do with his taxes?"

"Well, if he died within three years of making the gift, the government might claim he had only been trying to avoid taxes and take away his tax saving. But if he survived three years, the government couldn't question his motives—even if he thought he was on his deathbed when he made the gift."

"Boy," said Sam. "That really *is* the end. But you said he

wouldn't necessarily have to pay *any* gift tax. Don't tell me there's a way of getting out of *that*, too!"

"Well," said Mr. Prentice, "together, the professor and his wife could give six thousand dollars a year tax-free to as many people as they wanted. So if they started early, and gave six thousand dollars each to the three daughters and the nine grandchildren, in ten years they could give $720,000 without paying a penny of tax on it."

"Father," said Sam, "I don't remember your giving *me* six thousand dollars a year."

"Son," countered Mr. Prentice. "I don't remember *making* ten million dollars."

"Look, Dad. The way you describe it, the estate tax rates *look* tough—but nobody pays what those rates seem to call for."

"That's about what it comes down to," said Mr. Prentice.

"Well, why did Congress bother to put the rates in there in the first place?" asked Sam.

Sam's question is more than rhetorical. On their face, the estate tax rates—a severe 77 percent at their highest—appear to be the act of a Congress as devoted as the most ardent Liberal Society member to breaking up huge fortunes as they pass from one generation to another.

But, as with the income tax rates, all is not as it seems, as the following table shows:

Gross Estate Size	Tax per Rate Schedule*	Actual Tax†
$500,000–$1,000,000	29–33%	15.3%
$1–2,000,000	33–38%	18.2%
$2–3,000,000	38–42%	19.3%
$3–5,000,000	42–49%	21.2%
$5–10,000,000	49–61%	23.3%
$10–20,000,000	61–69%	24.4%
$20,000,000 and over	69%+	15.7%

* What would be paid if the rate schedule in the tax code applied to the entire gross estate.

During the past two decades, the estate tax rates have remained unchanged, but the fine print has not. On the contrary,
while the income tax has been biting more and more heavily into
more and more people's pockets, Congress has been opening up
new means by which the transfer of wealth could be shielded
from the rates appearing in Section 2001 of the tax code.

Neither the estate tax nor the means of avoiding it can
properly be appraised without taking into account its supposed
purposes which, in the tax history of the United States, have
been two: first, to raise revenue and second, to curb the passing
on from generation to generation of great wealth and the economic power that goes with it.

Prior to the twentieth century, the revenue-raising aspect was
paramount: a death tax was sporadically enacted when war
crises demanded added tax collections, but invariably the tax
would fade with the crisis. Theodore Roosevelt was the first
President to expound the wealth-leveling purpose of an estate
tax. "No advantage comes," he said in 1907, "either to the
country as a whole or to the individuals inheriting the money
by permitting the transmission in their entirety of . . . enormous
fortunes." A graduated death tax would, he thought, "preserve
a measurable equality of opportunity for (future) generations."

Twenty-eight years later, another Roosevelt spoke in a similar
vein: "Inherited economic power," said FDR in 1935, "is as
inconsistent with the ideals of this generation as inherited
political power was inconsistent with the ideals of the generation
which established our Government."

This view of the estate tax has not been confined to the
political progressives. No less a conservative than Herbert
Hoover viewed the tax as a means of striking at the "evils of
inherited economic power," and of "thaw[ing] out frozen and
inactive capital and the inherited control of the tools of produc-

---

† The *actual* average tax paid in 1958 (latest available data). Both
columns indicate tax as percent of gross estate.

tion." And Andrew Carnegie, the self-made steel magnate, must have sounded like a traitor to his class when, in 1889, he asked, "Why should men leave great fortunes to their children? If this is done from affection, is it not misguided affection? Observation teaches," he said, that "generally speaking, it is not well for the children that they should be so burdened." The "thoughtful man," said Carnegie, would as soon leave to his sons "a curse as the almighty dollar."

This was hardly the view of most persons in Mr. Carnegie's income bracket. Most prominent foe of the estate tax was Treasury Secretary Andrew Mellon who during the 1920's led a one-man campaign for the repeal of the tax, predicting that as things were going, it might be "only two or three generations until private ownership of property would cease to exist." And when, in 1924, Congress raised the estate tax rates, the Under Secretary of the Treasury, Garrard B. Winston, darkly prophesied that "we shall have more golf players and fewer Henry Fords and Thomas Edisons."

Congress itself has seemed to suffer a certain ambivalence about the estate tax, for despite the apparently stiff progressive rate schedule in the law, the estate tax laws are, in practice, more Mellon than Roosevelt.

Although the income tax has been transformed from a class tax into a mass tax (44 percent of adult Americans now pay income tax, compared with only 4 percent in 1939), the estate tax "club" has consistently remained highly exclusive: only the top 1 percent belong. This is due principally to Congress' decision that the first $60,000 of anyone's property left at death should not be subject to tax. Thus, most people don't even have to file an estate tax return; and even among the 38,000 who did pay tax in 1958, a fourth of their wealth was placed beyond the reach of the tax collector by reason of the $60,000 exemption.

This exemption is, of course, most helpful to the smaller estates. Vastly more important to the larger estates is the so-called "marital deduction," the privilege of leaving half one's property tax-free to one's wife or husband—which attorney Louis Eisenstein has characterized as "an exemption which is felicitously called something else." It is, of course, available to all estates, no matter how large. In fact, the larger the estate, the larger the exemption (causing great anguish to adherents of the "ability to pay" school of taxation). For the married, then, the top 77 percent rate does not apply to estates of over $10 million, as the rate schedule in the law seems to indicate, but to estates of over $20 million. At the lower end of the scale, the marital deduction has the effect of doubling the $60,000 exemption and enabling a married person to leave property of $120,000 tax-free.* All told, it removes more than $2 billion of wealth— nearly a fifth of the total wealth reported on estate tax returns —from Internal Revenue's immediate reach.

Defenders of the marital deduction point out that it does not offer a *permanent escape* of tax on the amount left to the wife, but merely a *temporary postponement* until the unhappy day when she too passes on. But, in fact, there is a considerable *net* tax saving. In the case of the hypothetical chemistry professor and his $10 million estate, without a marital deduction, the tax would be $6 million at his death. But the marital deduction permits splitting the estate into two separately-taxed bundles, on which the total tax is only $5 million (twice $2½ million of tax on each bundle), *for a net saving of one million dollars.*

Moreover, the very postponement of the tax on the wife's share is not to be sneezed at, since as long as she lives, she can enjoy the use of the $3½ million that otherwise would have been swallowed up by the U.S. Treasury at the time of her husband's death. Assuming this money would earn the professor's wife a 4 percent return, if she outlived him by ten years, the delay in paying the tax on her half of the estate would be worth just under $1,700,000.

---

* The first $60,000 because of the exemption, another $60,000 via the marital deduction.

As our hypothetical tax attorney, Joseph Prentice pointed out, however, it takes a trusting husband to make full use of the marital deduction, since under the law, his wife must be given a no-strings-attached power to dispose of his bequest when she dies. On the other hand, the incentives for a trusting attitude on the part of a man with a $10 million estate are considerable: a $3½ million immediate (though temporary) saving, a $1 million permanent saving.

The adoption of the marital deduction in 1948 lowered estate tax revenues by about a third. According to President Truman's unavailing veto message, the annual quarter of a billion dollars this cost the Treasury redounded to the benefit of "only about 12,000 of the most wealthy families."

The marital deduction has its roots in the distinction between the "common law" states and the so-called "community-property" states under whose laws (of Spanish and French descent) half a husband's property legally belongs to the wife. Thus, in community property states, only *half* a husband's property was subject to tax at his death.

In 1942, Congress in effect overrode the community-property principle and ended the death-tax advantages previously enjoyed by citizens of the eight community-property states. A few fringe discriminations remained, but some experts feel these could have been solved by minor changes in the 1942 law. Nevertheless, in 1948, along with marital income-splitting (see Chapter 4) Congress enacted the estate-tax marital deduction. Thus, the eight-state tail wagged the forty-state dog, but since this resulted only in lower taxes for those in the lucky forty, and no increase in the remaining eight, taxpayer complaints were handily avoided. The only injured party was the United States Treasury, which lost roughly $2 billion from income-splitting plus the quarter-billion dollars via the marital deduction.

The estate tax has never recovered, either as a revenue raiser or as a purported leveler of wealth, from the body blow of the marital deduction. The Treasury Department, in the last official effort to overhaul the estate and gift taxes (in 1950), failed to recommend repeal of the marital deduction, and its proposed estate tax rate increases fell far short of the pre-1948 levels.

The skipping of whole generations of estate taxes is a tax-saving plan that enjoys a particular vogue among the well-to-do. A special Treasury survey in 1945 (the last such study published) showed that among those with fortunes of $500,000 or over, nearly half their wealth was left on a "skipped-generation" basis. Of this, a third by-passed two or more generations of taxes. In 1957, the president of one of the largest trust companies in the United States, noting the dramatic growth in generation-skipping trusts in his own company, told *Fortune* magazine, "Uncle Sam *isn't* taking the big estates" these days.

The naïve college professor conjured up at the outset of this chapter might have saved nearly a million dollars by skipping two generations of estate taxes, using just $3 million of his $10 million estate.* The method of achieving this would be to leave the $3 million in the hands of a trustee (perhaps a bank or trust company) with instructions that the *income* from the $3 million was to be paid to his children during *their* lifetime, then to the grandchildren during *their* lifetime. At the grandchildren's death, the $3 million itself† would pass to the great-grandchildren. An estate tax *would* be paid at the time of the professor's death, but none would be paid either at his children's or his grandchildren's demise. The tax savings (assuming the $3 million passes, each time, to an only child): $622,000 by skipping one generation, nearly a million by skipping two generations. Looked at another way, the use of the "trust" device would leave the great-grandchild more than twice as much wealth—i.e., $1,768,000 instead of $787,000.‡

---

* The other $7 million being judiciously left, tax-free, to his wife and to charity.

† Assuming no rise in the price of the stocks left in trust.

‡ Assuming, again, no price rise and assuming no use is made of the $60,000 exemption.

Tax experts believe that over the years, estate tax revenues could be increased by $100 million if the United States were to tax each generation-to-generation transfer of wealth, as the British do.

But, some ask, suppose a father chooses to leave his property to his grandson, in effect by-passing his son: is it proper, in that event, to impose a tax, when the son dies, on the transfer of property *he never really owned?*

Advocates of the British system have a two-fold answer. First, they say, to an important extent he *does* own the property. He has complete enjoyment of one of the most vital aspects of ownership (the use of the income) and, especially if he serves as a trustee of his own trust, he may have an important, if not controlling, voice in how the property itself is managed and used during his lifetime. Hence, it *is* fair to impose some tax when he dies.

Second, property left "in trust" is, traditionally, conservatively managed. Therefore, it is argued, from the point of view of fostering a dynamic economy through venturesome investment, the tax system should discourage rather than encourage "trust" arrangements. To do so (perhaps by a tax on each generation-to-generation transfer) would admittedly present technical problems, but experts believe these would not be insurmountable ones.

Here again, it is not just the traditional liberals who look askance at generation-skipping. Herbert Hoover's voice may once again be summoned, warning, as it did in 1932, that "fortunes have become so large and lawyers so cunning that they can freeze them into trusts extending over more than three generations."

But there is really no need to go to all the bother and legal expense of creating "trusts" and leaving money to as yet unborn grandchildren. Substantial savings are to be had simply by giving money away during one's lifetime—so great in fact

that *with a $2 million gift, our hypothetical chemistry professor
could have saved $1,400,000 in taxes.* *

What accounts for this enormous saving? For one thing, the
gift tax rates themselves are one-fourth lower than the estate
tax rates. But because of a vital difference in the way the two
taxes are computed, the tax advantage is actually greater than
one-fourth. For a man in the top estate tax bracket (77 percent)
and the top gift tax bracket (57 percent), for example, a $157
out-of-pocket outlay (including taxes) toward his son *during
his lifetime would mean less than half the tax and leave his
son with nearly three times as much after taxes* as the identical
outlay, by will, would after his death. It works out this way:

	Gift During Lifetime	Gift After Death
Total out-of-pocket outlay	$157	$157
Tax	$ 57	$121
Tax as percent of total outlay	36%	77%
Amount left for son after tax*	$100	$ 36

* The difference is that the 57 percent gift tax applies to the gift alone,
not including the tax, whereas the 77 percent estate tax applies not only
to the transfer itself, *but also to the tax on it.*

The *Journal of Accountancy* has published an illustrative
example of a $5 million gift wherein *the estate tax would be
more than five times the gift tax!*

Apparently, though, human nature rebels against parting
with property during one's lifetime, for despite the large tax
savings to be realized, "living gifts" amounted to only 6 per-

---

* This is merely the estate tax saving. In addition, as was pointed out
on pp. 77-80, there are substantial income tax savings to be realized—via the
glories of income-splitting—by giving money in trust to children. The
pain of such a gift, incidentally, is considerably lessened by the fact that
the father can, legally, still retain substantial, if not complete, control over
the investment and use of the donated funds—just as if he continued to
own them himself.

cent of transfers at death among those covered in the special 1945 Treasury Department survey. Even the wealthiest, who presumably had most to gain, gave only 13 percent of their property during their lifetime.

Nevertheless, recognizing the clear temptation to avoid taxes through "living gifts," especially among the ill or morbid to whom death seems imminent, the law has always held that gifts made "in contemplation of death" should be subject to the higher estate tax rates.

But when a person makes a large gift, how can it be established whether or not he is "contemplating" his demise? What was the state of mind, for example, of one Oliver Johnson who, at the advanced age of 90 years and 4 months, gave his children $200,000 in real estate? The Tax Court, apparently impressed with his ability to make "a large percentage of ringers" in horseshoe pitching and, more particularly, with his practice of jumping "into the air and click[ing] his heels together two or three times before descending to the floor," ruled that death was not on his mind when he made the gift.

In 1950, even while acknowledging that "undoubtedly many gifts have escaped the estate tax" due to the government's inability to prove tax-avoidance motives, Congress eased the path of tax-saving through "living" gifts, in order, it was said, to end the previous legal uncertainties. Under the 1950 law (still in effect), for any gift made more than three years prior to death, the government is precluded from claiming "contemplation of death," even in the most flagrant circumstances (e.g., a donor believing he was on his deathbed when he made the gift). As the law is now worded a wealthy person has everything to gain and nothing to lose by making substantial "living gifts" in his later years. Even if he dies within three years and his gift motives are successfully challenged, the total tax is still slightly less than if he had not made the gift.* And if he survives for three years, handsome tax savings are his beyond challenge.

---

* See Appendix note.

About the only truly satisfactory solution to this thorny problem (proposed by Treasury Secretary Snyder in 1950) would be to weld the gift and estate taxes into a single tax, with one rate schedule (the property left at death being considered the last in a chain of lifetime gifts). That way, the size of the transfer tax would no longer depend on whether the transfer occurred before or after death.

The tax laws enhance the "joys of giving" in two other respects: first, for a married person, the initial $60,000 of "living gifts" are exempt from taxation. More important, every married couple is also permitted to give $6,000 a year tax-free to as many people as they choose.* Thus, one as blessed with wealth, longevity and direct descendants as John D. Rockefeller (who had thirty-seven living children, grandchildren and great-grandchildren when he died at age 97) could, if still married, make tax-free gifts of $228,000 a year without even going outside the immediate family. Few, of course, are as amply endowed, either with wealth or descendants. But it would not be surprising to find an affluent couple with three children (and their three spouses) and nine grandchildren, on whom a total of $90,000 of gifts could be lavished, tax-free, each year.

While it would be unduly burdensome, both for taxpayers and the government, to require keeping track of, and paying tax on, every small, casual gift, some may wonder whether benefactions of $3,000 or $6,000 a year fit into the "small" or "casual" category. For the skeptics, however, Congress has provided a lucid explanation: the large annual exemption was needed "to cover, in most instances, wedding and Christmas gifts."

As any enterprising life insurance salesman will be glad to tell you, at the drop of his hat on your desk, one of the best

---

* This, incidentally, is another tax incentive to matrimony, for a bachelor or spinster may only give the first $30,000 and $3,000 a year tax-free.

ways to use your "wedding and Christmas gift" tax-free gift privilege is to pay $6,000 a year in life insurance premiums and give the policies to your children, since the proceeds will go to them tax-free when you die. Louis Eisenstein once estimated that if you started such a program at age 40, you might easily leave each child $900,000 of insurance, totally untouched by the tax collector. Ordinarily a taxable estate of $900,000 would pay $288,700 in taxes.

Prior to 1954, such an arrangement was barred by the so-called "premium payment test," under which, if you paid the premiums, the insurance proceeds could not pass tax-free at your death, even if you had given your children complete ownership of the policies. But, said some, there is no estate tax on other property completely owned by an heir—why discriminate against insurance? Congress, persuaded by this reasoning, abolished the "premium payment test" in 1954. (The insurance industry was not slow in seizing on this new selling point in promoting greater insurance purchases. As early as November, 1954, a scant three months after the passage of the 1954 tax law, Eisenhower Administration officials were reportedly "annoyed with the life insurance industry" for so "strenuously 'selling' the new provision"—which had had the Administration's blessing—and driving up the revenue cost to the Treasury.)

Opponents of this change contend that life insurance is not like other property; by its very nature it is like a bequest left in a person's will. If, say these critics, a man wishes to give the $3,000 or $6,000 to his wife or children and leave to *them* the decision of whether or not to buy insurance, that's one thing. But if *he* makes the decision himself, and simply buys the policy for them, he is merely providing for their welfare after his death and should pay estate taxes accordingly.

For all but a handful, "living" tax-deductible gifts to charity during one's lifetime are limited to 20 or 30 percent of the donor's income annually. No such ceiling applies to wills, and a few wealthy persons have chosen to leave their entire taxable estate to charity, thus paying no estate tax whatever. While generally such large charitable gifts further one major purpose of the estate tax (to break up large concentrations of economic power), that is not necessarily the case. Sometimes, gifts of voting stock in a family-owned business to a family-controlled charitable foundation can be a useful means of perpetuating the business in family hands (see p. 244).

A program of estate and gift-tax reform would not only render those taxes more effective and rational, but would contribute roughly a half a billion of added revenues which could be applied toward a lowering of income tax rates. Priority points in such a reform might include abolishing the marital deduction (perhaps allowing a widow to postpone a tax on her half of the estate until her death, but applying rates that would mean no permanent *net* tax saving); doing away with generation-skipping; reinstating the "premium payment" test for life insurance policies; and reducing the $3,000-$6,000 annual tax-free gift-tax privilege to true "Christmas-and-wedding-gift" proportions.

The controversy over estate taxes, though quiescent of late, is of ancient vintage. Pliny the Younger, for example, complained that the death tax "was an 'unnatural' tax, augmenting the sorrow of the bereaved." A similar lament was heard two thousand years later, when Senator William V. Allen of Nebraska wondered, in the United States Senate, whether it is "right . . . to stand with the widow and children at the graveside of a dead father to collect a tax."

In recent decades, it has become more customary to assail the estate tax because of its supposed effects on the incentives and productivity of the living and, hence, on the private enterprise system. Andrew Mellon was a prime exponent of this viewpoint, decrying the tax for forcing the liquidation of securities, depressing stock prices and "destroying" capital. The breaking up of large estates, he believed, would violate the "theory upon which the country was founded . . . equality of opportunity."

It is precisely here that Mellon collides head-on with the advocates of a steep estate tax, who picture large inheritances as not only perpetuating but magnifying economic inequalities. According to one economist, such inequalities are caused by three main factors: unequal ability, unequal luck, and unequal inheritance.

Philosophers as well as economists have argued for a steep estate tax. John Stuart Mill (like Andrew Carnegie after him) favored a death tax that would set a limit on "what anyone may acquire by the mere favor of others without any exercise of his faculties." If "he desires any further accession of his fortune," said Mill, "he shall work for it."

Adding a political note to the controversy, Roger Babson expressed inability to "see why the control of ten or twenty thousand men should descend by inheritance through the death of some manufacturer, any more than the control of a city or a state should pass on to the son of a mayor or governor."

Congress, for its part, has apparently had difficulty choosing between the philosophy of the Carnegies, the Roosevelts and the Babsons on the one hand and that of the Mellons and the Plinys on the other. Thus confronted, it has chosen both: a Rooseveltian rate schedule largely vitiated by Mellon-sized "loopholes."

15 /

Old "Loopholes"
Never Die, They Just
Get Bigger

On October 9, 1942, Stalingrad was under Nazi siege, and American heavy bombers were staging their greatest daylight raids in Europe and striking hard at both ends of the Pacific fighting line. In the Senate of the United States, Robert La Follette was waging his own battle to prevent the Senate from "extending special [tax] privileges in time of war." "Apparently," he said, "the Senate . . . wants to see that everyone comes through the war entirely whole, except the poor devils who have to go out and fight."

His target in this instance was an effort to add "ball and sagger clay"* to the list of tax-favored minerals enjoying a percentage depletion allowance. "We are vesting interests which will come back to plague us," he warned the Senate. "If we are

---

* A type of clay used especially in the manufacture of porcelain. Lest anyone doubt its essentiality, Tennessee's Senator Kenneth McKellar assured the Senate that it was "very essential. Every time we eat a meal we have to use cups and saucers and other kinds of crockeryware." He then added that small amounts of the clay were also used by one Tennessee firm to make porcelain used in military radios.

to include all these things, why do we not put in sand and gravel?"

At the time, granting percentage depletion to encourage exploration for these two relatively plentiful and easy-to-find minerals must have seemed as ridiculous as Senator La Follette sought to portray it (as one senator later put it, "You only have to stub your toe to find gravel"). Yet a bare nine years later, depletion for sand and gravel was not ridiculous; it was the law of the land. Not only that; oyster shells and clam shells had joined the depletion family. Senator Hubert Humphrey was horrified. "How far shall we go? Where shall we draw the line?" he asked the Senate. "If we are to give depletion allowances to sand and gravel and oyster and clam shells I do not see any reason why we should not give depletion . . . to anything that can be taken from the earth."

Three years later, Congress came perilously close to making his intended exaggeration into a prophecy by awarding depletion to a long list of new minerals. As noted in Chapter 2, so swollen did the depletion list become that Congress felt obliged specifically to *exclude* "soil, sod, dirt, turf, water, mosses, minerals from sea water, the air or similar inexhaustible sources."

But the chain did not end even there. In 1963, a federal district court ruled that depletion could even apply, in certain circumstances, to *water*.

If anyone is surprised or indignant about these apparent absurdities, it is merely because he does not fully apprehend the principle of "equity" in taxation. Judging from congressional behavior, one can almost imagine this principle, as perceptively worded by Louis Eisenstein, framed in a sampler on the wall of the Ways and Means and Finance committee rooms:

EQUITY IS THE PRIVILEGE
OF PAYING AS LITTLE
AS SOMEBODY ELSE.

That is, once a tax concession has been granted to one group, it becomes inequitable to deny the same favor to anyone else who can successfully claim to be "similarly situated."

As soon as this principle is properly understood, the case for percentage depletion for sand and gravel ceases to be ridiculous; it becomes irrefutable. Consider this argument presented to Congress in 1951 by the National Sand and Gravel Association:

> Percentage depletion has been granted to many non-metallic minerals. Sand and gravel are nonmetallic minerals. Therefore, "it seems to us an unreasonable discrimination against our industry to continue to be denied the benefit of a taxation policy already extended to other members of the nonmetallic minerals family." (Q.E.D.)

This line of reasoning seemed eminently sensible to the Ways and Means Committee, which concluded that the then-excluded nonmetallics "have just as good a claim" for percentage depletion as those already enjoying this favor. (Senator Douglas of Illinois had the unkindness to point out that the committee "does not say they have a *good* claim. It says they have *just as good* a claim as those which [had] been [favored]."

In 1951, therefore, sand and gravel were awarded a 5 percent depletion allowance. But equity had still not been achieved. Just three years later, the Sand and Gravel Association was back before Congress, asserting that since sand and gravel are sold in competition with such products as limestone, which enjoys a 15 percent depletion allowance, the 5 percent rate was clearly inadequate to "eliminate this competitive inequality."

Limestone, in turn, had come to be honored with a 15 percent depletion rate when the two senators from Texas pointed out that it competes directly with such 15 percent road-building materials as rock asphalt. And how had rock asphalt ascended to its favored position? Thereby, as the saying goes, hangs a tale which helps illuminate our guiding principle that "Old 'Loopholes' Never Die . . ."

Go back to October, 1942, in the United States Senate. Senator Elmer Thomas of Utah had run into heavy weather in his effort to confer percentage depletion on rock asphalt as well as ball and sagger clay. He resorted to the ultimate senatorial weapon. To "clarify the issue," he told his brethren that if the clay-asphalt amendment should be defeated, he intended to propose the repeal of percentage depletion for *all* minerals save the sacred oil and gas. Then, glowering at his critics, he began to lash them with the list of depletion-favored products in their own states: timber in La Follette's Wisconsin, copper and iron mines in Senator Prentiss Brown's Michigan. Apparently the lesson was not lost on other senators, for rock asphalt and ball and sagger clay were voted into the pending tax bill, war or no war.

The next round of depletion-blessed minerals, approved in 1943, gave a stirring demonstration of the imperishability of tax preferences. Although the 1943 depletion grants were destined, by statutory decree, to perish with the end of World War II, when peace came Congress quickly (and with little opposition) resurrected them—and even added a few new minerals just for good measure. Today, these "temporary" depletion war babies are twenty years old, and show no signs of fading.*

Since 1942, the list of tax-favored minerals has become all-encompassing, and there is likely not a single state without its own built-in pro-depletion lobby. Thus, by meticulously hanging together,† the beneficiaries of depletion have brilliantly avoided hanging separately.

---

* The same durability was exhibited by the tax deduction for personal medical expenses. When it was initially enacted, in 1942, it was supposedly to last only during the "emergency." Not only has it survived; like all good tax preferences, it has been expanded. Annual revenue cost today: $1.4 billion.

† In asking for a 15 percent depletion allowance, for example, the Sand and Gravel Association went to repeated pains to emphasize to the Senate

In the case of oil and coal, the spreading of equity (and federal largesse) reached a state of exquisite logic. On the one hand, Congress gave the oil and gas industry a massive injection of percentage depletion to spur exploration and development, but this proved to have an unhappy side effect: the expansion of the industry and the prodigious use of oil and gas for fuel and energy drove the coal industry into a state of chronic illness. To Congress, the prescription was clear: simply double the dose of depletion for coal.

In the field of capital gains, the rendering of equity has also tested Congress' ingenuity, but the lawmakers have proved themselves up to the test. During World War II, for example, supposedly to induce businessmen to replace used machinery and equipment, Congress enacted the so-called "one-way street," which operated in an inventive manner: a machine sold at a *profit* was considered a "capital asset" and the profit taxed at the favorable 25 percent capital gains rate. But if the selfsame machine were sold at a *loss*, it suddenly ceased to be a "capital asset," so that the loss could be deducted at the much higher regular income tax rates (then 31 percent for corporations and up to 82 percent for individuals). One senator called this the "heads-I-win-tails-you-lose" provision. *

Some years later, a dispute arose between Internal Revenue and the courts as to whether sales of livestock "held for draft, breeding or dairy purposes" were entitled to capital gains treatment. In 1951, in order to end all doubt, the Senate Finance Committee herded all such livestock into the warm shelter of the

---

Finance Committee that "we do not wish to be regarded as asking, here, any reduction in the percentage depletion rate [for other minerals] provided for in the bill which passed the House."

* Although the "one-way street" was originally justified as helping achieve victory in total war, it too, proved durable enough to survive some fifteen years after the war's end. Not until 1962 was it partially repealed, but even then its most munificent aspect—its application to real estate—remained very much in force (see Chapter 8).

"one-way street" provision, and, always on guard against unfair discriminations, carefully included turkeys in the definition of "livestock." On the Senate floor, Minnesota's Senator Edward Thye sought a broader justice: if turkeys were worthy, why not chickens? There followed this exchange:

SENATOR DOUGLAS: Would the Senator from Minnesota consider the possibility of adding ducks, angora cats and dogs to his amendment?
SENATOR THYE: There would be some justification for adding the ducks, though ducks are not equal in importance to either turkeys or chickens with respect to the national income. The senator has an argument there, but when one goes too far down the ladder . . . he may get into a category which causes someone possibly to look upon the proposition as ridiculous.

Finance Committee Chairman Walter George apparently also feared the Senate was on the brink of the ludicrous. "I certainly cannot [accept] the chicken amendment," he told the Senate. "Turkeys were included somehow, I do not know how . . . I cannot conceive that Congress ever had in mind [according capital gains treatment] to assets which are purely transitory." Senator Williams of Delaware quickly jumped to Senator George's aid with an amendment to deny capital gains treatment to livestock which, he said, were clearly "transitory." But he apparently overstepped the bounds of helpfulness, for Senator George ungratefully rebuffed his proposal. "It would be a dangerous thing indeed," he intoned, "to say that the whole [livestock capital gain] section should be impaired" by so lowly a creature as a chicken or turkey. The turkey amendment, incidentally, perished at the hands of a heartless House-Senate conference committee, but the livestock provision is still in the law, bringing tax joy to many a movie star and other top-bracket taxpayer (see pp. 139-141).

Still another chain of dispensations sprang from Congress'

rectifying a supposed inequity regarding timber. Prior to 1943, if timberland owner A caused his trees to be cut and *then* sold them, he paid regular income tax rates while his neighbor, B, who sold the timber without cutting it, paid only the favorable 25 percent capital gains tax—a clear discrimination against A. So Congress proceeded to apply the customary and approved remedy: lower A's taxes to the level of B's. (So disturbed were the lawmakers about this particular discrimination that they made the remedy retroactive some 30 years—back to 1913.)

Later, in 1951, Congress felt a need to bestow tax relief on coal royalty recipients whose contracts had unforesightedly neglected to tie the royalty payments to the rising price of coal. The chosen *form* of tax relief for this "hardship" was to confer the special capital gains rate on coal royalty income. The chosen *rationale*: coal royalties would simply be receiving "the same treatment as timber royalties." Sidelight: Although the alleged "hardship" was suffered only by past royalty contracts, the remedy was made available to *future* contracts as well. To discriminate between the two would, of course, have been inequitable.

In granting capital gains treatment to coal royalties, however, Congress had created still another inequity which cried out for correction: it had denied comparable tax treatment to iron ore royalties. The Kennedy Administration perceived the discrimination and proposed the unorthodox remedy of repealing the favorable treatment enjoyed by coal royalties. This, however, did not accord with the congressional sense of justice; in 1963 instead of repealing the coal provision, the House Ways and Means Committee simply extended it to cover iron ore.

In 1951, Congress decreed that crops standing on farm land at the time it is sold should, like timber, be shaded by the capital gains umbrella. Thus, a farmer can time the sale of his land just before harvest time and have the proceeds of his year's work taxed at the 25 percent rate instead of his regular tax rates.

The last link in the chain (to date, at least) came in 1954, when Congress corrected an apparent ambiguity: capital gains for timber, the law now assures all and sundry, definitely *includes* the sale of "evergreen trees which are more than 6 years old at the time severed from the roots and are sold for ornamental purposes"—which, as we have seen, is the legally acceptable way of describing a simple Christmas tree.

If the specially-tailored Louis B. Mayer amendment (p. 44) struck you as an unwarranted tax favor, it was only because you had not been properly indoctrinated in "the new equity," under which it would have been heartless and unfair to treat Mr. Mayer any other way. It may be recalled that rather than waiting for the year-by-year share of M-G-M profits to which he was entitled after leaving the company, Mr. Mayer wished his money all in one lump. In asking that Mr. Mayer be spared the tax consequences of this wish (via being permitted to pay only a 25 percent capital gains tax on the lump-sum settlement), his attorney appealed to precedent and to Congress' sense of fairness: "The justice of this approach," attorney Alvord pointed out, "has already received congressional approval" in permitting capital gains taxation of lump-sum *pension* pay-outs. Judging from the way the Mayer amendment was finally tailored (see p. 48), there was just enough merit in Mr. Alvord's argument to cover Louis B. Mayer, but no others.

One guiding principle of taxation seems to be that one good tax favor deserves another. Social security and railroad retirement benefits, for example, have always been tax-free, but the pensions of federal, state and local employees are taxable. "Discrimination!" cried the teachers, the policemen and firemen. "Discrimination!" answered Congress in 1954, by enacting the retirement income credit (pp. 210-211). Current annual cost to the Treasury: $135 million.

In 1948, the blessings of income-splitting (joint return filing) were bestowed on married people, but plainly the chain of tax concessions could not end here. What, for example, of the bachelor supporting his mother, brothers and sisters—is he not entitled to tax relief? Of course he is, Congress was compelled to conclude, although only half as much as, say, a less-burdened childless married couple. (Might we one day witness a bachelors' march on Washington in search of "tax equity"?) And what of the suddenly-bereaved widow or widower—did Congress really intend to add to the blow by abruptly withdrawing the marital tax dispensation? Clearly not, and so they were given a two-year cushion to soften the impact.

And what is a doctor or lawyer or small-business owner to think when corporations are permitted tax-deductible contributions to employee pension plans, but the self-employed are denied comparable tax-deductions in providing for their old age? Ask the spokesmen for the American Bar or Medical Associations or for groups as diverse as the National Funeral Directors Association or the Society of American Florists and Ornamental Horticulturists—groups which for years besieged Congress with cries of "discrimination." In 1962, at long last, they prevailed in part (see p. 220). But, as with most "creeping preferences," the country has not heard the last of this one, for many self-employed groups are not covered by the 1962 measure. "I have no doubt," said Senator Smathers of Florida, principal senatorial sponsor of the bill, "that sooner or later we are going to make this type of [tax deductible] pension program available to anyone who is not otherwise in a position to get into such a program . . . In my opinion, it is a matter of time before this goal is achieved."

And so it goes, with each tax concession containing the seeds of still others, in a process that is strikingly unidirectional. As Senators Long of Louisiana and McCarthy of Minnesota once put it, "the principle seems to be that if inequity is *extended*, justice is achieved." And Senator Albert Gore of Tennessee comments: "It seems never to occur to some that provisions of law can be equalized by *taking away* some benefits . . ." (Such a thought did occur, briefly, to the Ways and Means Committee when in 1961 it tentatively voted to repeal a tax deduction enjoyed by life insurance but not casualty insurance companies. But the displeasure of the life insurance companies was such that the vote was later reversed. The Senate Finance Committee's thinking was more in keeping with tradition: it voted to extend the tax deduction to casualty *as well as* life insurance companies. But this happy solution was postponed, pending further study.)

Where will the process lead and end? Already imaginative pleas have been entered for the enlargement of the percentage depletion family. The National Patent Council, for example, has suggested that depletion be bestowed on inventions since patents "can last only 17 years," after which inventions, like oil wells, are depleted of their value. The Jockeys' Guild of America has made what one senator called a "rather strong case" for granting depletion to racing jockeys "since their capabilities are in part physical, their average riding life is less than four years" and since, therefore, "their assets deplete."*

Outlandish? Far-fetched? Senator La Follette apparently thought that percentage depletion for sand and gravel was far-fetched. And what would he have said if someone had suggested to him, in 1942, that depletion would be granted in a few years to oyster shells and clam shells—and even water—or that turkeys would come within a feather of joining the capital gains family?

Randolph Paul once observed that "most of the inequities in the tax structure . . . are men who came to dinner and do not mean to go home."

Even since he wrote those words in 1955, the dinner table has become considerably more crowded.

---

* This was a facetious characterization by Senator Eugene McCarthy of Minnesota who, in the same speech, said "perhaps we should extend the depletion allowance to U.S. senators."

16 /

The Heavy Odds
Against Reform

The year is 1951. The Korean war is at its height. Billions of added revenue are needed to finance the war effort. In Room P-15 of the Capitol—a small, velvet-curtained room near the House of Representatives' chamber—five senators and six congressmen are grouped around a green felt-covered table resolving the differences between the House and Senate versions of a major revenue-raising bill.

On point after point, the lawmakers argue, bluff, trade, negotiate, compromise, until they come to the depletion allowances to be granted a broad array of new minerals. Then one legislator hits on a time-saving device: where there are differences on depletion between the two bills, why not automatically approve the more generous of the two versions? In a matter of seconds, the depletion question is resolved. The senators and congressmen are delighted. As one observer later described it, "A holiday mood prevailed."

Years later, an official who had seen the tax-writing process at first hand said of this incident, "Well, that's par for the course."

Tax favors are not usually bestowed so jovially; yet the history of the tax laws—and especially the history of percentage depletion since its adoption nearly forty years ago—confirm that this episode is "par for the course" in essence, if not in detail. Over the years, percentage depletion has been broadened to include a smörgåsbord of minerals and chemicals. Even at the crest of his New Deal power, with lop-sided Democratic majorities in Congress, Franklin Roosevelt was unable to get even a committee of Congress to make the slightest dent in the depletion provisions, which now cost the taxpayers a billion and a half dollars a year.

Of course, the broadening of tax preferences has by no means been confined to depletion. Even a cursory look at the tax laws confirms that they contain today far more preferences, exceptions, exclusions and advantages than existed five years ago, or ten or twenty—this despite an occasional tax-tightening here or there.

Judging by that evidence, the deck is heavily stacked against tax reform. Turning up a few of the cards in the deck discloses why: THE PRO-REFORM FORCES: diffuse, inarticulate, politically impotent (who ever heard of an anti-depletion "lobby"?) . . . THE ANTI-REFORM FORCES: highly focused, intensely vocal politically powerful . . . THE TAX-WRITING POWER IN CONGRESS: tightly held by two carefully chosen committees . . . THE COMPLEXITY OF THE TAX LAW: supremely technical, it confounds many lawyers, perplexes most congressmen, totally baffles the public . . . THE TAX EXPERTS AND LOBBYISTS: often they alone can find their way through the legal and verbal fog, which can shroud their actions from public understanding and scrutiny.

Each of these cards turns up not once but many times as a tax bill works its way through the legislative maze.

A major tax measure* enters the maze through the east door of the capacious hearing room belonging to the Committee on Ways and Means of the House of Representatives, in which body, the Constitution stipulates, all revenue measures must originate.

The measure makes its formal entrance when the Secretary of the Treasury steps through the east door, takes his seat before the twenty-five members of this tax-writing committee arrayed above him on a semi-circular dais, and presents the tax recommendations of the prevailing Administration.

A committee member interested in "loophole-closing" will do well to pay close attention to the Treasury Secretary, for as the ensuing weeks of hearings drone tediously on, there will be few other voices urging a tightening of the tax laws. For the most part, the committee will be bombarded by a procession of spokesmen for this industry, that company, this labor union— viewing with alarm or cautioning against an Administration proposal or, as often, seeking a widening of an existing preference to accommodate their supposedly unique tax problem.

For example, in 1963, the Ways and Means Committee allotted four days to hear witnesses on the Administration's proposals on oil and gas and other resource industries. In those four days, the committee heard from 67 officials, individuals or organizations (including 13 governors and 10 members of the House) regarding the Administration's principal proposal—*but not one of the 67 favored the reform*. It did receive support, in passing, from Columbia Professor Roy Blough, from the American Veterans' Committee, the National Farmers' Union and

---

* I.e., one that deals with broadly applicable portions of the tax code, as distinct from minor measures addressed to a particular industry problem or technical difficulty. Major "reform" measures—and the extensive hearing procedures described here—are by no means annual events. They occur whenever the Administration in power is moved to press for substantial tax revision (e.g., the Eisenhower Administration in 1954 and 1958 and the Kennedy Administration in 1961 and 1963).

three unaffiliated individual witnesses, but otherwise the proposal was entirely friendless. Even George Meany, president
of the AFL-CIO, made no mention of the oil proposals in his
statement to the committee, although a single sentence in an
appendix to the statement did acknowledge the depletion-
tightening recommendations were "desirable." Opposing witnesses ranged from the U.S. Chamber of Commerce and the
Manufacturing Chemists' Association to the San Joaquin Valley
Oil Producers Association of California.

To list these organizations is not to criticize them for presenting their view of the national interest, but simply to reinforce
the view expressed by Dr. Roy Blough that "general public
interests are not adequately represented in the pressures that
are brought to bear by taxpayer groups on Congress." Continues
Dr. Blough, a leading student of (and, as a former top Treasury
official, a first-hand participant in) the tax-writing process:
"[the] concentration of producer interests, and particularly of
business interests, in the proposals brought to Congress . . . make
it difficult for the members of the taxing committees to secure a
balanced view either of what is in the general interest, what the
public wants or what the public would want if it were informed
of the facts."

Even such a political orphan as foreign aid will find extra-
Administration support, at a congressional hearing, from such
groups as the League of Women Voters, the National Congress
of Parents and Teachers, the American Association of University
Women and a number of important church groups. But at a
tax hearing, those organizations are not in evidence. Even the
American Bar Association, which prides itself on dealing "with
tax questions on the basis of public interest alone," letting "the
chips fall where they may," is apt to be silent. In fact, Assistant
Treasury Secretary Stanley Surrey, writing as a Harvard law
professor, told how "many a lawyer representing a client seeking a special provision could without much difficulty obtain
American Bar Association or local bar association endorsement

for his proposal. He could then appear before Congress and solemnly exhibit the blessing of the legal profession."

Here and there, the witness list will include a college professor, a maverick tax attorney or accountant or, perhaps, the AFL-CIO or ADA, speaking up for a tax-tightening proposal. But by and large, the Treasury Department is the principal voice of tax reform.* While it can and does use the threat of a presidential veto to block or soften individual "loophole" bills, the Treasury possesses little of the political power that Washington responds to. Unlike the Labor or Agriculture Departments, it lacks the political leverage of a constituency of its own. In fact, the inherent posture of the Treasury is poorly calculated to win friends and influence congressmen since, in order to protect the revenues, the Department is chronically opposed to the special favors many lawmakers believe should be granted. Many congressmen thus come to think of the Treasury not as representing the collective interests of all taxpayers, but as a stiff-necked, theory-minded bureaucracy insensitive to the real-life problems of "flesh and blood" taxpayers.

Still, weak reed or strong, the Treasury is virtually all that the "loophole closers" have to lean on.

When the public hearings are finally concluded, the Ways and Means Committee descends from its dais and assembles around a U-shaped table to begin fashioning the tax bill it will recommend to the House.

The commodious room in which it labors—by far the largest of any House hearing room—attests the fact that Ways and Means is the House's most powerful legislative committee.

---

* Louis Eisenstein observes that even the Treasury Department may be a weaker reed than "ability to pay" adherents might imagine or wish, since "the precise views of the Treasury depend on those who occupy its seats of authority." Thus, "ability to pay" proponents might be equally unhappy with the Eisenhower Treasury for championing the dividend credit (see pp. 197-204) and with the Kennedy Treasury for espousing a lower capital gains tax rate.

Looking down from the pale green walls are the portraits of former Ways and Means chairmen, three of whom (Polk, Fillmore and McKinley) later ascended to the White House. But as Chief Executive, their power on tax matters could hardly have been greater than when they were in Congress. To illustrate: at the southwest corner of the committee hearing room hangs the portrait of Robert L. ("Muley") Doughton, who in 1949 suffered the indignity of having his committee approve, by a one-vote margin, a bill inimical to his North Carolina tobacco constituency. Shaken but not downed, Mr. Doughton successfully insisted that the President of the United States not only reverse the official Administration position on the measure, but that he telephone a pro-Administration committee member and request him to change his vote.

Ways and Means derives its power from three main sources. First, its Democratic members are endowed with the authority to grant or withhold politically-vital committee assignments for their Democratic colleagues. Second, the most politically-sensitive bills—tariff and social security as well as tax measures —fall under its jurisdiction. Third, Ways and Means maintains a particularly tight rein on the passage of all such bills and amendments in the House: by House procedure, no amendment to a major tax, tariff or social security bill may be made during floor debate without the assent of Ways and Means; and by committee practice, any "minor" tax or tariff bill desired by a *non*-committee member to aid a favored constituent has little chance of passage without the active support—preferably, the co-sponsorship—of a Ways and Means member.

But if this can be enlisted, the bill is virtually assured committee approval, thanks to an institution known as the "member's bill." At selected intervals each year, at closed-door committee meetings and without any public hearings, each Ways and Means member is permitted to call up a bill of his own choosing which, by gentleman's agreement and in a spirit of mutual helpfulness, generally wins unanimous committee approval. Usually, though not invariably, a member's bill is addressed to (or at least springs from) the tax problem of a lone taxpayer—such as the estate of a Charles Merrill, perhaps, or a Mrs. Gerard Swope (pp. 49 and 50). Generally, it is opposed by the Treasury Department, although this fact is held close to the bosom of the committee: the government agency comments (usually made public and frequently a tip-off that all is not as it should be) are conspicuously absent in the committee reports on member's bills—unless the comments are *favorable* to the bill.

The tight committee control over tax legislation is a crucial card in the "stacked deck," for it permits those who wish to block "loophole-closing," as well as those seeking special tax favors, to concentrate on a limited target. If they can win the favor of the few "swing" votes on Ways and Means, they can, by and large, ignore the other 400-plus members of the House. The impregnability of the depletion allowance is a case in point. It is generally assumed that depletion advocates can rely on at least ten Republican votes* so that no more than three Democratic votes are needed to carry that day. Since the Democratic leadership generally decides who should fill Ways and Means vacancies and since for twenty-one years Texas' Sam Rayburn *was* the Democratic leadership, the oil industry had little reason to be concerned.

One recent candidate for Ways and Means was "approached" (he declines to say by whom) for a commitment in favor of oil depletion and was told that all the other contestants for the seat had declared themselves pro-depletion, just as all prior-year candidates had. "If that's true," he replied, "the oil people certainly don't need *my* vote." He refused to commit himself one way or the other and was denied the Democratic leadership blessing he had hoped to receive.

---

* Ways and Means is one of three House committees that maintains a fixed party ratio—15–10—no matter what party line-up is in the House as a whole.

"Ways and Means is the strangest of all the House committees—and the hardest to understand," comments one reform-minded Democratic congressman. "Judging by the voting records of its members on the floor of the House, the liberals *ought* to have darn near a working majority. But their public *voting* records and their '*operating*' records in the committee, behind closed doors, are two different things."

A labor union lobbyist confirms this. He cites statistics compiled by the AFL-CIO showing that twelve of the fifteen Democrats on the Ways and Means vote "with labor" on major issues more than two-thirds of the time, eight of them more than nine-tenths of the time. Yet, he declaims angrily, few of them, in closed-door committee sessions, will vote to tighten "loopholes" against the well-to-do, as organized labor would like them to (and as consistency with their usual voting pattern would lead one to expect).* For example, *The New York Times* reported that the Kennedy proposals for curtailing the oil depletion allowance were initially defeated in Ways and Means "by a near-unanimous voice vote" in what the *Times* termed "a defeat for organized labor and liberals."

Says the union lobbyist: "These guys like to play games with the fat cats on tax issues. And they get away with it by voting with us often enough on other issues so the labor guys back home won't get sore at them. Besides," he adds, "I'm lucky if I can cover a couple of basic points on our 'must' list with these guys. We can't hold their feet to the fire on *everything*."

Not only union lobbyists are roaming the House Office Building corridors as Ways and Means works on a tax bill. Industry or company spokesmen are also making the rounds, making sure that committee members fully understand their clients' needs and views. One Republican Ways and Means member points

---

* One factor that may contribute to the discrepancy is the rareness of a name-by-name vote in closed committee sessions, and the practice of not officially announcing who voted how, even when such a roll is called. Thus, closed-door committee votes cannot be invoked against a candidate in an election campaign.

out, however, that the pressure-group spokesmen who seem to dominate the public hearings and the private buttonholing are barred from the closed-door committee sessions where the final arguments are heard and the decisions made and where Treasury Department officials, by long-standing practice, are present.

After weeks of labor, Ways and Means ultimately gives birth to the bill, for the cursory consideration of the House—cursory in part because of the "closed" or "gag" rule forbidding "outsiders" to offer amendments during House debate; cursory, too, because, as Louis Eisenstein has observed, "a vote on a tax bill . . . is an act of faith." So arcane is the field of taxation, so obscure the language in which tax laws are couched that few members of Congress comprehend what is in them.

Consider, for example, this passage, chosen at random from the Internal Revenue Code:

> If the allowance of a deficiency dividend deduction results in an overpayment of personal holding company tax for any taxable year, credit or refund with respect to such overpayment shall be made as if on the date of the determination 2 years remained before the expiration of the period of limitation on the filing of claim for refund for the taxable year to which the overpayment relates.

Clearly, the tax code amply deserves Eisenstein's characterization as "a remarkable essay in sustained obscurity" having "all the earmarks of a conspiracy in restraint of understanding." Admittedly, much of the tax code's intricacies are inherent in the difficulty of its assignment (trying to foresee and fairly accommodate the infinite variations in a modern economy). Nonetheless, this very complexity is a vital card in the "stacked deck" against tax reform, for it endows the experts and the "insiders" with unusual powers, and robs even the most vigilant congressman or newsman of his normal powers of scrutiny. What casual observer, for example, would be able to spot a bill innocuously entitled, "A bill to amend Part III of Subchapter O of the Internal Revenue Code of 1954" as being a bill to provide substantial retroactive tax relief to the Hilton Hotel chain (and, potentially, nineteen other unsuccessful defendants in anti-trust proceedings)?

Congressman Patman of Texas has observed that "the tax laws are passed with the Members not knowing exactly what they mean." Representative Jenkins of Ohio, a high-ranking Republican member of Ways and Means, said of his party's pride and joy, the tax bill of 1954, that it was "entirely too complicated to be mastered in detail in the time that we [the House] have in which to study it."

Perhaps then, some say, little is lost by the "closed rule" depriving the comparatively uninformed non-committee members from offering amendments during House debate, and there is a fear that opening the bill for amendment would result in endless horse-trading of one special provision for another. Because of this no-amendment rule, after brief debate and little or no change, a tax measure is passed by the House and sent to the tender mercies of the Senate Finance Committee.

Senate Finance has been variously called "the citadel of conservatism" and the "happy hunting ground" for tax pressure groups. At times, such as the early fifties, political "liberals" have had no representation on the committee; at best, they have been an impotent and frustrated minority. This is not entirely accidental: the two current windmill tilters, Senators Albert Gore of Tennessee and Paul Douglas of Illinois, both say they had great difficulty gaining their Finance Committee posts. According to Robert Engler, in *The Politics of Oil*, at one point in 1955 a committee vacancy thought sure to go to Douglas (a leading critic of the depletion allowance) was pre-empted by Majority Leader Lyndon Johnson who, later in the session, handed on the seat to former Vice President Alben Barkley, again stymying Douglas. It was only on Barkley's death that Douglas finally won his Finance Committee seat.

Whereas Ways and Means has, of late, been headed by two staunchly reform-minded chairmen (Jere Cooper of Tennessee and Wilbur Mills of Arkansas), Senate Finance has for decades been dominated by a procession of men in whose hearts "loop-hole-closing" kindled no great flame: Reed Smoot (of Smoot-Hawley Tariff fame) of Utah; Pat Harrison of Mississippi; Walter F. George of Georgia; Eugene Millikin of Colorado and Harry F. Byrd of Virginia.

As with all congressional committee chairmen, these men have possessed great power. For example, the fact that soft drinks were one of the few items that wholly escaped any excise tax during World War II, was not, according to knowing observers, wholly unrelated to the fact that the giant of the soft drink industry, Coca-Cola, has its headquarters in Senator George's home state. It is also said that the 3 percent "floor" on medical deductions was eliminated for those over 65 shortly after the elderly Senator George found that he could not deduct his own medical expenses one year, since they came to less than 3 percent of his income. When this waiver-for-the-aged amendment (estimated revenue cost: $15 million) came up in a closed-door Finance Committee session, one new staff member whispered surprise that the Treasury spokesman present did not speak up against the amendment. "He can't oppose this one," was the reply. "This one is old man George's amendment."

Because all tax bills must originate in the House, and because Ways and Means does not make an actual text of such bills available for public comment until after the public hearings have been concluded, Senate Finance sits as a court of appeals from the actions of the House. The Treasury, of course, has its opportunity to appeal from Ways and Means' rejection of its tax-tightening proposals. But, as in the House hearings, the preponderance of pleas come from private-interest spokesmen, protesting such "reforms" as the House did enact (or seeking added tax concessions), and it is rare that a reform bill emerges from Senate Finance stronger, from Treasury's viewpoint, than when it passed the House.

Although it deals with one of the most technical of governmental subjects, the Finance Committee, unlike Ways and Means, has not one single professional staff member to advise it on tax matters. To aid its deliberations, it relies instead, by long-standing practice, on the staff of the Joint Committee on Internal Revenue Taxation*—and, more particularly, on its chief of staff, Colin F. Stam.

A felicitous and perceptive article on Stam by E. W. Kenworthy of *The New York Times* is entitled "A Study in Anonymous Power." Both words are appropriate to this bald-pated, cardigan-sweatered man (who looks for all the world like a Franciscan monk) for his anonymity, outside the tax fraternity, is exceeded only by his power on tax matters. One lawyer told Kenworthy, with perhaps a touch of hyperbole, that this power has been greater, over the years, than that of the President, the Secretary of the Treasury and the chairmen of the tax-writing committees, separately or combined.

Stam's influence, which many feel has passed its crest, has derived in considerable measure from his encyclopedic knowledge of the tax law and its history, initially gained through ten painstaking years (1929-39) of consolidating a welter of separate tax laws into the Internal Revenue Code of 1939, and added to by his twenty-five years of subsequent service as Chief of Staff of the Joint Committee. Whereas the Treasury Department invariably imports a battery of specialists to committee sessions, each able to speak in a particular field, the committees may—and do—turn to Stam for background or advice across the whole spectrum of taxation, and he is frequently able to

---

* The Joint Committee, established in 1926, to oversee the operation, effects and administration of the Internal Revenue laws, technically consists of the five senior members of the Ways and Means and Senate Finance Committees. But to all intents and purposes, the Joint Committee is its professional staff of 7 lawyers and 5 economists which provides technical advice on tax matters both to Ways and Means and Finance.

keep committees or individual lawmakers from stubbing their
toes on hidden technicalities.

But his role is far more than that of a mere technician. Roy
Blough, for example, states that Stam has had "a profound influence over tax policy decisions."

Passages from a single week's hearings before Senate Finance
in 1951 illustrate the reliance placed on Mr. Stam's counsel. A
succession of witnesses was seeking special excess profits relief
amendments:

> *July 23*—SENATOR MILLIKIN (to a witness—former Sen-
> ator Joseph H. Ball of Minnesota—seeking an amendment
> on behalf of the Association of American Shipowners):
> Senator Ball, have you talked to Mr. Stam on it? . . . May
> I suggest you get in touch with him and have a talk with
> him . . .
>
> *July 24*—SENATOR TAFT: May I ask, Mr. Stam . . . do you
> see any particular reason why it [the requested relief
> provision] should not be done?
>
> *July 26*—SENATOR KERR: I would like to have Mr. Stam's
> reaction to that.
>
> *July 26*—SENATOR HOEY: Mr. Stam, what do you say
> about that?

As these passages suggest, a nod or a shake of Stam's head
can profoundly affect the fate of any proposed amendment—
especially in the closed-door sessions of the Senate Finance
Committee, where his influence reaches its full height—and
Colin Stam's office is a "must" call for many a Washington-wise
attorney seeking tax relief for his client.

How has Stam used his great influence? As with all powerful
men, opinions differ sharply and feelings run high. "Completely
objective," says a high-ranking Ways and Means Republican.
"That man has cost this country a hell of a lot of money," says a
Senate Finance Committee Democrat.

The main criticism leveled at Colin Stam is that he has no

philosophy of taxation, no fixed star to guide his path. One former Treasury official has seen Stam expound one line of argument in the House and the exact opposite in the Senate, accommodating himself to the conflicting views of the respective chairmen. When the committee chairmen have backed revenue-raising reforms, such as wage withholding in 1943, Stam has, too. But when they have opposed changes (as with the dividend and interest withholding in 1962), Stam has followed suit. To the extent he reveals any personal predilections in private conversation, they seem closely akin to the conservatism of Senate Finance Chairman Harry F. Byrd.

One former Stam staff member, while no admirer of Stam's, believes any criticism should be shifted to Stam's principals: the congressmen and senators he serves. "He gives them what they want. He doesn't argue with them—some think he ought to argue more than he does, but that's not the nature of the job." Stam himself seems to agree: he is there to serve the lawmakers, not the Treasury Department. Thus, if a Senator George looks with favor on bestowing tailored tax relief on a Louis B. Mayer, Colin Stam will—as he did in the Mayer case—draft the appropriate provision.

The Constitution prohibits the Senate from originating revenue bills (hence Finance has no "member's bill" procedure, as such) but it does not prevent the Senate from appending to a House-passed tax bill a wholly extraneous tax provision favored by one or other Senator. (As one committee member once put it, "What's the good of being on this committee, if you can't get through a little old amendment now and then?") For example, the Leo Sanders provision, bestowing hundreds of thousands of dollars of retroactive tax relief on an Oklahoma City contractor (p. 50), was tacked on to a House bill dealing with the transfer of patents between related persons. The sponsor of the Sanders provision, the late Senator Robert S. Kerr of Oklahoma, had a reputation as one of the most skillful and frequent exploiters of this technique. Recalls one fellow Finance Committee member: "Bob had a special way of explaining his 'innocent little amendments' so you'd be convinced you were just voting for 'simple justice.' But after it was all over and you'd find out what you'd really voted for, he'd cackle and say, 'Well, you know me—I'm against any conspiracy I'm not in on.'"

Says another Finance Committee senator: "It's in the last couple of hours of our work on a big tax bill—after all the Treasury proposals have been disposed of—that the 'little old amendments' begin pouring into the bill, so fast it's hard to keep track of them." At least two committee members were not even aware that the special retroactive provision for Howard Knipp (see p. 57) had been added to the 1962 tax bill by Senate Finance. One of these senators feels handicapped in spotting and objecting to these special provisions by the fact that Finance is one of the only Senate committees that denies its members the privilege of bringing their own personal staff members into closed-door sessions, to help with research, memoranda, special data. "Sometimes," he says, "we're just operating blindfolded."

Once Senate Finance has completed its work, it sends a tax measure to the Senate floor for debate, where the power of the Committee and, more particularly, of its chairman, are on full display.

While Senate rules do not prohibit the offering of "outsiders'" amendments, Senate custom decrees a high mortality rate for such provisions unless they are acceptable to the Finance Committee, which, understandably, the Senate regards as its expert agent in tax matters. In 1951, for example, a group of "outsiders," led by Minnesota's Hubert Humphrey, offered a series of "loophole-closing" amendments; each was defeated by at least a two-to-one margin.

Traditionally, the chairman of Senate Finance is the sole arbiter of the acceptability of "outsiders'" amendments, and senators may frequently be heard to plead, plaintively, "I am asking the chairman . . . whether he is willing to accept this amendment." Consistency is not required in the chairman's screening of desired provisions. Harry Byrd may, for example, righteously rebuff an effort by Vermont's Senator Ralph Flanders to bring tax relief to a particular Vermont citizen, on the ground that "this would establish a very dangerous precedent . . . attempting to pass a general law for one specific purpose"—while, on that same day, Chairman Byrd himself had shepherded through a measure tailor-made to bestow up to $4 million of tax relief on the estate of Mrs. Gerard Swope (pp. 49-50).

Frequently, "loophole-closing" amendments are either voted by the Senate or "accepted" by the chairman of the Finance Committee, only to perish shortly in the House-Senate conference committee named to reconcile the differences between the House and Senate versions of a measure. Senate liberals darkly suspect conservative Senate conferees of yielding too easily in the bargaining with the House. When in 1959 a Senate repeal of the dividend credit (by a 47-31 vote) failed to survive the House-Senate conference, Senator Douglas was prompted to liken the fate of such "loophole-closing" actions "to the fate of the two young princes of England who put their trust in Richard the Third, who went into the Tower of London under very good promises but were strangled by Richard the Third and never emerged from the Tower."

The closing days of Congress provide an unusually apt climate for the passage of specially-tailored tax relief provisions. The usually desultory machinery of Congress springs to life, and bills whose passage would ordinarily require weeks or months begin to skim through with only the most superficial consideration (viz., the special bill for Congressman Cannon mentioned on pp. 53-54, which cleared the congressional obstacle course in less than two days).

An end-of-session case study is that of the "Bridgeport Brass"

amendment, fashioned to bring excess profits tax relief to the
Connecticut company, which came before the Senate in the
closing days of the 1952 congressional session. Senator Douglas,
alerted to the tailor-made nature of the provision, objected to
its passage, but not before two other made-to-order provisions
had been added to the measure—one specifically for the Budd
Company of Philadelphia and the Sangamo Electric Company
of Springfield, Illinois, the other, offered by ancient Senator
McKellar of Tennessee, making a favorable adjustment in the
coal depletion allowance.

Poised in the Senate gallery were the representatives of
Bridgeport Brass. Upon Douglas' objection, they made a beeline
for him and, aided by their home state senator and the ideological ally of Douglas, William Benton, they entered their plea.
Finally persuaded their case had merit, Douglas was troubled
now by the other two special provisions that had become part
of the bill. Based on the assurances of a reform-minded Ways
and Means member that he would do all possible to scuttle
these two provisions in the House-Senate conference, Douglas
withdrew his objection. The "par for the course" outcome: all
the provisions—for Bridgeport Brass, for the Budd Company,
for Sangamo Electric and for Senator McKellar's constituents—
were approved by the conference committee and became law.
But there is an ironic postscript: due to a quirk in the wording
of the Bridgeport Brass provision, the company did not get the
relief intended for it.

The specially-tailored relief provisions are, by and large, the
mark left on the tax laws by the Washington tax lobbyist.
Typically, he is a lawyer, but he is probably less sought after
for his legal acumen than for his intimate knowledge of what
makes the legislative and political wheels go round and, particularly, for his contacts and entrees on "the Hill." Thus, he
might well be a former senator or congressman or, perhaps, an
ex-congressional staff aide. One former Treasury official tells of

witnessing the Ways and Means Committee approve a tailor-made relief bill for a company represented by a former Ways and Means staff member—on the ground that "we've got to do something to help out old _____."

The Washington lobbyist is likely to be generously rewarded for his efforts—his fee may run into the hundreds of thousands if his assigned mission is special relief legislation—but this is not astonishing in view of the considerable tax savings involved. The Louis B. Mayer provision, for example, saved Mayer $2 million; and a Washington lawyer matter-of-factly mentioned in a sidewalk conversation that his success in changing a single date in one tax measure meant a $3 million saving for his client, and that the insertion of such a technicality as a parenthetical cross-reference in another statute brought comparable savings to a second client.

Sometimes the introduction of special-relief legislation will help a lobbyist secure a favorable ruling for his client from Treasury or Internal Revenue. One Washington attorney, whose request for a ruling was rejected by Treasury, persuaded a top-ranking Ways and Means member to introduce a relief-giving bill. Not long thereafter, the ruling he had been denied unexpectedly arrived in the morning mail. Reason: Treasury, discovering the particular case that prompted the congressman's bill, and preferring a one-case ruling to a generally applicable law, had beat a strategic retreat and reversed its stand. (This was precisely the procedure used by Wisconsin Representative John Byrnes, top-ranking Republican on Ways and Means, to secure reversal of an Internal Revenue ruling adverse to a Wisconsin insurance company in which, it was later revealed, Mr. Byrnes then acquired a stock interest.)

Given their special power, the chairmen of Ways and Means and Finance are clearly the most advantageous "Hill" contacts —both for the lobbyist and for his client. None, perhaps, has attained the success, in this line, of Ellsworth C. Alvord, the attorney who, acting as official spokesman for the United States

Chamber of Commerce, successfully appealed for special relief for his personal client, Louis B. Mayer. Alvord was known to be on the most cordial terms with Chairman George of the Finance Committee. Lest anyone doubt the intimacy of Mr. Alvord's relationship with the committee, those attending a Finance hearing might frequently see the tall, striking frame of Mr. Alvord appear in the private committee-room entrance supposedly reserved for senators, stand poised in the doorway surveying the audience, and then disappear into the private recesses of the Finance Committee chambers.

You are not likely to find the tax lobbyist registered as such on Capitol Hill under the lobbying law—Alvord, for example, did not register as a representative of Mr. Mayer.*

There is little talk in Washington of personal venality among the senators and congressmen who sponsor special tax amendments, but campaign contributions are another matter. One high-ranking Senate Finance Committee member, asked by a newsman about his uncharacteristic sponsorship of several pro-insurance company amendments, explained, in an unguarded moment: "This is the way we finance our campaigns. Hell, I wish there was a tax bill up every year."

The astute lobbyist seeks to minimize the Washington pressure and maximize the "back-home" influences. One Ways and Means member tells of receiving a call on behalf of the oil depletion allowance from a friend and business associate who was also the local representative of a major oil company. The friend acknowledged frankly that he was only calling at the behest of company headquarters in the state capital.

To bolster congressional support for a bill making an exception for DuPont's court-ordered sale of all its General Motors stock, DuPont and General Motors each sent letters to their millions of stockholders throughout the country urging them to

---

* Many attorneys take the view that the vaguely-worded lobbying statute does not apply to the particular activities in which they happen to engage.

write their congressmen and senators on the bill's behalf. The response was impressive.

Ordinarily, mail from constituents has little effect on a legislator's vote. But when it comes in torrents, it can be decisive—as it was in the case of the mail blitz credited with the defeat of tax withholding for dividends and interest (see pp. 168-172). This blitz had its origins in private dining room No. 4 of the Palmer House in Chicago on March 26, 1962, according to James McCartney of the *Chicago Daily News*. There, the "legislative subcommittee" of the U.S. Savings and Loan League—the trade association of savings and loan companies—resolved, after a four-hour debate, to organize a massive letter-writing campaign by the thirty million users of savings and loan institutions.

Four days later, a mailing went out to the League's 4,800 member institutions, with sample "Dear Saver" form letters to send to their customers. Treasury officials recall with bitterness what they feel was an erroneous implication, in these mailings, that the proposed withholding plan involved a *new* tax, and not merely the payment of a tax that had been due all along. A typical "Dear Saver" letter said: "If you agree that *this proposed withholding tax* is unfair then you can do something about it . . . [tell] the senators so, in your own words, and preferably in your own handwriting."* (Emphasis added)

Reports McCartney: "Soon the deluge began to fall on the Capitol, first in letters by the handful, then by the box, then by the cartload, then by the carload. Before it was over Paul Douglas had received 75,000 letters, Senator John Sherman Cooper [of Kentucky] got 60,000. Nobody in the Senate remembers anything quite like it."

At the time of the Palmer House meeting in Chicago, a Savings and Loan League expert estimated "we didn't have the

---

* Some of the anti-withholding newspaper advertisements were even blunter about the "new tax" idea. One in Oak Park, Illinois, for example, warned, in large type, about a "threatening new 20 percent tax."

votes in the Senate" to kill the withholding plan. But after the
blitz, the vote in Senate Finance was 11 to 5 and in the Senate
as a whole 66 to 20 against withholding.

Mail blitzes such as this operate in only one direction: they
sometimes defeat but they never rescue a tax-tightening proposal; on the contrary, reform-minded congressmen report they
get almost no "pro-reform" mail to spur them on—another of
the cards that help to stack the deck.

The same ingredients that endow the opponents of "loophole-
closing" with vitality and articulateness also divide and mute the
forces of reform. "You would expect us labor guys to go all out
to tighten up on expense account high living," says one top-
ranking AFL-CIO official. "But we had Actors Equity and the
hotel and restaurant and bartenders' union on our necks telling
us that an expense-account crackdown would ruin the theaters
and the restaurant and hotel business. So while we went on
record for the tighter rules, we couldn't mount an all-out
campaign."

The voice of the Treasury can also be muted. Congress makes
no effort to conceal its distaste for outspoken Treasury re-
formers. During World War II, Randolph Paul, the dean of tax
reform and then a top Treasury official, took to the speech
circuit to defend the Roosevelt tax program. This incurred the
displeasure of the Chairman of Ways and Means and the
speech-making came to a prompt halt. And President Kennedy's
appointment of Stanley Surrey, Harvard law professor and
apostle of tax reform, as top Treasury tax official, "spurred a
vigorous effort by oil companies and other groups to block the
appointment," the *Wall Street Journal* reported. Surrey was subjected to a merciless grilling by Senate Finance, and only an
assurance by Secretary of the Treasury Douglas Dillon that he,
not Surrey, would decide tax policy, clinched Surrey's Senate
confirmation.

Reform proposals can easily fall by the wayside at any point in the legislative obstacle course. For example, in 1958 and 1959, a panel of legal experts worked long and hard, at Congress' invitation, to devise reforms in the field of estates, trusts and partnerships. Their proposal was approved by Ways and Means, passed by the House, cleared Senate Finance and seemed close to passage. But somehow the measure could not find a place on the agenda of Senate debate and died. Why? Because, it is commonly believed, its provisions for tightening up on tax avoidance through multiple trusts (see p. 79) were distasteful to the prevailing Senate Democratic leaders. The reform has never since been revived.

Faced with a continuous uphill struggle, reform-minded legislators are apt to lose their zeal over the years. Minnesota's Senator Eugene McCarthy, who twice led the effort in the Senate to repeal the dividend tax credit, noted a severe attrition of his allies on the second go-round. His explanation: "A lot of senators came to me and said, 'I took a lot of heat for my vote the last time—and anyway,' they said, 'it's futile.' "

But it isn't entirely futile. Many efforts to enact new "loopholes" are rebuffed; and Congress does, from time to time, abolish or constrict tax preferences.* It should not be short-changed on the credit due it. Nor should anyone underrate the staggering difficulty of the task confronting congressional tax-writers, for theirs is easily the toughest legislative job Congress undertakes. And, as acknowledged by even such a congressional critic as Stanley Surrey, "its accomplishment in this field may be measured favorably against the tax systems of other countries."

Nevertheless, over the years, the exceptions and the preferences in the tax laws have grown rather than diminished in number, and if this chronicle of the tax-writing process is incomplete—as any, especially of this length, must be—it is because it has deliberately focused on those factors underlying this almost unarguable fact.

---

* Examples: The stricter taxation of life insurance companies in 1959; and of American businesses overseas in 1962.

Virtually all these factors—the lop-sided parade of witnesses at the public tax hearings . . . the member's bill procedure . . . the tight control of power in the two tax-writing committees . . . the power of the experts and the tax lobbyists . . . the one-sidedness of constituents' letters on tax matters—all are symptomatic of a basic cause: either the public doesn't understand about tax preferences or doesn't care about them, or both.

One member of Ways and Means, the most vocally reform-minded of the twenty-five, thinks it's the latter. "The average American," he says, a bit regretfully, "doesn't mind other people having their own 'loopholes'—he only cares about getting his. So you shouldn't blame Congress or the committees about what the American people don't want. If we don't vote tax reform, it's simply because there's no pressure for it."

17 /

What Should Be Done About "The Great Treasury Raid"?

Why is there no public pressure for "loophole-closing"?

Is it because the public doesn't *care* about taxes? Not likely; rare is the man who can honestly say he doesn't care how much tax he pays.

More probably it's because tax reform debates have, by and large, been conducted in such a way that the public can't participate. In part, the issues have been posed and debated in terms that mean little or nothing to the taxpayers, who have never been given much reason to feel that *they* had enough to gain from "loophole-closing" to warrant a pro-reform letter to a congressman.

By way of illustration, take one of the capital gains "loophole-closing" proposals in the 1963 Kennedy reform program. Suppose the Gallup Poll asked:

Do you think coal royalties should receive capital gains tax treatment?

The response could easily be somewhat as follows:

What is capital gains tax treatment?	21%
What are coal royalties?	19%
How should I know?	60%

Or the response might well be, "Why should I care?" After all, this particular "loophole" only means, at the best, a few cents a year on the average person's tax bill.

Suppose, on the other hand, the question of capital gains taxation were posed more broadly. Suppose a taxpayer were asked to match his entire year's earnings—let's say $6,000—against an identical amount his neighbor made by selling some stock at a $6,000 profit. Suppose the question were then to be posed this way:

Dollar for dollar, your neighbor's $6,000 will do just as well as yours when it comes to buying food, or clothes—or a new car or a Florida vacation.

Why won't it do just as well when it comes to paying taxes?

Why should he pay less taxes on his $6,000 than you do on your $6,000?

When a tax reform debate begins posing questions like that, then the public can join the discussion.

Or, take another of the 1963 Kennedy reform proposals, dealing with percentage depletion for oil. Suppose the question were asked:

Do you believe oil investors should be allowed to carry over their excess deductions or group their properties so as to raise the 50-percent-net-income ceiling?

It would not be surprising if the response were a glazed look of total non-comprehension. But suppose the question were framed thus:

Do you believe the oil industry should be allowed tax deductions for non-existent investments?

Do you believe we should be spending $1½ billion every year to subsidize oil exploration when Texas oil wells are deliberately being held to less than 30 percent production—and when they can't even sell that much oil?

Those, too, are questions a taxpayer can discuss. There are others he might be induced to write his congressman about, such as:

Why should *earned* income be taxed more severely than *unearned* income? That is, why should the tax system penalize those who work for a living? (See pp. 235-236.)

Why should even one person—much less five—have $5 million of income and pay no taxes? (See p. 4.)

Why should the government pay more of a rich man's than of a poor man's medical expenses or charitable gifts— or, for that matter, fender-fixing costs? (See p. 221.)

Why should the average multimillionaire pay less taxes, proportionately, than others with but a small fraction of his income? (See pp. 5-6.)

Suppose, moreover, the taxpayers were told that an across-the-board "loophole-closing" program *would pave the way for a 45 percent cut in all tax rates*—that is, for a rate schedule ranging from 11 percent to 50 percent, instead of the 20 percent to 91 percent that prevailed through 1963? Then, perhaps, they might feel there was something in it for *them.**

---

* True, the Kennedy 1963 reform program was supposedly tied to the "carrot" of a $10 billion tax cut. But it was clear throughout that the two

Unhappily, though, tax reform programs have not posed such questions or offered such stakes. They have, instead, been tailored to the "politically possible." Yet that phrase must have a hollow and ironic ring to those who survey the wreckage of what they had fashioned to fit the boundaries of political reality.

These past reform programs could be likened to an effort to put partial patches over the punctures in a worn out old tire. Yet, while supposedly designed with an eye to the "politically practical," this partial-patch approach suffers two political weaknesses. First, it implies that there is nothing wrong *in principle* with a leaky tire or with the punctures themselves; it's just that some of them are a little too large. (Thus, the debate centers around fringe technicalities, rather than basic questions, and the public is relegated to the sidelines.) Second, so long as *some* groups continue to enjoy tax favors, "loophole-closing" will have trouble winning friends and influencing congressmen. It is not surprising, for example, that even such a reform-minded senator as Maurine Neuberger, from the timber-laden state of Oregon, should have opposed the Kennedy proposal to end capital gains treatment for timber. "How could I vote for a tax crackdown on timber," she asks, "as long as the oil industry still has its depletion loophole?" In a similar vein, AFL-CIO President George Meany opposed ending the $100-per-week tax-free "sick pay" provision (see p. 219) on the ground that to eliminate this tax concession "in the name of equity would hardly be fair when so many glaring loopholes available to the wealthy are still tolerated."

Apparently, then, if there is a "politically practical" way out of the tax-preference maze (and many believe none exists) it does not lie in the partial-patch approach, but in starting afresh —with a wholly new tire, of modern design.

---

were not tied, and that the Administration was prepared to jettison the reform (which only accounted for about a third of the tax-cut "carrot" anyway) in order to get its true goal—the "economic stimulus" of a massive tax cut.

It is, of course, a violation of every political axiom—and of common sense, too—to suggest that where a partial "loophole-closing" program has proved unattainable, a more far-reaching request would fare better. Perhaps the only answer is that a fresh approach could not fare much worse; and if it were a program the public could take the measure of, and respond to, it might do better.

Herewith, then, a suggestion for a simplified income tax—a tax which more nearly approaches the concept suggested by the Sixteenth Amendment, taxing income "from whatever source derived," in a uniform manner—*but at rates only half as high as those in effect prior to 1963.*

Under this system, making out your tax return would be far simpler and faster than it is today. It would, in essence, be a three-step operation:

Step One: Add up all your income for the year—that is, everything you received that gave you an ability to buy things (more below about what this includes).

Step Two: Subtract from this:

(a) a certain amount (to be set by Congress) for yourself and each dependent*

(b) any costs you incurred in getting your income (just as you do now on your tax return)†

Step Three: Taking the above result, compute your tax from the following rate schedule:

The word "income," in Step One, means all those things that give you what economists term "control over economic resources"—or, in layman's language, ability to buy things. This

---

* This exemption, similar to that now in the tax law, is based on the premise that there is a minimum level below which the tax system should not reach. It achieves the same effect as putting a zero-bracket in the rate schedule except that it takes into account differences in family.

† The return of your capital outlays would continue to be non-taxable, as at present. Percentage depletion allowances would be ruled out, however, and mineral industries placed on the same deduction basis (i.e., original cost) as other industries.

If Income Is:		Tax Would Be:*	
Under $2,000		11%	
	This	Plus this %	Of excess over
$2–4,000	$220	12%	$2,000
$4–6,000	$462	14%	$4,000
$6–8,000	$748	16.5%	$6,000
$8–10,000	$1,078	19%	$8,000
$10–12,000	$1,452	21%	$10,000
$12–14,000	$1,870	24%	$12,000
$14–16,000	$2,343	26%	$14,000
$16–18,000	$2,860	27.5%	$16,000
$18–20,000	$3,410	29%	$18,000
$20–22,000	$3,993	31%	$20,000
$22–26,000	$4,609	32%	$22,000
$26–32,000	$5,907	34%	$26,000
$32–38,000	$7,953	36%	$32,000
$38–44,000	$10,010	38%	$38,000
$44–50,000	$12,375	40%	$44,000
$50–60,000	$14,751	41%	$50,000
$60–70,000	$18,876	43%	$60,000
$70–80,000	$23,166	45%	$70,000
$80–90,000	$27,621	46%	$80,000
$90–100,000	$32,241	48%	$90,000
$100–150,000	$37,026	49%	$100,000
$150–200,000	$61,501	49.5%	$150,000
$200,000	$86,251	50%	$200,000

* *This rate schedule is basically illustrative.* It does not take into account the impact on various income groups of the elimination of various preferences. It is simply constructed on the assumption that the elimination of various tax preferences would add $40 billion to the $50 billion of revenue now derived from the personal income tax, and that therefore a 45 percent cut in all tax rates could be accommodated without any loss of revenue.

would include, of course, your wage and salary income, including those fringe benefits paid for by your employer and actually received by you;* your social security and other government benefits (now non-taxable); and *all* your interest income, including interest on state and local bonds† and on life insurance savings.

You would, of course, report *all* your capital gains (instead of just half, as at present). This would include those gains in your investment portfolio at the time of your death. You would, however, be allowed full deductions of all your capital *losses*, at your regular income tax rates, and there would be an averaging device (See Glossary) that would permit "bunched" income of various sorts—not merely capital gains—to be taxed as if it had been received over a period of years.

The benefits of marital income-splitting would be ended, but without reverting to the chaotic conflict between the community-property and the common-law states that obtained prior to 1948‡ (see p. 71). The new tax law would also have to contain safeguards to prevent the artificial splitting of income within family units (through such devices as controlled trusts, family partnerships, and the like).

Strict, logical adherence to the criterion of "ability to buy things" would require taxing such things as gifts, bequests and life insurance proceeds as they are received, as well as such income-equivalents as the return on your investment in your home (or car), the free services provided by your bank in lieu of interest payments on your deposits, the food and fuel produced and consumed on farms, and others. Some of these (e.g.,

---

* To the extent these can be practically and accurately measured on a taxpayer-by-taxpayer basis. Under this standard, some "income in kind"—such as an occasional free meal furnished by an employer—would not be taxed.

† Congress might well wish to accompany this with a direct subsidy program that would keep state and local borrowing costs down to their present levels. See pp. 193-194.

‡ This would be accomplished by continuing to permit the filing of joint returns by married couples, but providing a separate rate schedule for the joint-return filers with brackets twice as wide as those applicable to unmarried taxpayers. This would put single and married taxpayers on a par.

bank services, food and fuel) are not susceptible to an accurate taxpayer-by-taxpayer measurement, and an effort to tax them would not be worth the administrative and compliance headaches it would cause. Some say this is also true of the rental-equivalent of owned homes, and to tax imputed rental income and not other kinds of "imputed" income would present a troublesome inconsistency. Besides, with all outlays for interest and taxes no longer deductible, the principal discrimination now suffered by home renters would be eliminated. As to gifts, bequests and insurance proceeds, an effective gift-estate tax structure, as suggested in Chapter 14, would subject most of these to tax at the time of their transfer.

The subtraction side of your tax return might well include deductions for *major* medical expenses and casualty losses (i.e., those in excess of, say, 5 percent of your income), on the dual ground that such expenses are irregular and therefore cannot be planned for in family budgeting, and that they uncontrollably deprive a taxpayer of much of his "ability to buy things."

There might also be a tax incentive to charitable giving*— although if you crack the tent an inch, a dozen (or more) camels' noses will present themselves, each with a claim on the tax system to foster this or that publicly-beneficial activity (isn't home ownership, for example, almost as unarguable a virtue as charity?). Other techniques for encouraging philanthropy should therefore be explored before invading the tax system for this purpose. In England, for example, an individual's gift is matched by a gift from the government to the same charity. Thus, the charity is benefited, but the tax tent remains tightly closed.

---

* If such a concession is granted, it should certainly be in the form of a tax *credit* (see Glossary) instead of a deduction, so that a like portion of each person's generosity, be he rich or poor, would be borne by the government.

The skeleton plan suggested here does not purport to deal with all the problems involved in the fashioning of any tax system. But surely such problems as would arise in the design of a simplified income tax system, as here suggested, would be no more intricate than those with which the technicians must wrestle under the existing "house of horrors" (as Representative Wilbur Mills has characterized the present tax code). In fact, with capital gains taxed on a par with other income, and with the institution of an averaging device for "bunched" income, many existing problems would either become far simpler or would disappear entirely.

Most tax experts have no doubt that a simplified system of this sort would work. Their doubts concern its congressional acceptability, not its workability.

The advantages of such a simplified plan are many. It would mean a fairer tax system—in that everyone would pay taxes more nearly according to a uniform rate schedule. No system of taxation can be expected to render Solomon-like justice for each of forty-eight million individual taxpayers. But any departures from this ideal flowing from a simplified, broadly-based tax plan would surely not be as massive as the existing discrimination against those whose income is wholly earned (especially the high-paid professionals), or as flagrant as the anomaly of the average multimillionaire paying less taxes, proportionately, than taxpayers with a fraction as much income (see pp. 5-6).

A no-preference tax system would mean an end to high top-bracket rates. Not only do these muffle incentives; they provide a rationale and an acceptability for many of the existing tax preferences. That the government should take 70 percent—or, prior to 1964, 75, 80 or 90 percent of a man's dollars is offensive to many who are not even subject to those rates, and their indignation over a tailor-made Louis B. Mayer amendment may be tempered by the thought that without it, he would have had to pay nearly 90 percent of his termination pay to the Treasury.

With lower rates, decision-making in American business would be less dominated by the "tax angle," and there would be less cause for the valid complaint voiced by *Life's* chief editorial writer, John K. Jessup, that this "tax angle" has "distorted business judgments, discouraged innovation and diverted millions of expensive man-hours from productive work."

Under a general no-preference rule, in instances where government action is called for, there would be more disposition to look to other more direct and efficient governmental means of fostering particular social or economic activity, and less ready resort to the usually clumsier and costlier techniques the tax system offers. (For example, it required $2.5 *billion* of federal revenue loss, via the "investment credit" and the more liberal 1962 depreciation rules, to stimulate an added $1.1 *billion* of business investment, which means there was more than a 50 percent "slippage," or waste.)

Finally, a simplified tax plan would mean a more *forthright* tax system, in which each citizen would have greater reason to believe that the rate schedule he finds on his tax return means what it says and applies uniformly to others, not just to himself.

There is no intention here to exaggerate the happy effects that would flow from a simpler, more broadly-based tax system, or to suggest that it would magically create a Utopian society in which every man shared Justice Holmes' pleasure in paying taxes in order to "pay for civilized society." The "tax angle" would still be with us, just as it has always been; high top-bracket rates are not its only *raison d'etre*. There were massive tax preferences long before high rates were enacted.* Nor did the low tax rates of the twenties (top rate, 25 percent) diminish the avidity with which tax avoidance was pursued. The very architect of those gentle rates, Andrew Mellon, when he resigned as Secretary of the Treasury, was careful to take with

---

* Three of the most conspicuous tax favors—tax exempt bonds, oil depletion, and the preferential capital gains rate—all became law when the top rates were comparatively low (7, 58 and 25 percent, respectively).

him, as his tax adviser in private life, the Treasury Department's top expert on tax avoidance techniques.

There is no reason to expect the future to differ markedly from the past. Nonetheless, as things now stand, the very possibility of escape creates its own pressure. Block off the major escape routes (especially the capital gains route) and you tap much of that pressure.

Thus, the combination of lower rates and fewer avenues of escape would not end but would lessen the thrust for tax preferences.

Anyone in high public office who seriously proposes a no-preference tax system should be prepared for the air to be filled with black predictions of catastrophe. Without oil depletion (it would be said) oil exploration would come "to a standstill"; without mortgage interest deductions, home-buying would plummet; without a special capital gains tax, the sources of capital would wither; the economy would flounder and the Treasury, far from gaining revenues, would be starved for the dollars to run the government.

No one should minimize the economic impact of a major revision of the tax structure. There would have to be many economic adjustments and some dislocations as the tax supports now underpinning many areas of the economy were removed. Yet such changes would be in a direction that should be applauded by the United States Chamber of Commerce and the National Association of Manufacturers. There would be less government interference (via tax subsidies) with private decision-making, and a greater role for the free play of private forces in the market place. Perhaps there *would* be less drilling for oil. But when Texas oil production is deliberately held to less than 30 percent of capacity and the bountiful supplies of foreign oil are intentionally denied entry into America, isn't there at least a suggestion that there has already been too much oil exploration? If the fast-depreciation-capital-gains-tax advantages of real estate were ended, perhaps there would be less building of apartments and offices in major cities. But with vacancy rates growing in, say, New York, isn't there evidence that this tax subsidy has encouraged some over-building? Wouldn't the economy be better off, in the long run, with a free play of market forces regulating the allocation of capital and resources—determining, for example, the level of oil exploration and real estate construction? And wouldn't the economy clearly be better off without incentive-stifling high top-bracket rates? What is more, those who decry "back-door" government spending should rejoice in the elimination of tax subsidies—the most insidiously invisible of all drains on the federal Treasury.

While taxes can have a profound effect on economic activity, there is a tendency to endow them with vastly more power—to heal as well as to injure—than they actually possess. For example, the low tax rates of the twenties, which Andrew Mellon said would be the salvation of free enterprise, were followed by the greatest economic calamity in the nation's history. Conversely, from 1942 to 1964, the top income tax rate has been as high as 94 percent, and never below 82 percent, and yet there has been no such catastrophe; in fact, the past two decades have been an era of general prosperity and growth.

There is also a tendency to underrate the resiliency of the American economy, which took in stride such fiscal shocks as a $7 billion tax increase bill in 1942 and, more significantly, a $94 billion drop-off of government purchases between 1945 and 1948. Surely such an economy can withstand a rearrangement of the tax system *that does not involve any over-all change in federal revenues.*

The need for a thorough overhauling of our tax system . . . is one of our most pressing national problems . . . We should develop as soon as possible a long-range, integrated, well-balanced, equitable and simplified scheme of taxation.

—Statement by Republican Members of the House Ways and Means Committee

We can no longer afford to defer serious, large-scale efforts to revise our federal tax system.

> —Democratic Rep. Wilbur Mills of Arkansas, Chairman of the Ways and Means Committee

I do not believe we can continue much longer under our present tax structure. It is eroding faster every day.

> —Republican Rep. Thomas B. Curtis of Missouri, third-ranking Republican member of that same committee.

The first of those statements was made in 1943, the second two in 1958. Yet the years have rolled by, and the sweeping tax reform of which these congressmen spoke so urgently is still a thing of the future. Meanwhile, as Randolph Paul put it, "the income tax . . . is a wasting asset of the Nation."

> [The] process of erosion and patchwork amendment must stop somewhere [Paul continued]; otherwise the statute, even now almost hopelessly complicated will "approach the ridiculous," and taxpayers will spend more and more of their time and energy on the job of keeping their tax liability to a minimum.

Some will point out that America's is probably the most effective tax system in the world, that we collect the greatest revenues the most efficiently, with by far the greatest degree of voluntary compliance by taxpayers. This is all true, and no reader should conclude from this book that everything about our tax system is wrong. Nor, however, should even the most impassioned Fourth of July orator be lulled into thinking that all is right with the system either, and the bill of complaint is a long one: the anomaly and inequity of five men with $5,000,000 income paying *no* tax, while millions with but a thousandth as much income contribute a portion of their incomes to their government . . . the deceptiveness of a tax system which ostensibly calls for taking 90 percent of a multimillionaire's income but actually takes less than 25 percent . . . the discrimination against wage earners and professionals, whose earned income enjoys no tax favor . . . the special dispensations to the Louis B. Mayers, whose principal claim for tax relief is their access to a lobbyist or a member of Congress . . . the effect of these anomalies and inequities on taxpayer compliance in a country where the government relies on each citizen to report his income honestly . . . the chain-reaction of tax favors, whereby one preference furnishes the justification for the next . . . the tenacity of tax preferences, whereby even the most "temporary" become permanently embedded in the system . . . the waste of energy and talent drained off in the frantic quest to "beat the tax game" . . . the danger that the existing high-rate, low-base structure will not prove flexible enough to meet the needs of a national emergency . . . the erosion, not only of the tax base, but also of public morality as "tax avoidance" becomes the norm and as each tax preference whets the appetite for more . . . most of all, the helplessness of the uninformed public to understand the chipping away of the tax system that goes on behind an impenetrable screen of technicalities.

We come full circle—to the appearance of James C. Carter before the Supreme Court in 1895 quoted, in part, in the first chapter. Describing the inevitable tendency of humans to "relieve themselves" from "the burdens of taxation," Mr. Carter said:

> One class struggles to throw the burden off its own shoulders. If they succeed, of course, it must fall upon others. They also, in their turn, labor to get rid of it, and *finally the load falls upon those who will not, or cannot, make a successful effort for relief.* [Emphasis added.]

It is to this latter group that this book is addressed.

Appendix

Acknowledgments

Never again will I skip lightly over the acknowledgments in a book, for the past twelve months have made me acutely and gratefully aware of the extent to which kind and patient friends can rescue an author from paths of error and add perspective and balance to his work.

Especially is this true when an untutored layman such as myself presumes to set foot in what I referred to in the preface as that dark and tangled jungle, the Internal Revenue Code. If it is foolhardy to enter in the first place, it is even more hazardous to take more than a step or two without the guiding hand of an expert. I have been blessed with many guiding hands, both among the able and dedicated staff of the Internal Revenue Service and the Treasury Department, and among the community of Washington tax attorneys. They have given generously of their time, not only in helping me to gather information and to understand the complexities of their trade, but also in reading manuscripts and winnowing out my transgressions. I shall not embarrass them by seeming to link them publicly by name with what many might consider my radical views, even though these views are purely my own. Instead, let me absolve them of any errors that may have stubbornly remained in the manuscript, despite my conscientious efforts to avoid them; and express to them (they know who they are) my deeply felt gratitude for their patience and endurance.

For these latter two qualities, two friends deserve whatever laurels can be heaped upon them: Norman Ture of the National Bureau of Economic Research and Joseph A. Pechman of the Brookings Institution, both of whom were infinite sources of facts, wisdom and guidance. If they ever tired of answering my endless stream of questions, they were kind enough not to show it.

Two cherished friends in New Orleans, Thomas B. and Stephen B. Lemann contributed invaluably by permitting no premise or statement to pass unchallenged, thereby either revealing to me the error of my ways or obliging me to revise or sharpen my own thinking and exposition.

Other friends, non-professionals in the tax field, read portions of the manuscript and offered valuable advice: Lillian Cohn, Louis G. Cowan, Dore Schary, and, in particular, Robert P. Burroughs. A characteristically perceptive comment by Dr. Gene Gordon on one of the earliest chapters was an indispensable guideline in writing the rest of the book. Special thanks are due, too, to David Aaronson, to Professor David Weaver of the George Washington University Law School, and to Mrs. Doris Van Wagner and others in the Treasury Department Library, who, with unfailing kindness, steered me to the most helpful among the many helpful tomes on taxation that line the shelves of that library.

The thoroughness of the source footnotes in the Appendix is a credit to the painstaking work of Jay Baraff, who meticulously sleuthed every fact to its source, never losing his considerable sense of humor in the process.

I am also indebted to Louis Eisenstein and his delightful book, *The Ideologies of Taxation,* whose verbal and analytical virtuosities are frequently and unashamedly called into service throughout this book.

The typing of a manuscript is a task of unimaginable arduousness under the best of circumstances; but when an author with procrastinating tendencies and a firm publisher's deadline waits until the final week to complete half the manuscript, only a Gertrude N. Callander, loyally aided and abetted by her husband, Charles, would have the fortitude and competence to complete the task—and remain cheerful to boot. My gratitude to them both cannot be properly expressed here.

Finally, a special medal for my favorite five—Henry, Michael, Holly, David and Eve—for tolerating and understanding a frequently absent or uncommunicative (and sometimes growly) father during the past year. Their mother did that, too—and so much more besides. To her fell the unhappy lot of wading through early drafts of manuscripts, when thoughts were still struggling to be born, not to mention reviewing second, third and fourth versions of the same material. Managing, somehow, to tread that narrow path between unhelpful charitableness and unhelpful severity, the batting average of her suggestions would earn her a place in any Authors' Wives' Hall of Fame. If the subject of tax "loopholes" has indeed been made intelligible, it is she who deserves the credit.

WASHINGTON, D. C.   PHILIP M. STERN
SEPTEMBER, 1963

Glossary

"Ability to pay"—As used in this book, "ability to pay" is a short-hand name for the basic philosophic concept underlying the graduated income tax (under which higher incomes are subject to stiffer tax rates than lower incomes).

This concept is based on the premise that as a person's income rises, he is "able to pay" to the government a greater share of each additional dollar of income. Thus, under pre-1964 rates, a married man need only pay 22 cents of his four-thousand-and-first dollar of taxable income, but on his four-*hundred*-thousand-and-first dollar of taxable income, he is deemed "able to pay" 91 cents.

Accelerated depreciation—See *Depreciation.*

Adjusted gross income—A taxpayer's income before taking his exemptions and personal deductions.

More specifically, it is his total dollars received, minus (a) those items he does not have to report on his tax return or include in computing his tax (such as interest on state and local bonds, social security benefits, etc.); (b) his business expenses;

and (c) one-half of all his long-term capital gains (see Glossary description of capital gains).

Averaging—See *Income averaging.*

"Bunched" income—Refers, generally, to the uneven receipt of income—peaks in some years, valleys in others—in such a way that in peak years, the taxpayer is pushed into an artificially high tax bracket.

Thus, he is obliged to pay more taxes than another taxpayer who receives the same number of dollars spread evenly over the same number of years.

Capital gains—Profits made on the sale or exchange of a share of stock, or a machine, building or other "capital asset" which a person has owned for more than six months and which is not regularly used in his trade or business or held by him primarily for sale to customers. (There are some kinds of income which do not involve the sale of a capital asset—such as, for example, coal royalty income or lump-sum pension benefits—but which the law taxes as if they were capital gains.)

Only half of a person's capital gains are included in his taxable income; the other half escapes tax entirely. The maximum rate on the included half is 50 percent—making the top capital gains rate 25 percent (50 percent tax on half the gain). But the capital gains rate may be less than that: if, for example, an individual's own top-bracket rate is 38 percent, then his capital gains rate is only 19 percent (38 percent tax on half the gain). The tax bill approved by the House in 1963 provided that on capital assets held for more than two years, only 40 percent (rather than half) of capital gains are included in taxable income, and the top capital gains rate is 21 percent.

Collapsible corporation—A device for transforming "ordinary income" into a capital gain through an early liquidation (or "collapsing") of a corporation.

Example (taken from the days when these were in vogue in the movie industry and were nicknamed "Hollywood corporations"): A special corporation would be formed to produce a motion picture. When the picture was completed, but before it was distributed, the corporation would be "collapsed" and the rights to all future income from the movie sold. The difference between the original stock price and the sale price would be taxed as a capital gain. Such corporations must now, under the law, be in existence at least three years (or until the bulk of their income has been realized) before they can be "collapsed" and thus are no longer in great use in Hollywood. They are, however, still used in the real estate industry.

Depletion; depletion allowance—A tax deduction that may be taken by the owners of oil and gas wells, minerals and other natural deposits.

There are two forms of depletion: "cost depletion" (limited to the original cost of the mineral property and similar to depreciation) and "percentage depletion," which is not based on, or limited to, original cost, but is computed each year as a percentage of the gross income from the mineral property. It cannot, however, exceed 50 percent of the net (after-expense) income from the property. For example, oil and gas are accorded a 27½ percent depletion allowance, which means that for an oil property with $100,000 of *gross* income per year, the depletion deduction would be $27,500. If, however, the *net* (after-expense) income from the property were $40,000, the depletion allowance would be limited to half that, or $20,000. Only oil and gas enjoy the 27½ percent depletion rate; other minerals have a 23, 15, 10 or 5 percent depletion allowance.

Depreciation—An annual tax deduction designed, in general, to recognize the wearing out of a capital asset such as a machine or building with the passage of time, and to permit the owner to recover, tax-free, his original capital investment in that asset over its "useful life." The "useful lives" of various kinds of assets are suggested by guidelines issued by the Treasury Department.

"Straight-line" depreciation consists of uniform deductions taken during each year of the asset's "life." For example, on a $100,000 asset with a ten-year "life," the annual deductions would be $10,000.

"Accelerated" depreciation may follow various formulas, but in essence it permits greater-than-average deductions in the early years of the asset's life, gradually shrinking until they become smaller-than-average in the later years. That is, in the case of the $100,000, ten-year asset referred to above, the early-year deductions would be greater than $10,000, the later-year deductions less than $10,000.

Dividend tax credit—A provision of law enacted in 1954 permitting those who receive corporate dividends to reduce the amount of tax they owe the government by 4 percent of their dividend income.

Example: A person with $1,000 of dividends who would pay $2,040 in taxes, but for the dividend credit, is permitted to reduce his taxes by $40 (4 percent of $1,000) and thus pay $2,000 in taxes. (The tax bill approved by the House in 1963 provided for the repeal of this tax feature.)

"Double taxation"—This usually refers to the fact that a dollar of corporate dividends is subjected to taxation twice: once in the hands of the corporation and again in the hands of the corporate shareholder. There are numerous other instances of "double taxation," such as the payment of an excise tax with dollars that have already been subject to an income tax.

Estate tax—The tax imposed on the transfer of property after a person's death. Only amounts above $60,000 are subject to this tax.

Exclusions—Income a taxpayer does not have to include in computing his tax.

This would include such items as various government payments (social security, railroad retirement and veterans' benefits), interest on state and local bonds, and all money received by gift or inheritance.

Gift tax—A tax that may be imposed on the giver when he transfers property to another person during his lifetime.

Each taxpayer is permitted to give $3,000 per year ($6,000 a year for married couples) tax-free to as many people as he may choose. Over and above that, each taxpayer is permitted to make $30,000 of tax-free gifts ($60,000 for married couples) during his lifetime.

Head of household—An unmarried person who supports a relative as part of his household, or his father or mother even if they are not part of his household.

Heads of household are taxed according to special tax rates which lie roughly midway between the rates applicable to unmarried taxpayers and those applicable to married joint-return filers.

Imputed income—Income you receive in some form other than cash.

For example, your bank provides you certain services free, in lieu of paying you interest on your deposits. The value of those services is "imputed income," as is the value of the housing you get from your owned home, over and above your expenses. Generally speaking, imputed income is not taxed in the United States, but in some countries the imputed rental income on owner-occupied homes is or has been taxed to the owner (see page 214).

Income averaging—A means of alleviating the so-called "bunched" income problem (described elsewhere in Glossary) by permitting a taxpayer, in effect, to smooth out the peaks and valleys of his income and compute his taxes as if the income had been received more evenly over a period of years.

For example, under the tax bill approved by the House in 1963, anyone whose income has varied more than one-third in a five-year period could, in effect, lop off his above-average income in the fifth year and have it taxed as if it had been spread evenly over the prior four years.

Income-splitting—Refers to various means by which a given amount of income may be split up into smaller and separately taxed "bundles," thus avoiding the high tax rates that would apply if the income were taxed as a single "bundle."

The best-known and most widely-used method is the filing of

a joint tax return by married couples, which permits the husband's income to be taxed as if it were two half-sized "bundles." Thus, under pre-1964 rates, $100,000 of a bachelor's taxable income would be subject to a top rate of 89 percent and result in $67,320 of tax. But if taxed as two $50,000 "bundles" (as in the case of joint-return filers), the top rate drops to 75 percent and the tax to $53,640. If, through the creation of separately-taxed trusts or a family partnership, the $100,000 can be split into three "bundles," the top rate becomes 65 percent and the tax $45,980. Split four ways, the top rate is 59 percent and the tax $40,600.

"Ordinary income"—Income that is subject to the regular income tax rate schedules, as distinct from "capital gains," which are accorded a special 25 percent rate.

Percentage depletion—See *Depletion.*

Retirement income credit—A provision easing the taxation of those over 65.

Under this provision, an elderly person's tax bill may be reduced by an amount equal to one-fifth of his first $1,200 of pension, annuity, dividend, interest or royalty income. For example, it gives a person over 65 with $1,000 of pension income a $200 tax cut. However, the basis for the tax reduction is reduced by one dollar for every dollar (over $1,200) of either social security benefits or income earned from a job. For example, an elderly person with a job paying $1,500 a year would have the basis of his retirement tax credit reduced by $300. Thus, his credit would come to $180 (one-fifth of $900). Those over 75 may earn as much as they like without any reduction of their tax credit.

Spin-off—A device used for transforming a corporate dividend payment from "ordinary income" into a capital gain.

Example: Corporation A might "spin off" some assets into a specially-created Corporation B, and give stock in B to its shareholders in lieu of a cash dividend. When the B stocks rises in value, the shareholders can sell it and pay only the capital gains rate on the profit. "Spin-offs" were more frequently used before

1954, when the law and the regulations placed restrictions on them.

Stock option—The right granted a corporate officer or director to buy company stock at a fixed price within a certain period of time.

Example: An executive, given a five-year option (or right) to buy 5,000 shares of his company's stock at $25 per share, later exercises that right and still later sells the stock, whose market price has gone up to $50 per share. If his company's option plan meets certain requirements in the tax law, his $125,000 profit is taxed at the 25 percent capital gains rate.

"Straight-line" depreciation—See *Depreciation*.

Taxable income—The amount left after a taxpayer has claimed all his exemptions and deductions; i.e., the amount actually subject to tax.

Tax Court—A special court made up of sixteen judges whose function is to resolve disputes between taxpayers and the Internal Revenue Service.

Although headquartered in Washington, individual judges hear cases all around the country. Tax cases may also be considered by the regular district courts of the United States and by the Court of Claims. Appeals from decisions of the Tax Court may be taken to the appropriate federal Circuit Court of Appeals.

Tax credit—A subtraction from the amount of *tax* a person owes. (This is different from a tax deduction, which is a subtraction from the amount of a person's *income* that is subject to tax.)

A tax credit works this way: Suppose an elderly person has a $125 retirement income credit (see page 210). He figures up his tax bill, which happens to come out to $625, and then subtracts $125 from that. The tax he owes the government is thus reduced to $500. Under a tax credit, all taxpayers receive the same dollar advantages, no matter what their tax bracket—which is not the case with a tax deduction (see below). Examples of tax credits: the "retirement income credit"; the dividend tax credit.

Tax deduction—A subtraction that reduces the amount of a person's *income* that is subject to taxes.

Example: Suppose a taxpayer in the 59 percent tax bracket has $50,000 of income that would otherwise be taxable. If he takes a $1,000 medical expense deduction, his taxable income is reduced to $49,000. If he had not been permitted to deduct the $1,000 (if, say, he had bought a mink coat with it), $590 of the $1,000 would have gone to the government. *In this sense, Uncle Sam has paid $590, or 59 percent of the deducted amount.* The higher your tax bracket, the greater portion the government pays. For a person on the 26 percent bracket, for example, the government pays only $260 of a $1,000 medical bill.

Tax "shelter"—Generally speaking, any device or plan which "shelters" a person's income from the regular income tax rates.

Trusts—A legal—*and separately taxable*—arrangement with respect to property or wealth in which one or more "trustees" hold title to the property and manage it for the benefit of one or more beneficiaries.

For example, a father may put property in one trust—or several—for his minor son, to be managed by trustees until the son reaches a certain age. Since each trust is, in most cases, separately taxable, this offers the possibility of considerable tax savings through "income-splitting" (see elsewhere in Glossary).

Notes and Sources

EXPLANATION OF ABBREVIATIONS

BTA—Decisions of the Board of Tax Appeals (predecessor to the Tax Court); 38 BTA 516 refers to Volume 38 of the reports of the Board's decisions, at page 516.

CR—Congressional Record; 100 CR 12312 refers to Volume 100 of the permanent, bound Congressional Record at page 12312. The notation "(daily)" means the reference comes from the non-permanent Record, whose page numbers are different from the permanent record.

Cum. Bull.—The Cumulative Bulletin containing published Treasury Department and Internal Revenue Service regulations.

Compendium—Refers to "Tax Revision Compendium: Compendium of Papers on Broadening the Tax Base," a three-volume collection of papers on a broad range of tax policy, collected and published by the House Ways and Means Committee in 1959. 2 Compendium 875 means Volume 2 of the Compendium, at page 875.

Economic Indicators—Monthly statistical publication prepared by the President's Council of Economic Advisors.

Eisenstein—Refers to tax attorney Louis Eisenstein's book, the *Ideologies of Taxation*. Copyright © 1961 The Ronald Press Company.

FY—Fiscal Year, the government's accounting year, which ends June 30. FY 1962 refers to the twelve months ending June 30, 1962.

F. 2d; F. Supp.—Federal Reports, Second Series; Federal Supplement —series of volumes reporting decisions of federal courts. 220 F. 2d 890, 895 means that the case quoted begins in Volume 220 of the series at page 890, but that the particular quotation in question appears at page 895.

H. Doc.—House Document. These frequently contain Presidential messages, including veto messages. H. Doc. 43, 80-2 refers to House Document No. 43 of the Eightieth Congress, Second Session.

H. R.—Designates a bill introduced in the House of Representatives. Senate bills bear the prefix S.

H. Rep.—House Report—the report accompanying a bill issued by the committee of the U.S. House of Representatives that handled the bill. H. Rep. 491, 81-2 refers to House Report No. 491 of the Eighty-first Congress, Second Session.

IRC—Internal Revenue Code, the basic tax law of the United States. IRC Sec. 1237 refers to Section 1237 of the Code.

HWM—House Ways and Means Committee. 1951 HWM 2328 refers to 1951 tax hearings before the committee, at page 2328.

JCER—Congress' Joint Committee on the Economic Report. 1955 JCER 412 refers to page 412 of the collection of papers on "Federal Tax Policy for Economic Growth and Stability," compiled by the Joint Committee and issued Nov. 9, 1955. 1955 JCER Hearings refers to panel-discussion hearings on that same subject, also held in 1955.

SFC—Senate Finance Committee. 1950 SFC 1315 refers to 1950 tax hearings before the committee, at page 1315.

SOI—"Statistics of Income," published annually by the Internal Revenue Service. Unless otherwise stated, reference is to volumes on individual income tax returns (separate volumes are published for corporations' and for trust, gift and estate tax returns). 1960 SOI 34 refers to the 1960 "Statistics of Income" (for individual tax returns), at page 34.

S. Rep.—Senate Report (see H. Rep.). S. Rep. 485, 84-1 refers to Senate Report No. 485 of the Eighty-fourth Congress, First Session.

Stat.—The General Statutes of the United States. 70 Stat. 43 refers to Volume 70 of the General Statutes, at page 43.

TC—Refers to decisions of the Tax Court of the United States. 25 TC 512 refers to Volume 25 of those decisions, at page 512.

U.S.—The United States Reports, containing decisions of the U.S. Supreme Court. 215 U.S. 425 refers to Volume 215 of those reports, at page 425.

Page

Preface

viii   *Stanley Surrey:* 70 Harvard Law Review 1175 (1957).

xi   *Learned Hand:* Commissioner v. Newman, 159 F. 2d 848 (1947).

Page

1. *The Tax Deviates*

4   *Five Americans with over $5 million income paid no taxes:*
     1963 SFC 280. Income includes 100 percent of capital gains.

4   *One American enjoyed nearly $20 million income, paid no
     tax:* 1961 HWM 107. Income includes 100 percent of capital
     gains.

4   *Thirty-seven paid less than 25 percent tax and paid less than
     comes over $500,000 paid no tax:* 1961 SOI (Preliminary) 14
     and 16. Income means adjusted gross income.

4   *Real estate corporation in New York: The Wall Street Journal,*
     July 17, 1961.

4   *Mrs. Horace Dodge: Fortune,* Nov., 1957, p. 238.

4   *Thirty-seven paid less than 25 percent tax and paid less than
     half, proportionately, etc.:* 1963 SFC 279.

5   *Americans paid taxes on less than half their incomes:* Eco-
     nomic Indicators, Oct., 1963, p. 4 (data on personal income);
     1960 SOI 4.

6   *Table:* First column shows tax computed according to pre-1964
     rate schedule in Section 1(a) of the tax code for the average
     taxpayer in each income group, as if his "adjusted gross in-
     come" plus his presently untaxed capital gains were all taxable.
     This does *not* take into account tax-free interest, or deductions
     for depletion and intangible drilling expense. The second
     column shows actual taxes paid by the average taxpayer in
     each income group as a percent of total income, including
     presently untaxed capital gains. Statistics from 1960 SOI.

6   *Four real-world men:* All are single, with no dependents. Taxes
     computed according to pre-1964 rates.

8   *Number of non-taxable persons with incomes over $1 million:*
     SOI Table 1 versus Table 4 permits comparison of total versus
     taxable returns in this income group.

8   *"Discriminatory and inequitable":* 1963 HWM 51.

12   *Interest deductions cost Treasury nearly $3 billion a year:*
     Interest deductions for 1963 were estimated at $10.5 billion,
     for an estimated revenue loss of $2.7 billion.

12   *Texas oil wells held to less than 30 percent of capacity:* The
     Wall Street Journal, Sept. 20, 1963, reported that the Texas
     Railroad Commission, which determines production from Texas
     wells, had fixed it for October, 1963, at 28 percent of capacity.

12   *Four-fifths of the elderly non-taxable:* 1962 Report to the
     President of the Federal Council on the Aging, p. 87.

14   *James C. Carter before the Supreme Court:* Pollock v. Farmers'
     Loan & Trust Co., 157 U.S. 429, 516 (1895).

15-16   *Table:* Figures on "shrinkage" of the tax base are based on latest available government statistics or estimates as to the current gross magnitude of each item, reduced by the extent to which it is estimated that the item affects non-taxable persons. The conversion of this "base shrinkage" figure to a revenue loss figure is either based on current expert estimates or on the conversion factor used by Joseph A. Pechman in his paper, "What Would a Comprehensive Income Tax Yield?", at 1 Compendium 279.

2. Ah, To Be an Oil Man

17   *Amanda Bailey's taxes:* Computed from then-existing tax rates and tables.

18   *Amerada Petroleum profits:* Moody's Industrials, 1945, p. 1872.

18   *Corporations paid 55 percent taxes:* President's Economic Report, Jan., 1961, p. 192.

18   *Individual oil operator's taxes:* 109 CR 23230-2 (daily), Dec. 12, 1963.

19   *Individual D, with $26 million income and no taxes:* 109 CR 23230 (daily), Dec. 12, 1963. In 1960, this operator sold an oil reserve for a profit (long-term capital gain) of $26,203,307. After taking into account other income items (including an impressive $852,639 of taxable interest, and an intriguing $18,150 of "salary"), offset by his oil exploration and development expenses (principally for dry holes) and overhead expenses not allocated to specific business operations, the Treasury Department lists his "total reported economic income" at $26,440,776. He managed to avoid paying any federal income taxes (and, in fact, to report a *loss,* for tax purposes) principally by doing the following: (1) The $26 million oil reserve sale was on an installment basis, with $10,872,449 being received and, under the law, reported for tax purposes in 1960. (For more about this, see below.) Yet, since this was a long-term capital gain, only *half* of this ($5,436,224) was includable in taxable income (see Glossary under Capital Gains). (2) After percentage depletion deductions (i.e., the excess of such deductions over the regular cost-basis deductions permitted in other industries) of $686,642 and intangible drilling expense deductions of $1,609,530, his oil operations netted him a *loss* (for tax purposes) of $762,090. (3) His oil exploration and development deductions and his unallocated "overhead" expense deductions (see above) came to $2,276,-156. (4) He listed farming losses—possibly due in part to cattle operations described on pages 139-41—of $276,368.

(5) His tax losses carried over from prior years—mainly due to oil operations—came to $3,934,047.

Some may argue that since he actually received only about $11 million of the $26 million on the installment sale of his oil reserve, it is unfair to call the entire $26 million "income"— even "economic income"—for that year. Yet, Treasury officials contend, he consummated the sale of the entire property in that year—i.e., he parted with $26 million worth of oil, and he had control over the full $26 million of resources. Were he, under the sale agreement, to draw interest on the unpaid $15 million (as is often the case in installment sales), it could be said he was merely lending this money to the purchaser of his oil. Moreover, it is argued, if he wanted immediate enjoyment of the unpaid $15 million, he could always bank the note (or mortgage) he had received—although at the expense of a certain bank discount, and at the possible expense of having the proceeds subject to tax in the year he receives them.

19   *Five million income in one year without tax:* 97 CR 11724-5 (1951).

19   *Individual oil company profits:* Moody's Industrials, 1962, p. 2618, 2650, 2313 and 1490.

19   *Corporations paid 49 percent taxes in 1961:* Economic Indicators, Nov., 1963, p. 7.

19-20 *Company W and Company A profits and taxes:* 105 CR 11915-6 (1959).

20   *1957 oil company taxes versus other corporations:* 1 Compendium 300.

20   *Eighty-three percent of depletion deductions emanate from oil and gas:* 1 Compendium 296.

21   *Percentage depletion costs the Treasury $1.5 billion annually:* "The Federal Revenue System: Facts and Problems" (1961 publication of the Joint Committee on the Economic Report), p. 98. See also papers by Pechman and Hellmuth at 1 Compendium 251-281 and 283-316.

21   *Texas oil production held to less than 30 percent of capacity:* See note from p. 12.

21   *Leading oil proponent:* Senator Russell Long of Louisiana, quoted at Eisenstein 129.

21   *J. Paul Getty statement:* Newsweek, July 15, 1963, p. 48.

21   *H. L. Hunt, Hugh Roy Cullen:* New York Times Magazine, Oct. 20, 1957; Holiday, Feb., 1957, p. 55.

22   *Murchison-Richardson:* Holiday, Feb., 1957, p. 56.

22   *Dr. Martin Miller; Michael Benedum:* Fortune, Nov., 1957, p. 176.

Page

22   *Bob Hope, Bing Crosby, et al: Time,* Oct. 10, 1949.

22   *Industrialist confided to* Wall Street Journal: Engler, *The Politics of Oil,* p. 158.

23   *Houston oil expert's investment advice:* 105 CR 11915 (1959).

24   *The three advantages of oil investments:* Based on analysis by Louis Eisenstein, *The Ideologies of Taxation,* Chapter 6.

25   *One student of the oil industry:* J. P. Jackson, "Tax Planning Before Drilling," 27 *Tulane Law Review* 21 (1952).

26   *Depletion deductions equal 19 to 200 times those permitted other industries:* 1 Compendium 296.

29   *Savings from computing depletion on basis of processed products:* 106 CR 13220 (1960).

29   *Morton Salt case:* Morton Salt Co. v. U.S., 63-1 USTC Paragraph 9468 (1963).

29   *1960 Congressional measure:* Public Law 86-564.

30   *Aramco, Standard Oil of New Jersey, Socony Mobil:* Engler, *The Politics of Oil,* p. 225.

30   *33 major oil companies:* 105 CR 17240 (1959).

31   *Aramco royalty payments:* Engler, *The Politics of Oil,* p. 224.

31   *Senator Mike Monroney:* 105 CR 11914 (1959).

32   *1926 Senate study:* 67 CR 3768, 3772, 3777 (1926).

32   *History of 27 1/2 percent oil depletion figure:* 30 *Indiana Law Journal* 406; 67 CR 3762, 3776-8 (1926).

32   *One court held it did not:* F.H.E. Oil Co. v. Commissioner, 150 F.2d 857 (1945).

33   *Congress directed Internal Revenue:* IRC Sec. 263 (c).

33   *Percentage depletion extended to 85 minerals:* IRC Sec. 613 (b).

33   *Court upheld depletion claim on underground water:* Marvin Shurbet v. U.S., 63-2 USTC Paragraph 9528 (1963).

33   *Corporate depletion deductions quadrupled:* 1946 corporation SOI, p. 8; 1956-57 Corporation SOI, p. 6.

34   *"World glut" of oil: Life,* Aug. 24, 1962.

35   *Laying out $1.18 per barrel, getting 80 cents in depletion:* "The Oil Depletion Issue" (publication of the Petroleum Industry Research Foundation, Inc.), p. 96 (1959).

36   *Court rulings on "double deduction" question:* U.S. v. Dakota-Montana Oil Co., 288 U.S. 459, 462 (1933); F.H.E. Oil Co. v. Commissioner, 147 F.2d 1002, 1003 (1945) and 150 F.2d 857, 858 (5th Cir. 1945).

36   *Oil companies keep two sets of books:* 1953 HWM 11996.

Page

36   *Dun's Review:* from *Dun's Review and Modern Industry,* March, 1955, p. 33-5.

37   *Thirty-three oil companies saved a billion in taxes:* see note on p. 20.

38   *Concentration of depletion deductions in large corporations:* 1958-59 corporation SOI, Tables 4 and 45.

38   *One of your most ardent senatorial supporters:* Senator Monroney of Oklahoma, 97 CR 11726 (1951).

38   *Drilling record of five largest oil companies:* Oil and Gas Journal, Vol. 57, No. 16, cited at 2 Compendium 975.

38   *"Your own oil-industry witness":* General E. O. Thompson of the Texas Railroad Commission, 1950 HWM 248.

39   (Footnote) *Taxpayer's peccadilloes:* See Eisenstein 139.

39   *Distinction on 35 minerals:* IRC Sec. 613 (b)(2)(B).

42   *Twenty-four hundred years supply of coal:* Eisenstein 144.

42   *Most coal discovered prior to 1913:* Fay, "The Discovery Clause in Income Tax Laws," Engineering and Mining Journal Press, Feb., 1924, p. 243.

3. Ah, To Be Louis B. Mayer

45   *Sec. 1240 saved Mayer $2,000,000:* 70 Harvard Law Review 1147 (1957).

47   *Description of Mayer provision:* Louis Eisenstein, *The Ideologies of Taxation,* p. 156. Copyright © 1961 The Ronald Press Company. Reprinted with permission of The Ronald Press. Inner quote from S. Rep. 781,82-1, p. 50 (1951).

47   *Alvord appearance as Chamber of Commerce representative:* 1951 SFC 1451, 1478.

48   *Revenue loss "negligible":* S. Rep. 781, 82-1, p. 50 (1951).

48   *1954 re-enactment of Mayer provision:* 1954 SFC 1985, 2002-3; S. Rep. 1622, 83-2, p. 115 (1954).

48   *The "Hollywood Rajah":* Taken from the title of Bosley Crowther's book, *Hollywood Rajah: The Life and Times of Louis B. Mayer* (1960).

48   *Merrill provision:* Eisenstein 159.

50   *Sanders case and provision:* Leo Sanders et al v. Commissioner, 21 TC 1012 (1954); 225 F.2d 629 (1955), cert. denied 350 U.S. 967 (1956); S. Rep. 1941, 84-2 (1956); 102 CR 7795 (1956); H. Rep. 2253, 84-2 (1956), p. 5; Public Law 84-269, 70 Stat. 404.

52   *L. R. McKee:* L. R. and Lulu McKee v. Commissioner, 18 TC 512 (1952).

Page

52   *Universal Oil Products Co.:* Universal Oil Products Co. v. Root
        Refining Co. 328 U.S. 575 (1946).

53   *Clarence Cannon bill:* S. Rep. 1283, 84-1 (1955); 101 CR
        12655, 1287 (1955).

54   *Fort Wayne Journal-Gazette and Owens-Corning Fiberglas
        provisions:* 5 National Tax Journal 58 (1952).

55   *Budd, Sangamo Electric and Bridgeport Brass Companies:* 98
        CR 9072-76 (1952).

56   *Bill for DuPont-General Motors:* H. R. 8847, 87-1 (1961);
        Public Law 87-403 (1962).

56   *Hilton Hotel Corporation:* H. Rep. 1269, 85-1, p. 18 (1957);
        see also 109 CR 4172 (daily), Mar. 18, 1963.

57   *Twin Cities provision:* 108 CR 17076 (daily), Aug. 30, 1962.
        Previously vetoed bill: H.R. 8652, 87-1; S. Rep. 1101, 87-1;
        107 CR 21552 (1961).

57-8   *Howard F. Knipp provision:* Knipp's Estate v. Commissioner,
        25 TC 153 (1955); 244 F.2d 436 (1957); H. Rep. 632, 86-1;
        S. Rep. 1002, 86-1; 105 CR 8478 (1959).

60   *Stanley Surrey statement:* 70 Harvard Law Review 1170
        (1957).

60   *Senators Humphrey and Lausche:* 108 CR 17076 (daily),
        Aug. 30, 1962.

61   *Prof. Walter Blum:* 1955 JCER 259.

61   *"It has been observed . . .":* Harvard Law Review, May, 1957,
        p. vii.

61   *William L. Cary:* 68 Harvard Law Review 745 (1955); 1955
        JCER 264.

4. Your Wife May Be Worth a Million

62   *$10,000-a-year salary:* All calculations on pages 62 and 63
        assume that salary (or income) is equivalent to adjusted gross
        income, and that the taxpayer takes personal deductions of
        10 percent thereof.

63   *Seven million, 15 million married men:* 1960 SOI 41.

64   *97 percent of benefits went to top 5 percent:* Eisenstein 45;
        Treasury Department release, Apr. 14, 1948.

64   *Couple A's benefits 319 times Couple B's:* Assumes respective
        incomes of $5,000 and $100,000 and respective tax of $38 and
        $12,108.

65   *Cash value table:* Husband's income means his adjusted gross
        income.

66   *Ludwig S. Hellborn:* 1951 National Tax Proceedings 310-314.

Page

68   *Congressional Democrats of the day:* H. Rep. 1274, 80-2, p. 67 (1948).

72   *Paysoff Tinkoff:* Tinkoff v. Commissioner, 120 F.2d 564 (1941).

72   *Stanback brothers:* T. M. Stanback et al v. Commissioner, 183 F.2d 889 (1950).

73   *1939-48 growth in partnerships:* 96 CR 14106 (1950).

73   *Questions to partner-wife:* Redd v. Commissioner, 5 TCM 528 (1946) (A), Transcript, p. 63.

73-4   *Pre- and post-1951 rules on family partnerships:* Commissioner v. Culbertson, 337 U. S. 733 (1949); 96 CR 19677-8 (1950).

74   *Safeguards against income-shifting:* The father must receive a reasonable salary for the services he performs for the partnership, and the rate of return on his contribution of capital must be approximately the same as that for other family partners.

74   *Uneeda Doll Company case:* Sklarsky v. U. S., 153 F. Supp. 796 (1957).

75   *West Coast construction company:* Walberg v. Smyth, 142 F. Supp. 293 (1956).

75   *734 separate corporations and others:* 163 HWM 158ff., esp. 178.

76   *88-corporation construction company:* Shaw Construction Co. v. Commissioner, 35 TC 1102 (1961).

76   *Alphabet-corporation case:* Aldon Homes v. Commissioner, 33 TC 582 (1959).

76-7   *Revell plastic models:* Revell, Inc. v. Riddell et al, 273 F.2d 649 (1959).

77   *$120 million cost of multiple corporations:* 1963 HWM 63.

78   *Dr. Boyce:* Boyce v. U. S., 190 F. Supp. 950 (1961).

78   *1937 Roosevelt Message; Stranahan family savings:* Hearings, Joint Committee on Tax Evasion and Avoidance, 75-1, June-July, 1937, p. 278ff.

78   *Two members of the New York bar:* Joel I. Friedman and Henry L. Wheeler, Jr., cited in 36 Taxes 588 (1958).

79   *"Congress was once on the brink":* H. R. 9662, 86-2; H. Rep. 1231, 86-2; S. Rep. 1616, 86-2 (1960).

79   *Dan Throop Smith:* Smith, Federal Tax Reform 291 (1961).

79-80   *Doubling of number of trusts:* 1958 SOI (Fiduciary, Gift and Estate Tax Returns) 30.

5. The Great Capital Gains Trial

83   *Situation No. 1:* Compare IRC Sec. 1221 (3) with IRC Sec. 1235. Novelists who spend more than two years writing their

Page

book are allowed to "spread" the book's income over a period of years, and the House tax bill passed in 1963 affords them certain additional "spreading" advantages, but they are still prohibited from capital gains treatment of their income.

84   *Congress' reason for giving capital gains to inventors:* S. Rep. 2375, 81-2, p. 44 (1950).

84   *Situation No. 2:* IRC Sec. 631 (c).

84   *Congress admitted no real capital gain involved:* H. Rep. 749, 88-1, p. 93 (1963).

84   *Congress on coal-royalty "hardship":* H. Rep. 586, 82-1, p. 31-2; S. Rep. 782, 82-1, p. 42 (1951). Coal royalty owners who get capital gains do not, at the same time, get a percentage depletion allowance.

86   *General counsel of Ford:* William T. Gossett; from *Fortune,* Dec., 1958, p. 202.

88   *Figures on capital gains tax returns:* 1960 SOI Tables 1, 3, 8.

88   *Situation No. 6: "more than two pages of the tax law devoted . . .":* Subdivider denied capital gains treatment by IRC Sec. 1237.

92   *Wife can sell and pay no capital gains tax:* IRC Sec. 1014.

93   *$12 to $13 billion escapes tax:* 1963 SFC 307.

93   *"One tax expert figured out . . .":* Merle Miller, 1958 HWM 2318-21.

93-4   *Portion of incomes in capital gains:* 1963 SFC 279. Average excluded capital gains comes to $3,140,892, so total capital gains would be twice that.

94   *Stanley Surrey:* 2 Compendium 1203.

94   *Tax code on "collapsible corporations":* IRC Sec. 341.

99-100   *Capital gains tax history:* National Tax Journal, 1949, p. 12 ff.

103   *Summary of findings of Harvard Business School professors:* Walter W. Heller, at 1955 JCER 389, summarizing findings of Butters, Thompson and Bollinger, Effects of Taxation: Investments by Individuals (1953).

104   *1922-33 capital gains statistics:* Seltzer, *Nature and Tax Treatment of Capital Gains and Losses,* p. 156 (1951).

105   *Stock issues only 4 percent of 1962 corporate fund needs:* Department of Commerce, Survey of Current Business, July, 1963, p. 29, Table 34.

105   *The words of the tax law itself:* IRC Sec. 62 (a).

107   *Justice Brandeis:* Quoted by Merle Miller at 1958 HWM 2321.

Page

6. Living High at the Taxpayers' Expense

110   *J. S. Seidman statement:* 1961 HWM 1685-6.

111   *Early history of expense accounts:* 2 Compendium 1061, 1076.

111   *Mortuary, island resort, yacht, etc:* 1962 SFC 299 ff.

112   *Expense account practices in the 1930's:* 2 Compendium 1082.

112   *"I haven't paid for my lunch in thirty-one years":* New York Times Magazine, Mar. 20, 1960, p. 62.

112   *Business giving practices:* Reporter Magazine, Dec. 25, 1958; Spirits (magazine), October, 1960; 1962 CR 16730 (daily), Aug. 27, 1962.

113   *U. S. News and World Report:* Jan. 26, 1960, pp. 52-4.

113   *Eastern Steel company executives:* Wall Street Journal, Oct. 11, 1962.

113   *One large oil company:* 1961 HWM 1662.

113   *African safari case:* Sanitary Farms Dairy, Inc. v. Commissioner, 25 TC 463 (1955); 1961 HWM 168.

114   *Olivia de Havilland:* Olivia de Havilland Goodrich v. Commissioner, 20 TC 323 (1953).

114   *"A brewing company . . .":* Cleveland-Sandusky Brewing Co. v. Commissioner, 30 TC 539 (1958); 1961 HWM 168.

114   *"One district judge . . .":* Thomas v. Patterson, 189 F. Supp. 230 (1959); 289 F.2d 108 (1961); *Racing handicapper:* 1961 HWM 170, Charles J. McLennan v. Commissioner, TC Memo, Op. Docket No. 4757 (June 25, 1945).

116   *1040 pennant case:* Robert Lee and Betty Jane Henry v. Commissioner, 36 TC 879 (1961).

116   *"An estimated $100 million of added revenue . . .":* 108 CR 20548 (daily).

117   New York Times *editorial:* June 26, 1963.

117-8   *Internal Revenue regulations on business-pleasure trips:* Regs. 1.2744 (e) (5) (i) and (iii), from Federal Register of June 25, 1963, p. 6506-7.

121   *Manhattan restaurateur Vincent Sardi:* 1961 HWM 1618, 1625.

121   *"Another theatre expert":* J. S. Seidman, at 1961 HWM 1685-6.

121   *National Restaurant Association:* 1961 HWM 1627.

121   *Sardi explanation:* 1961 HWM 1620.

121   *Entertainment "as American as apple pie":* New York Times, Feb. 1, 1962.

121   *"An industrialist seemed to regard . . .":* George F. Newman, Iowa Manufacturers Association, at 1961 HWM 1655.

Page

121 *"Another defender of deductions . . .":* Frank V. Olds, Controllers Institute of America, at 1961 HWM 1636.

122 *"A* Wall Street Journal *survey":* Wall Street Journal, Oct. 11, 1962.

122 *Senator Smathers:* 108 CR 16997 (daily), Aug. 29, 1962.

122 *"Some Congressmen pointed out":* 108 CR 16997 (daily), Aug. 29, 1962.

122 *"One Congressional witness . . .":* Vincent Sardi at 1961 HWM 1612.

122 *J. S. Seidman:* 1961 HWM 1686.

123 *"One moderate-income taxpayer . . .":* U. S. News and World Report, Jan. 25, 1960, p. 51.

123 *Vincent Sardi:* 1961 HWM 1619.

123 *Gifts used to gain special favors:* 1961 HWM 1691.

124 *Clarence Randall:* Dun's Review, August, 1960.

125 The New York Times: Editorial, June 26, 1963.

7. How "Show Biz" Wards Off the Tax Collector

127 Variety *headlines:* April 27, 1955, Nov. 24, 1948, Dec. 29, 1948, Mar. 16, 1955.

127 *Jack Benny sale:* 12 Tax Law Review, p. 33-5; Variety, Dec. 22, 1948.

127 *Amos 'n' Andy sale:* Variety, Sept. 1, 1948, Sept. 28, 1948.

128 *"You Bet Your Life"* sale: Julius H. (Groucho) Marx v. Commissioner, 29 TC 88 (1957).

128 *Irving Berlin:* Irving Berlin v. Commissioner, 42 BTA 668 (1940).

128 *Fred MacMurray:* Fred MacMurray et al v. Commissioner, 21 TC 15, 30-31 (1953).

128 *Anatole Litvak:* Anatole Litvak v. Commissioner, 23 TC 441 (1954).

129 *Mrs. Glenn Miller:* Helen D. Miller v. Commissioner, 299 F.2d 706 (1962).

129 *Jose Ferrer:* Commissioner v. Jose Ferrer, 304 F.2d 125 (1962).

129 *Edgar Bergen et al:* Variety, Dec. 29, 1948, p. 1.

130 *Sergeant York:* Jack Steele, Scripps-Howard newspapers, Jan. 13, 1958; New York Times, Apr. 20, 22, 1961.

130 *Jesse Lasky:* Bessie and Jesse Lasky v. Commissioner, 22 TC 13 (1954).

130 *Dwight D. Eisenhower:* Jack Steele, Scripps-Howard newspapers, Jan. 13, 1958.

Page

130   *Kathleen Winsor:* Herwig et al v. U. S., 105 F. Supp. 384 (1952).

130   *President Truman:* Jack Steele, Scripps-Howard newspapers, Jan. 13, 1958.

131   *Top stars form their own corporations: Variety,* Mar. 16, 1955.

131-2   *de Mille Productions:* Cecil B. de Mille et al v. Commissioner, 31 BTA 1161 (1935).

132   *Charles Laughton, Fontaine Fox:* Laughton v. Commissioner, 40 BTA 101 (1939); Fontaine Fox v. Commissioner, 37 BTA 271 (1938).

132   *Scripps, Block, Mellon companies:* 1937 Hearings before Joint Committee on Tax Evasion and Avoidance, p. 147-8.

133   *One tax-advisory service:* "What To Do About Personal Holding Companies" by Bruce H. Greenfield, in Prentice-Hall Tax Ideas, p. 7411.

133   *The actual case of Actor T:* 1963 HWM 359.

134   *Spate of new star-owned corporations: Variety,* Apr. 27, 1955.

134   *Lucille Ball, Sid Caesar, Perry Como, Jackie Gleason:* Marie Torre, *New York Herald Tribune,* Feb. 28, 1956.

136   *One privately-owned corporation:* 1963 HWM 361.

137   *Pat O'Brien corporation:* Pat O'Brien et al v. Commissioner, 25 TC 376 (1955).

138   *Americans who shielded their incomes abroad:* 1963 SFC 222.

140   *"Tax experts who are clever at mathematics:"* The break-even despite an $85.34 loss works out this way: On an 89-percent deductible expenditure of $100, the out-of-pocket outlay is $11. If the taxpayer gets back as little as $14.66, and keeps 75 percent of it, his net *intake* is $11, the same as his outlay. If the inflow is $100 and he keeps $75 of it, his profit is $64—or 582 percent of his $11 out-of-pocket outlay.

140   *Briarcliff farm example:* The tax advantages are effected roughly as follows: Brian Heathcliffe, a hypothetical matinee idol, buys 125 brood cows from Briarcliff Farms at $1,000 apiece. As Briarcliff lends him nine-tenths of this, his first-year outlay is $27,650—a $12,500 down payment plus $15,150 to Briarcliff to keep, feed and care for his cows (since his Manhattan apartment won't hold 125 brood cows). These are all tax-deductible—as is a "paper" depreciation deduction of $22,500. This paper deduction—involving no cash outlay— is the secret. His first-year tax deductions mean a tax saving to him of $32,230—nearly $5,000 greater than his cash outlay, so he ends up with a "tax profit" of nearly $5,000. In the second year his cash outlay is $17,190 but his tax saving is

$32,520, so he has a "tax profit" of more than $15,000. And so it goes, until at the end of the fifth year his "tax profit" totals $51,867. At that time, the herd is sold for $150,500, and since there is only a 25 percent capital gains tax to pay, the after-tax proceeds are sufficient to pay off his loan to Briarcliff Farms. And so Brian Heathcliffe walks away with his $51,867 "tax profit," not having risked a penny of his own. Only Uncle Sam is left shaking his head, for he is out $159,117. (All the above based on an analysis of an actual Briarcliff Farms prospectus.)

141 *Musician-conductor, manufacturer of chain-link fence:* 1963 HWM 456, 457.

141 *Pamphlet in ersatz Western lingo:* Prentice-Hall Executives' Tax Report, Feb. 4, 1963.

142 *Executive versus actor on $750,000 income:* The executive, with taxable income (after deductions and exemptions) of $65,000 a year, would pay, over the ten-year period, roughly $296,000; the actor would pay about $381,000—all computed at pre-1964 tax rates.

142 *Kirk Douglas: Variety,* Mar. 6, 1955.

8. How To Get Rich Quick in Real Estate— With Uncle Sam's Help

143 *Eight New York real estate corporations:* 1962 SFC 366.

143 *Kratter Realty Corporation: Wall Street Journal,* July 17, 1961.

144 *Providential Building nets $200,000 cash:* Assumes building cost of $5 million, land cost of $1 million, gross rents one-seventh the cost of land and building, operating expenses 40 percent of gross rent, interest and amortization equal to 8 percent of mortgage. Depreciation figure based on double-declining balance method.

146 *Yankee Stadium sale:* Prentice-Hall pamphlet, "Federal Tax Angles in Real Estate," p. 13 (1961).

147 Fortune *magazine:* Feb., 1960, p. 244.

147 *Transcontinental and Tenney:* 1962 SFC 366.

148 *Futterman:* Moody's Bank and Finance Manual, 1962, p. 1220, 1252.

148 *Eleven new corporate prospectuses:* 1962 SFC 366.

148 *One particularly helpful pamphlet:* Prentice-Hall, "Federal Tax Angles in Real Estate," p. 5.

150 *Daniel Friedenberg: Harper's,* June, 1961, p. 32.

152 Architectural Forum: "The Role of Depreciation," April, 1955, cited at 1962 SFC 354.

152 *One leading real estate expert:* Mark H. Johnson, 1961 HWM 1247.

153   *". . . low debt repayments in the early years":* An additional factor: the lender enjoys a cushion of security in the fact that the mortgage is usually not for the full *value* of the building, nor does it extend for the full useful *life* of the building, so that there is a leftover value in the building even after the termination of the mortgage.

154   *One real estate spokesman acknowledged to Congress:* Richard Swesnik, speaking on behalf of National Association of Real Estate Boards, 1961 HWM 1055.

157   *One real estate tax pamphlet:* Prentice-Hall, "Federal Tax Angles in Real Estate," p. 13.

157   *Recent Supreme Court decision:* Knetsch v. U. S., 364 U. S. 361 (1960).

158   *Federal Tax Angles in Real Estate:* Quoted with the permission of the publisher, Prentice-Hall, Inc.

9. Missing: $5 Billion

162   *Revenue loss of $4-5 billion:* See hearings on Gambling and Organized Crime before Senate Permanent Investigating Subcommittee, Aug. 22-25, 1961, p. 118.

162   *Breakdown of unreported $25 billion:* Speech by Internal Revenue Commissioner Mortimer Caplin, Des Moines, Iowa, Dec. 7, 1961.

163   *Figures on IRS employees, tax returns and audits:* Annual Report of Internal Revenue Service, FY 1962, p. 20, 32, 75.

163   *Justice Jackson:* U. S. v. Kahriger, 345 U. S. 22, 36 (1953).

163   *Dentist, doctor with thirty-five years' practice:* Internal Revenue Service.

164   *Use of fictitious or dead people as dependents:* Internal Revenue Service.

165   *Philippe of the Waldorf:* New York Times, Sept. 20, 1960, p. 80.

165   *Nearly a million unfiled returns:* Annual report, Internal Revenue Service, FY 1962, p. 41.

166   *TV commentator:* Internal Revenue Service.

166   *Farmer with $135,000 unreported oil income:* Internal Revenue Service.

167   *Real estate man, lawyer, with unreported interest and dividends:* 1961 HWM 111, 114.

167   *$400 million versus $10 million collections on gambling tax:* Hearings on Gambling and Organized Crime before the Senate Permanent Investigations Subcommittee, Aug. 23, 1961, pp. 94, 100, 101.

Page

167-8   *Proportion of taxpayer errors on returns:* 1948 Internal Revenue Survey.

168   *Would collect $650-880 million:* H. Rep. 1447, 87-2, p. 5; 108 CR 16712 (daily), Aug. 27, 1962.

169   *"Churches, synagogues," etc.:* Full-page advertisement in opposition to dividend-interest withholding in Lima (Ohio) *Citizen,* Mar. 9, 1962.

170   *Nearly 38 million wage earners over-withheld:* Internal Revenue Service, Annual Report for FY 1962, p. 19.

170   *Statistics on wage versus dividend-interest withholding:* 108 CR 17030 ff (daily), Aug. 29, 1962. Also IRS Annual Report (see above), p. 19. While the over-all average over-withholding on dividends and interest is $84 (the figure in the table), Treasury experts believe that for half of the two million affected persons, the amount of over-withholding would be $10 or less.

171   *"One in twenty . . . one in twelve"; top 1 percent receive over half . . . nearly a fifth:* 1960 SOI 36.

171   *"Dear Saver" letters:* undated letter from Garfield Federal Saving and Loan Association, Philadelphia; letter of Apr. 9, 1962 from Talman Federal Savings and Loan Association, Chicago.

174   *Less than a third of all returns audited:* Internal Revenue Service annual report for FY 1962, p. 32.

176   *$1 for enforcement staff brings $6 of revenue:* House Hearings on Treasury Appropriations for Fiscal Year 1963, p. 378.

177   *Justice Jackson:* U. S. v. Kahriger, 345 U. S. 22, 36.

10. The Favored Few

180   *Top 1 percent make more than $25,000, etc.:* 1961 SOI (Preliminary) 15.

180   *Savings from the three pertinent provisions:* See notes on Table, pp. 15-16. Although stock options save optioned executives an estimated $80 to $100 million, this does not represent a net revenue loss to the Treasury because option benefits, unlike salaries, are not deductible to corporations.

180   *Mrs. Horace Dodge, Sr.: Fortune,* Nov., 1957, p. 238.

181   *Charles Stewart Mott: Washington Post,* June 20, 1963; *Newsweek,* July 1, 1963; *Time,* June 28, 1963.

181   *E. R. Breech:* Lent and Menge, "The Importance of Restricted Stock Options in Executive Compensation" (mimeographed, Amos Tuck School, Dartmouth College), p. 8 (1962).

181   *George Romney:* American Motors Corporation prospectus, Jan. 29, 1962, p. 22.

Page

181   *Roger Blough:* Hearings on stock options before Senate Finance Committee (referred to hereafter as SFC Stock Option Hearings), July 20-21, 1961, p. 65.

181   *Options available in 1,500 corporations:* 1963 HWM 467-8.

181   *Average salary of optioned executives:* Lent and Menge (see above), p. 7.

181-2   *Thomas J. Watson, Jr.:* 1962 IBM proxy statement, p. 10.

182   *Manufacturing company president, electric company president, etc.:* 1961 SFC Stock Option Hearings, p. 88. The "profit" figures cited assume the market price remained stable during the six months these executives were required to hold the stock in order to be accorded capital gains treatment on the gain over the option price.

182   *"The Supreme Court has held":* Commissioner v. LoBue, 351 U. S. 243 (1956) in which the Court "held that the 'proprietary interest' test had no basis and that all employee options resulted in taxable compensation" (1963 HWM 466).

182   *Option benefits to Charles H. Percy, L. S. Rosenstiel, W. R. Stevens; over-all options averaged two-thirds salary:* Lent and Menge, pp. 8, 15.

183   *Potential option benefits from U. S. Steel, Ford, Alcoa:* Beller, "The Stock Option Scandal," AFL-CIO, 1959, pp. 10, 11, 13, 15.

183   *Option plans increased seven-fold:* 1963 HWM 467.

183   *Half optioned stock allotted to nine executives:* 1963 HWM 487.

183   *Thomas J. Watson, Jr. owned outright or in trust $40 million of IBM stock:* Securities and Exchange Commission, "Official Summary of Security Transactions and Holdings" (often called "Insiders' Trading Report"), Feb., 1962, p. 13.

184   *Over-all stock prices, 1950-62:* 1963 HWM 482.

184   *Thirty-eight pairs of matched companies:* 1963 HWM 483.

184   *(footnote) Bethlehem Steel, Westinghouse:* 1963 HWM 483.

185   *Alcoa-J. A. Livingston:* 1961 SFC Stock Option Hearings, p. 96.

185   *Sen. Albert Gore:* 1961 SFC Stock Option Hearings, p. 100.

187   *Two stock option authorities:* Daniel M. Holland and Wilbur G. Lewellen, "Probing the Record of Stock Options," *Harvard Business Review,* March-April, 1952, p. 149.

187   *Bethlehem Steel:* Ibid.

187   *1958-60 survey:* 1963 HWM 490.

188   *Large drug company, large metals company:* 1963 HWM 493.

188   *J. A. Livingston:* 1961 SFC Stock Option Hearings, p. 101.

Page

189   *Three Ford executives:* Lent and Menge (see above), p. 8.

189   *Henry Ford II on stock option values:* Harvard Business Review, July-August, 1961, p. 45.

189   *Dr. Herbert W. Robinson:* 1961 SFC Stock Option Hearings, p. 142.

191   *Ownership of state-local bonds:* Lent, "The Ownership of Tax Exempt Securities," National Bureau of Economic Research Occasional Paper 47.

192   *Individuals own about two-fifths of tax-free bonds:* Report of the Secretary of the Treasury, 1961, p. 625.

192-3 *Morgan Guaranty, First National of Chicago:* Wall Street Journal, July 8, 1963. Amount of tax-free income assumes an average 3 percent yield. The 38-45 percent tax rate is derived from 1962 Moody's Bank and Finance Manual.

193   *An important court test:* Atlas Life Insurance Co. v. U. S.; a ruling was made in the Northern District of Oklahoma (see 63-1 USTC, Paragraph 9452 [1963]). It has been appealed and, at this writing, is pending before the tenth Circuit Court of Appeals.

193   *Assurances given key governors:* 59 CR 1262 (1913). Cited at 1 Compendium 701.

193   *Most Secretaries of the Treasury:* 1955 JCER 300n.

194   *U. S. Treasury loses far more revenue:* Ott and Meltzer, "Federal Tax Treatment of State and Local Securities" (Brookings Institution, 1963), pp. 5-7.

194   *Average per capita debt:* 1 Compendium 726.

194   (footnote) *States would pick up $180 million:* Ott and Meltzer (see above), p. 7.

194-5 *Stylon Corporation:* Journal of Commerce, May 7, 1952.

195   *Cherokee, Alabama:* "Municipal Industrial Planning," pamphlet published by the Investment Bankers Association, p. 10.

195   *Opelika, Alabama:* The Weekly Bond Buyer, Sept. 10, 1962.

195   *Investment Bankers Association:* pamphlet, "Municipal Industrial Planning" (see above); also Barron's, June 19, 1961.

196   *Borg-Warner:* Release by Allied Industrial Workers of America Milwaukee, Mar. 15, 1961.

196   *Lyon, Inc.:* United Auto Workers press release, July 12, 1961.

196   *Deming, New Mexico:* Business Week, Aug. 9, 1958.

197   *"The Supreme Court has all but resolved":* Helvering v. Gerhardt, 304 U. S. 405 (1939), in which the court approved the Federal taxation of salaries paid by states and localities. Also see letter of opinion of Apr. 14, 1942, from Assistant Attorney

General Samuel O. Clark, Jr. to Randolph E. Paul, tax advisor
to the Secretary of the Treasury.

197   *"Cataclysmic view of one rhetorician":* 1941 statement of Henry
Epstein, Solicitor General of New York State; quoted at 1
Compendium 725.

198   *Statistics on ownership of corporation stock:* Eisenstein 112
(all figures cover only those shares owned by individuals as
distinct from those owned by institutions and corporations);
also 1963 HWM 268.

198   *Over half went to top 1 percent of taxpayers:* H. Rep. 1337,
83-2, p. B8 (1954).

199   *Eisenhower on 100 taxes on an egg:* Jacksonville, Fla., Sept. 2,
1952; also Warsaw, Indiana, July 15, 1962.

200   *Reps. Daniel Reed and Joseph Martin:* 96 CR 9238, 9386,
(1950).

200   *Dan Throop Smith:* 3 Compendium 1546.

201   *Table:* based on Treasury analysis, 1963 HWM 260.

203   *Post-1954 stock purchase and corporate financing patterns:*
1963 HWM 269-277. *Rep. Curtis' observation:* 1955 JCER
Hearings, p. 525.

203-4   *Figures on "Who benefitted":* 1960 SOI 32. Figures on "How
many actually received":* 1963 HWM 264.

11. The Favored Many

208   *Congress' reasons for tax advantages for the elderly:* H. Rep.
1274, 80-2, p. 20 (1948).

208   *Figures on low incomes of the aged:* Social Security Bulletin,
Jan., 1962, Table 4, p. 6; Social Security Administration Research Note 12, Sept. 27, 1961, p. 5.

208   *Government studies of living expenses:* Social Security Research Note 12 (see above), p. 9.

209   *Four-fifths of the elderly are non-taxable:* 1962 Report to the
President by the Federal Council on the Aging, p. 87.

209   *$10,000 couple saves only $66:* Assumes a 10 percent ($1,000)
personal deduction and two double exemptions (total: $2,400).

210   *Double exemption for the aged: $380 million cost:* 1963 HWM
217.

210   *Three-fifths of aged have incomes less than $1,200:* Social
Security Bulletin, Jan., 1962, Table 4.

211   *Paraphrase of one writer:* Groves, *Federal Tax Treatment of the
Family* (Brookings Institution 1963), p. 115 (preliminary manuscript).

211   *Three out of four elderly work:* 1963 HWM 213.

Page

212-13   *Tax-free imputed income on owned homes:* Department of Commerce, Survey of Current Business, July 1963, p. 39, Table 72. Amounts of imputed rental income on individual houses based on these rules of thumb: rental value, 10 percent of sale price; taxes, 25 percent of housing cost; maintenance and depreciation, 3 percent of sale price. Figures also assume mortgage of 50 percent of sale price, bearing 5½ percent interest.

214   (footnote) *British abandonment of rental-income tax: The Economist,* Apr. 6, 1963, p. 71.

215   *Paying $3 billion, six times Federal outlays for housing:* Richard Goode, "Imputed Rent of Owner-Occupied Dwellings Under the Income Tax" (Brookings Institution Reprint No. 50), pp. 509-10.

215   *Home ownership up 50 percent:* Goode (see above), p. 516. This applies to non-farm homes.

216   *$5 billion of imputed interest income:* Department of Commerce, Survey of Current Business, July, 1963, p. 39, Table 72.

217   *$10 billion of employer contributions, $1.4 billion trust fund earnings:* Social Security Bulletin, Apr., 1963, p. 8; Securities and Exchange Commission release 1902 (May 24, 1963), p. 3, Table 7.

217   *$5.6 billion contributions to health plans:* Social Security Bulletin, Apr., 1963, p. 8.

219   *Dan Throop Smith: Federal Tax Reform,* p. 58 (1961).

220   *Recent Treasury regulations:* See Rev. Rul. 61-157, 61-2 Cum. Bull. 67 and Rev. Rul. 63-108, 1963 IRB 23, p. 13.

220   *Senator Smathers:* 108 CR 17676 (daily), Sept. 6, 1962.

220   *Could cost $3 billion of revenue:* S. Rep. 992, 87-1, p. 60 (1961).

222   *A 1948 survey:* Kahn, Personal Deductions in the Federal Income Tax, 169n.

223   *Table on personal deductions:* 1944 and 1960 SOI; 1963 figures are Treasury Department estimates.

227   *1942 pessimism on charitable giving unwarranted:* Speech by Stanley S. Surrey, 109 CR 3683 (daily), Mar. 11, 1963.

227   *Millionaires' charitable contributions:* 1960 SOI 60.

229   *Bill for deductibility of fall-out shelters:* H.R. 104, 88-1 (1963).

229   *More than 100 bills on education deductions: Washington Post,* Mar. 25, 1962.

12. *Some Moral Preachments of Our Tax Laws*

232   *Nora Payne Hill:* Nora Payne Hill v. Commissioner, 13 TC 291 (1949); 181 F.2d 906 (1950).

233   *Scholarship income untaxed:* IRC Sec. 117.

Page

235   *Extra exemption for the blind:* IRC Sec. 151 (d).

235   *Depreciability of baseball players:* Rev. Rul. 54-441, 1954-2 Cum. Bull. 101.

236   *Earned income credit from times past:* This was in the law from 1924 to 1931 and from 1934 to 1943.

13. 'Tis More Blessed To Give—If You Work It Right

238-9   *Gifts of $39,400 of jewelry, a large number of paintings; water-front rights to lake-shore home:* Address by Mitchell Rogovin (Assistant to the Commissioner of Internal Revenue) to Sixth Biennial Conference on Charitable Foundations, New York University, May 21, 1963, pp. 28-9 (manuscript).

240   *Examples of dealer-appraisal practices: New York Times,* Jan. 17, 1962.

240   *Artist appraises her own paintings for $169,000:* Hilla Rebay v. Commissioner, TC Memo. 1963-42, Feb. 18, 1963. 1963 CCH Tax Court Reporter, Dec. 25,964 (M).

241   *$42,500 deduction on ancient jewelry gift:* Chester D. Tripp v. Commissioner, TC Memo. 1963-244, Sept. 11, 1963. 1963 CCH Tax Court Reporter, Dec. 26,298 (M).

242   *Commercial advertising of Pomona Plan; statement by Pomona College official: Wall Street Journal,* Sept. 16, 1960.

242-3   *Business purposes listed in 1960 law review article:* Howard Oleck, *Cleveland Marshall Law Review,* May, 1960.

243   Business Week *quote:* May 7, 1960.

243   *Kiplinger Tax Letter:* Sept., 1961.

243   *Fruehauf Trailer Company proxy contest:* 14 NYU Institute of Taxation 118 (1956) citing *Wall Street Journal,* Jan. 25, 1954.

243-4   *Murchison-Kirby proxy contest; Lewis S. Rosenstiel: Wall Street Journal,* July 10, 1961.

244   *Foundation making large loans, small grants:* Cummins-Collins Foundation v. Commissioner, 15 TC 613 (1950).

245   *"Bootstrapping":* Examples may be found in Clay B. Brown, 37 TC 461 (1961); Anderson Dairy, Inc., 39 TC 1027 (1963).

248   *"Nearly $20 million of income in one year" tax-free:* 1963 HWM 107.

249   *"Can be met without going far beyond the [30 percent] ceiling": The Journal of Accountancy* (Jan., 1963) cites the example of a taxpayer with a gross income of $200,000 paying $103,000 in federal taxes. For him, the regular 30 percent ceiling would permit charitable deductions of $60,000; meeting the 90 percent requirement would require, in this case, gifts of little more than that ($78,000).

Page

14. Precautions To Take Before You Die

254   *"Actual tax" figures in table:* 1958 SOI (Fiduciary, Gift and Estate Tax Returns), 59.

255   *Theodore Roosevelt:* 17 Works of Theodore Roosevelt (Memorial Edition), pp. 504-5.

255   *Franklin Roosevelt:* H. Rep. 1681, 74-1, Part 2, p. 643 (1935).

255   *Herbert Hoover:* 3 Memoirs 35-6.

256   *Andrew Carnegie:* Carnegie, *The Gospel of Wealth,* pp. 8, 9, 49, 50 (1933).

256   *Andrew Mellon:* Mellon, *Taxation: The Peoples Business,* p. 119 (1924).

256   *Garrard B. Winston:* 1925 National Tax Association Proceedings 249-51.

256   *Percent paying income tax:* Eisenstein 55.

257   *Louis Eisenstein:* 1955 JCER 838.

257   *Removes $2 billion of wealth:* 1958 SOI (Estate/Gift) 57.

258   *Truman veto message:* H. Doc. 589, 80-2, p. 4 (1948).

258-9   *Treasury Department in 1950:* 1950 HWM 24-5.

259   *Special Treasury survey:* 1950 HWM 75 ff.

259   Fortune *magazine:* Nov., 1957, p. 238.

260   *Herbert Hoover:* 3 Memoirs 136.

261   *Could have saved $1,400,000 in taxes:* Without the gift, his estate tax would be a little over $6 million. With the gift, he would pay about $550,000 *gift* tax, plus slightly over $4 million in *estate* taxes, for a total tax of about $4.6 million—$1.4 million less than he otherwise would have paid.

261   *Journal of Accountancy example:* Mr. A, during his lifetime, gives his son $5 million and pays a $1,800,000 gift tax. In order to convey the same amount of money ($5 million) to his son by will, after his death, an estate of $15 million would be required, involving an estate tax of $10 million. Thus the gift tax ($1.8 million) is less than one-fifth of the estate tax ($10 million).

262   *Oliver Johnson:* Estate of Oliver Johnson v. Commissioner, 10 TC 680 (1948).

262   *Acknowledgment of estate tax avoidance through "contemplation of death":* H. Rep. 2319, 81-2, p. 62; S. Rep. 2375, 81-2, p. 57 (1950).

262   *"Slightly less than if he had not made the gift":* In the event of such a successful challenge, the gift tax that has already been paid, serves a dually helpful purpose. First, since it *has* been paid, it is no longer a part of the decedent's estate, which means

Page

a death-tax saving. Second, it is applied as a credit against whatever estate tax *is* due.

263   *John D. Rockefeller: New York Times*, May 24, 1937, p. 10.

263   *Congress' lucid explanation:* H. Rep. 708, 72-1, p. 29; S. Rep. 665, 72-1, p. 41 (1931).

264   *Louis Eisenstein estimate:* 1955 JCER 812; also see 94 CR 7908 (1948).

264   *Eisenhower officials annoyed: Wall Street Journal*, Nov. 17, 1954.

265   *Pliny the Younger:* Schultz, *The Taxation of Inheritance*, p. 6 (1926).

265   *Sen. William V. Allen:* 31 CR 5081 (1898).

265-6   *Andrew Mellon:* Mellon, *Taxation: The People's Business*, p. 123 (1924).

266   *Three factors behind inequality:* Wedgwood, *Economics of Inheritance*, p. 81 (1929—Pelican edition).

266   *John Stuart Mill:* Mill, *Principles of Political Economy*, Book 2, Chapter 2, Section 4.

266   *Roger Babson:* Myers, *The Ending of American Hereditary Fortunes*, p. 255 (1939).

15. Old Loopholes Never Die, They Just Get Bigger

267   *Senator La Follette:* 88 CR 8017 (1942).

267   (footnote) *Senator McKellar:* 88 CR 8021-2 (1942).

268   *Senator Humphrey:* 97 CR 11812 (1951).

268   *Depletion could apply to water:* Marvin Shurbet v. U. S., 63-2 USTC Paragraph 9528 (1963).

268   *Worded by Louis Eisenstein: Ideologies of Taxation*, p. 176.

269   *National Sand and Gravel Association:* 1951 HWM 1539.

269   *"Have just as good a claim"; Sen. Douglas:* 97 CR 11811-2 (1951).

269   *1954 request of Sand and Gravel Association:* 1954 SFC 1267.

269   *Two Senators from Texas:* 100 CR 9043 and 9450 (daily), July 1, 1954.

270   *Senator Thomas of Utah:* 88 CR 8022-3 (1942).

270   *Survival of war-time depletion allowances:* Sec. 15, H.R. 4069, 80-1; 93 CR 997-8, July 24, 1947.

270   (footnote) *Medical expense deduction intended for duration of "emergency":* S. Rep. 1631, 77-2, p. 6 (1942).

270   (footnote) *Sand and Gravel Association:* 1954 SFC 1267.

272   *Douglas-Thye exchange; George-Williams exchange:* 97 CR 12336-7 (1951).

Page

273   *Capital gains for coal royalties:* Revenue Act of 1951, Sec. 325;
        S. Rep. 782, 82-1, p. 42 (1951).

274   *Attorney Alvord:* 1951 SFC 1478.

274   *$135 million cost of retirement income credit:* 1963 HWM 217.

275   *Groups in favor of H.R. 10:* 1959 SFC hearings on H.R. 10.

275   *Senator Smathers:* 108 CR 17675 (daily), Sept. 5, 1962.

275   *Senators Long and McCarthy; Sen. Gore:* S. Rep. 1615, 86-2,
        p. 47 (1960); 108 CR 17716 (daily), Sept. 6, 1962.

276   *Tax deduction for insurance companies:* see HWM Press Re-
        leases RR 61-56, July 19, 1961; RR 62-3, Jan. 24, 1962, S. Rep.
        1720, 81-2; H. Rep. 2413, 87-2 (1962).

276   *National Patent Council:* 1954 HWM 1191.

276   *Jockeys' Guild of America:* See Sen. Eugene McCarthy at 106
        CR 13225 (1960).

276   *Randolph Paul:* 1955 JCER 309.

16. The Heavy Odds Against Tax Reform

280   *Roy Blough:* Blough, *The Federal Taxing Process,* p. 41.

280   *Stanley Surrey:* 70 *Harvard Law Review* 1170 (1957).

281   (footnote) *Louis Eisenstein: Ideologies of Taxation,* p. 212.

284   *"Defeat for organized labor and liberals":* New York Times,
        June 7, 1963, p. 1.

285   *Passage from Revenue Code:* IRC Sec. 547 (b) (2).

285   *Louis Eisenstein: Ideologies of Taxation,* p. 215.

286   *Bill for relief of Hilton Hotel Corporation:* H. R. 7628, 85-1
        (1957), introduced by Rep. Noah Mason, Republican, of Illinois.

286   *Congressman Patman:* Eisenstein 215, 216.

286   *Douglas and the Finance Committee:* Engler, *The Politics of
        Oil,* p. 399.

288   *Kenworthy article:* appears in *Adventures in Public Service,*
        Vanguard Press, 1963.

289   *Roy Blough:* Blough, *The Federal Taxing Process,* p. 63.

289   *Passages from 1951 Finance Committee hearings:* 1951 SFC
        1446, 1558, 1669.

290   *"What's the good of being on this committee":* Stanley S.
        Surrey, 70 *Harvard Law Review* 1156 (1957).

292   *Byrd-Flanders episode:* 102 CR 14680 (1956).

292   *Sen. Douglas:* 105 CR 11910 (1959).

293   *Budd Company; Sangamo Electric:* 98 CR 9072-9076 (1952).

294   *Rep. John Byrnes: New York Times,* Nov. 10, 11, 18, 1963.

Page

296   James McCartney: *Chicago Daily News*, Oct. 8, 1962.

297   Opposition to Surrey appointment; Dillon letter: *Wall Street Journal*, Jan. 16, Apr. 13, 1961.

298   Reforms in estates, trusts, partnerships: H. R. 9662, Eighty-sixth Congress; H. Rep. 1231, 86-2; S. Rep. 1616, 86-2 (1960).

298   Stanley Surrey: 70 *Harvard Law Review* 1145 (1957).

17. What Should Be Done About "The Great Treasury Raid"?

303   George Meany: 1963 HWM 1962.

308   Wilbur Mills' "house of horrors": *Life*, Nov. 23, 1959.

309   John K. Jessup: *Life*, Aug. 24, 1962.

309   An added $1.1 billion of business investment: *Business Week*, Apr. 27, 1963.

309   Justice Holmes: Compania General de Tabacos v. Collector, 275 U. S. 87, 100 (1927).

309   Andrew Mellon: Schlesinger, *Crisis of the Old Order*, p. 63.

311   Andrew Mellon: Mellon, *Taxes: The People's Business*, pp. 17, 18, 69, 80.

311   Statement by Republican Ways and Means Members: H. Rep. 871, 78-1, Part 2, p. 7 (1943).

312   Mills and Curtis statements: Quoted in Scripps-Howard newspaper series on taxes by Jack Steele, January, 1958.

312   Randolph Paul: 1955 JCER 307.

313   James C. Carter: Pollock v. Farmers' Loan & Trust Co., 157 U. S. 429, 516 (1895).

Index

"Ability to pay," 68, 87; defini-
tion, 320
Alcoa, 183, 185
Alvord, Ellsworth C., 47, 48,
274, 294-295
Amerada Petroleum Company, 18
"Amos 'n' Andy," 127
Arabian-American Oil Company,
30
Art: tax-deductible charitable
gifts, 239-241; regulations to
correct abuse, 245
Authors: tax on novels, 83,
234; Eisenhower ruling and
"amendment," 130; Kathleen
Winsor, 130
Automatic data processing, 172-
176
Autry, Gene, 22, 134
Avoidance V. evasion, x

Ball, Lucille, 134
Bazelon, David T., quoted, x

Benedum, Michael, 22
Benny, Jack, 127
Berlin, Irving, 128
Block, Paul, 132
Blough, Roger, 181, 280, 289
Blum, Professor Walter, quoted,
61
Bonds, tax-free, 6, 15, 190-197;
beneficiaries, 180, 191-193,
revenue loss to Treasury, 193;
arguments for and against
eliminating exemption, 193-
197
Brandeis, Justice Louis, quoted,
107
Breech, E. R., 181
Bridgeport Brass Company, 55,
293
Budd Company, 55, 293
"Bunched" income, 90, 96, 97,
100-103
Byrd, Sen. Harry F., 290, 292
Byrnes, Rep. John, 294

Cannon, Rep. Clarence, 53-54, 292

Capital gains tax: cost to Treasury, 15, 93; oil depletion, 26; Mayer case, 44, 51, 274; v. regular income tax, 82-91; defined, 82, 321; distribution by income groups, 88; "bunched" income argument, 90, 96, 97, 100-103; holding period, 91; advantages to millionaires, 93-94; effort to close "loopholes," 95; need for abolition of, 96; history of separate rate, 97; "locked in" argument, 98, 101-103; proposal to put capital gains on par with regular income, 105-106; use in entertainment business, 127-142; in real estate industry, 148, 149, 152, 157; in stock-options, 182, 183, 190; unearned income advantage, 236; Pomona Plan to avoid tax, 241-242; one-way street provision, 271; livestock, 271-272; timber, coal, crops, 273; Christmas trees, 274; reform effects, 300-301, 306; as part of simplified tax plan, 306; definition, 321

Caplin, Mortimer, quoted, 124, 176

Carnegie, Andrew, quoted, 256

Carter, James C., 14

Cary, William L., quoted, 61

Casualty losses, deductible, 232; eliminated in simplified tax plan, 307

Charitable deductions: cost to Treasury, 223; criticism of present system, 226-228; donors benefit more than receivers, 238-250; unlimited deduction privilege, 248-249

Charitable foundations and trusts: Merrill, 48; Swope, 49; Clarence Cannon, 53-54; Pomona, 242; Fruehauf, Kirby, 243; Rosenstiel, 244

Christmas trees, capital gains treatment, 85, 274

Clay, depletion allowance, 29, 267, 270

Coal: lack of need for exploration subsidy, 42; royalties treatment, 84; depletion allowance, 271; capital gains treatment to royalties, 273, 300

Cohan (George M., expense account) rule, 119

"Collapsible" corporations, 94-95, 137-138, 151; definition, 321

Community property, 67, 71, 258-259, 306

Como, Perry, 134, 135

Congress: special tax-relief legislation, viii, 44-61; how tax legislation is handled, 277-299

Cooper, Rep. Jere, 53

Co-operative League of the U.S.A., 8

Corporation taxes: multiple corporations, 75-77; movie corporations, 131-137; "collapsible corporation," 137-138; real estate, 158, 159

Corporations: tax savings to, 18-20, 54-57, 75-77; multiple, 77-

79; "collapsibles" and "spin-
offs," 94-95; "bunched"-in-
come argument not applicable
to, 100; personal holding
companies, 132-138; real
estate, 143-159
Crosby, Bing, 22, 134
Cullen, Hugh Roy, 21
Curtis, Rep. Thomas B., quoted,
312

Death, failure to tax capital gains
at, 15, 92; revenue loss to
Treasury, 93; reform pro-
posal, 96; effect on "locked-
in" argument, 102
Deductions (personal): cost to
Treasury, 15, 221: 5-percent
"floor" proposal, 221, 223;
reasons for allowing, 221-223;
growth by type, 1944-1963,
223; for taxes paid, 224-225;
for interest paid, 225-226; for
gifts to charity, 226-228; for
medical expenses, 228; proposed additions, 229; un-
limited charitable deductions,
248-249; definition, 327
de Havilland, Olivia, 114
de Mille, Cecil B., 131-132, 133
Dependents: definition, 55-56;
income-splitting, 69-70; false
claims, 164
Depletion; depletion allowance:
cost to U.S. Treasury, 15;
minerals covered, 20; oil, 20-
42; processed products, 29;
reasons for and against, 33-
42; clay, 267, 270; sand and
gravel, 268, 269; limestone,
269; rock asphalt, 269, 270;

coal, 271; sought for inventions, 276; definition, 322 (see
also Oil)
Depreciation: machinery, 34-35;
real estate, 144-156; machine
over man, 235; definition, 322
Dividends from corporate stocks,
6, 16; unreported, 162, 166-
167; withholding proposal,
168; cost to Treasury, 180,
199; owners of stocks, 198
Dividend tax credit, 197-204;
"double-taxation" argument,
198-201; beneficiaries, 203-
204; definition, 323
Dodge, Mrs. Horace, Sr., 4, 180,
191, 197
Double taxation: arguments for
and against, 199-200; definition, 323
Doughton, Rep. Robert L., 53,
282
Douglas, Kirk, 131, 142
Douglas, Sen. Paul H., vii, 60,
269, 272, 286, 292, 293

Education deductions, 232-233
Eisenhower, President Dwight
D., tax ruling and "amendment," 130
Eisenstein, Louis, quoted, 14,
47, 234, 257, 264, 268, 281n,
285
Elderly persons: deductions, 7,
12, 15; tax advantages, 207;
low incomes, 208; medical deductions, 209; cost to Treasury of special provisions, 210;
retirement income credit, 210;
Kennedy reform proposals,

211; earned income limit, 233

Electioneering deduction, special provision, 56

Entertainment expenses (*see* Expense accounts)

Entertainment industry: use of capital gains, 127-130; stars' use of corporations, 131-137; "collapsible corporations,"137-138; "living abroad," 138-139; livestock-raising, 139-141

Estate taxes: Swope case, 49; relationship of capital gains, death and estate taxes, 92; bequests to family-held foundation, 244; how to avoid paying, 251-254; rates and actual tax by estate size, 254; history and reason for, 255; $60,000 exemption, 256, 263; marital deduction—cost to Treasury, 257-259; skipping of generations, 259-260; gifts during lifetime and after death, 261-263; life insurance gifts, 264; reform proposals, 265; arguments for and against reform, 265-266; definition, 323

Excess profits, wartime, 54-55

Excise taxes: cosmetics, gambling, cabaret, 167

Expense accounts: cost to U.S. Treasury, 15, 110, 125; "ordinary and necessary" expenses, 111, 113, in lieu of high salary, 112, 113; cost of gifts deducted by de Havilland and others, 114; "vacation-like"

conventions, 114-115; Kennedy reform proposal, 116; entertainment activities exception, 118; George M. Cohan "rule," 119; new law requires documentation, 119; accountants' problem eased, 119-120; arguments for entertainment expenses, 121-122; arguments for tighter rules, 123-125; "T&E" bribery cases, 124; labor support, 297

False-refund claims, 165

Family partnerships, 72-75

Family trusts, 49, 77-79; argument against, 260

Farmers: unreported income, 162, 166

Ferrer, Jose, 129

Finance committee, Senate: handling of tax bills, 287-292

Ford, Henry, II, quoted, 189

Foreign: oil investment, 29-31; oil imports, 40; residence to avoid income taxes, 138

Friedenberg, Daniel, cited, 150

Fringe benefits: tax treatment of, 217-220; cost to Treasury of non-taxation, 217

Freuhauf Foundation, 243

Futterman Corporation, 148

Gas (*see* Oil)

Gasoline tax deductions, 224

George, Sen. Walter, viii, 272, 287

Getty, J. Paul, 21

Gifts: deductible business, 112, 119; charity deductions, 226-228; how to avoid gift taxes,

253; $6,000 tax-free annual, 254, 263; gifts during lifetime and after death, 261-263; life insurance gifts, 264; as part of simplified tax proposal, 307; gift tax definition, 323

Gleason, Jackie, 134, 135

Gore, Sen. Albert, 185, 275, 286

Government payments to individuals, non-taxation of, 211-12

Hand, Judge Learned, quoted, x

Harrison, Sen. Pat, quoted, x

"Head of household," 53, 70-71; definition, 324

Health and medical benefits, 216-218; sick pay, 219-220

Hellborn, Ludwig S., 66

Hitchcock, Alfred, 140

Holding companies: personal, 131-137

Homeowners: tax advantages to, 212-216; expenses compared with renters, 213-215; cost to Treasury, 15, 214

Hoover, President Herbert, quoted, 255-256, 260

Hope, Bob, 22

Humphrey, Sen. Hubert, vii, 60, 268, 291

Hunt, H. L., 21

Imputed income, 212-216; as part of simplified tax plan, 306-307; definition, 324

Income, "bunched," 90, 96, 97, 100-103, 306, 308; definition, 321

Income, concentration of among top taxpayers, 179

Income, elderly, 208, 233

Income, unearned v. earned, 236, 302

Income, unreported: cost to Treasury, 16, 162; annuities, pensions, wages and salaries, 162; farmers, small business, 162, 163; farmers, 162, 166; interest and dividends, 162, 166-167, 168; dependents falsely claimed, 164; false-refund claims, 165; excises on cosmetics, gambling, cabarets, 167; automatic data processing, 172-176 (see also Withholding of taxes)

Income-splitting: married couples, 15, 63-80; multiple corporations, 75-77; trusts, 77; elimination of, 71, 306; definition, 324

Insurance: cost to Treasury on interest, 15; company-paid, 218

Insurance companies, taxation of, 276

Intangible drilling deductions, 20, 23-26, 32, 35, 36

Interest: cost to Treasury of deductions, 12, 223, 225; unreported, 162, 166-167; withholding proposal, 168; reasons for and against deduction, 225-226 (see also Bonds, tax-free)

Inventions: capital gains treatment, 83, 234; depletion sought, 276

Investment: oil, 29-31; v. speculation, 91; "locked-in" argu-

ment, 98-99, 103; investment
credit effect, 309
Investment Bankers Association,
195
Iron ore: depletion for, 28, 29;
capital gains treatment, 84,
273

Jackson, Justice Robert, quote,
162, 177
Jenkins, Rep. Thomas A., 286
Jessup, John K., quoted, 309
Joint Committee on Internal
Revenue Taxation, 288
Joint tax returns, 15, 63-69

Kennedy, President John F.: oil
depletion, 71; capital gains,
95; business entertainment
expenses, 116; dividend tax
credit, 199; retirement income
credit, 211; sick-pay, 219
Keogh, Rep. Eugene, 49-50
Kerr, Sen. Robert, 46, 50, 60,
289, 290-291
Kiplinger Tax Letter, 243
Kirby, Fred M., Foundation, 243
-244
Knipp, Howard F., 46, 57-58,
291
Kratter Corporation, 143

La Follette, Senator Robert,
quoted, 267
Lasky, Jesse, 129-130
Lausche, Sen. Frank, 60
Life insurance: cost to Treasury
on interest, 15; company-paid,
218; use of gift to avoid estate tax, 264
Limestone, 269

Literary works: tax on, 83; classified ordinary income, 84;
Eisenhower, Truman writings,
130; *Forever Amber* ruling,
130
Litvak, Anatole, 128
Livestock-raising: tax advantages, 139-141; expansion of
capital gains treatment, 271-
272
Livingston, J. A., quoted, 185,
188
Loans: interest on, 226; foundation use of, 244-245

Machrowicz, Rep. Thaddeus,
quoted, 121
MacMurray, Fred, 128
Marital deductions, 49n, 257
Martin, Tony, 134
Martin, Rep. Joseph, quoted,
200
Marx, Groucho, 128, 134
Matrimony: individual tax savings, 61-80; joint returns, 63-
69; income-splitting, 63-80;
cash value of wife, 65; "community property" laws, 67, 71
Mayer, Louis B., viii, 44-48, 274,
295
McCarthy, Sen. Eugene, 57, 60,
275, 298
McKee, L. R., 52
Meany, George, 280, 303
Medical: deductions for elderly,
209; company health plans,
217; cost to Treasury of deductions, 223; arguments for
and against deduction, 228-
229; as part of simplified tax
proposal, 307

Mellon, Andrew, 132, 193, 256, 265-266, 309, 311
Member's bill procedure, 282
Merrill, Charles E., 45-46, 48-49
Mill, John Stuart, quoted, 266
Miller, Mrs. Glenn, 128-129
Miller, Dr. Martin, 22
Millionaires, number untaxed, 8
Mills, Rep. Wilbur, 308, 312
Monroney, Sen. Mike, 31
Morton Salt Company, 29
Motion picture industry, 126-142
Mott, Charles Stewart, 181
Multiple corporations, 75-77
Murchison, Clint, 22

National Sand and Gravel Association, 269
National Tax Equality Association, 8
Neuberger, Sen. Maurine, quoted, 303

O'Brien, Pat, 137
Oil: subsidies, 11, 12; revenue costs to Treasury, 15, 21; tax savings, 18, 19; depletion allowances, 20-42; "intangible" drilling expenses, 20, 23-26, 32, 35, 36; production curbs, 21; tax advantages, 24; capital gains advantage, 26; Administration reform proposals, 27-28; property "grouping," 28; foreign investment advantages, 29-31, 40; royalty payments, 30, 31; depletion history, 31-33; court rulings, 32-33; reasons for and against depletion allowances, 33-42;

drilling outlays, 35; "double deduction" argument, 36; exploration risks, 36-38; drilling successes, failures, 38; deductions, by size of corporation, 38; wildcatters, 39; defense needs, 40; prices, 41; in personal holding companies, 138; pressures in Congress, 279, 283, 295; tax reform effects, 301-302, 310; definition of depletion, 322
Old-age deductions (see Elderly)
Owens-Corning Fiberglas Company, 54

Partnerships: Knipp case, 57-58; family, 72-75
Patman, Rep. Wright, quoted, 286
Paul, Randolph, 276, 297, 312
Pensions: unreported pension income, 162; tax treatment of, 217, 218-219; deductions for self-employed, 275 (see also Retirement)
Percentage depletion (see Depletion; Oil)
Percy, Charles H., 182
Personal holding companies, 131-137
Pomona Plan, college fund-raising plan, 241-242
Private laws for tax relief, 53-54, 57-60, 294
Professionals: unreported income, 162, 163
Profit-sharing plans, 218, 220
Property tax deductions, 224

Randall, Clarence, quoted, 124-125

Real estate: cost to Treasury of tax advantages, 15, 143, 158-159; depreciation, 144-156; tax "shelter," 147; capital gains, 148, 149, 152, 157; tax advantages, 148, 151, 153; "collapsibles," 151; Administration reform proposals, 153, 155; arguments for and against "recapture" proposal, 153-156; tax-saving devices, 156-159; reform effects, 310-311

Reed, Rep. Daniel, 49-50, 200

Rental income: used to avoid personal holding company tax, 135-136; imputed, 212-216, 307

Retirement income credit: cost of Treasury, 16, 274; inequities, 210; Administration reform proposals, 211; definition, 325

Revenue losses to U.S. Treasury: general, 15-16; percentage depletion, 21; Louis B. Mayer, 47-48; Leo Sanders, 52; "joint returns," 63-64; family partnerships, 72-75; multiple corporations, 77, 80; capital gains, 93; expense accounts, 15, 110, 125; overseas residents, 138; real estate, 143, 158-159; from absence of withholding tax, 168; tax-exempt bonds, corporate dividends, stock options, 180, 189; benefits to elderly, 210; homeowners, 214; fringe benefits, pension trust funds, 217; sick pay, 219; itemized personal tax deductions, 221, 223

Richardson, Sid, 22

Robinson, Dr. Herbert W., quoted, 189-190

Rock asphalt, 269, 270

Romney, Governor George, 181

Roosevelt, President Franklin D., quoted, 78, 255

Roosevelt, President Theodore, quoted, 255

Rosenstiel, Lewis S., 182, 244

Ryan, Phil, 137

Sales tax deductions, 224, 225

Sand and gravel, 268, 269

Sanders, Leo, 46, 50-52, 290

Sangamo Electric Company, 55, 293

Sardi, Vincent, quoted, 121, 123

Scripps, E. W., 132

Seidman, J. S., quoted, 110, 122-123

Sick pay: cost to Treasury, 15; tax-free plans, 219-220

Sinclair Oil, 19

Sixteenth Amendment, 3, 5, 31n, 168, 193, 304

"Skipped generations," to reduce estate tax, 259-260

Small business: unreported income, 162, 163

Smathers, Sen. George, 117, 122, 220, 275

Smith, Dan Throop, quoted, 79, 200, 219

Social security: cost to Treasury of non-taxation, 15, 210; role in retirement income credit, 210

Socony Mobil, 19, 30

"Spin-offs," corporation, 94-95; definition, 325

Stam, Colin F., 288-290

Standard Oil: (Cal.) 19, (N. J.) 30

State and local taxes, deductibility, 223-225

Statler Hotel Corporation, 147

Stevens, W. R., 183

Stewart, Jimmy, 22

Stock options: beneficiaries, 181; tax savings, capital gains treatment, 182, 183, 190; purpose of, 183; arguments pro and con, 184-190; no net revenue loss to Treasury, 189; definition, 325

Subsidies, 11, 12, 41-42

Sulphur depletion deductions, 26

Surrey, Stanley S., viii, 60, 94, 280, 297, 298

Swope, Mrs. Gerard, 46, 49, 50, 292

Tax credits—definition, 326 (see Dividends; Retirement)

Tax-exempt institutions (see Charitable foundations)

Tax "shelter": real estate, 147; definition, 327

Tax withholding (see Withholding)

Tenney Corporation, 147-148

Texaco, 19

Thomas, Sen. Elmer, 270

Thye, Sen. Edward, quoted, 272

Timber: capital gains for, 273; Christmas trees, 85, 274

Transcontinental Investing Corporation, 147

Transfer payments, 211-212

Travel expenses (see Expense accounts)

Treasury Department, 281, 283, 288, 290, 297

Truman, President Harry S, 67, 130, 258

Trusts: charitable, 48, 49; family, 77-79; use in skipping of generation, 259-260; definition, 327

Turkeys: capital gains amendment, 272

Twin Cities Rapid Transit Company, 57, 60

Uneeda Doll Company, 74, 75

U.S. Savings and Loan League, 296

Universal Oil Products Company, 52-53

Unlimited charitable deduction, 248, 249

Wages and salaries: unreported income, 162

Water, depletion for, 268

Watson, Thomas J., Jr., 181-182, 183

Ways and Means Committee: tax activities, 279, 281-286; Member's bill procedure, 282

Winsor, Kathleen, 130

Withholding of taxes: history, 168; cost to Treasury from lack of for dividends and interest, 168; arguments for and against dividend and interest withholding, 169-170

Workers: fringe benefits, 216-220; sick pay, 219-220

York, Sgt. Alvin, 129-130

Young, Robert R., 22

About the Author

PHILIP M. STERN, a Phi Beta Kappa Harvard graduate, has had varied experience in journalism, government and politics. After a year as reporter and editorial writer for the New Orleans *Item,* a Rockefeller fellowship brought him to Washington, where he served, successively, as legislative assistant to Congressman (now Senator) Henry M. Jackson and Senator Paul H. Douglas, as a 1952 campaign aide of Adlai Stevenson and as Director of Research for the Democratic National Committee. In 1957, he and three associates founded a daily newspaper, the *Northern Virginia Sun,* in Arlington, Virginia. After four years as editor and later as publisher, he served a year as a Deputy Assistant Secretary of State. He and his wife and five children make their home in Washington, D. C., where during the past two years, in addition to researching and writing *The Great Treasury Raid,* he has written articles for *Harper's, The New York Times Magazine, The Reporter, The New Republic* and *The Progressive.*